Michael Edwardes was born in 1923 and educated in England and in France at the Sorbonne, where he studied Indian languages and religions. Among his many books on India are *Battles of the Indian Mutiny, Plassey: The Founding of an Empire, British India* (the basis of a ten-part television documentary), and a political biography of Jawaharlal Nehru. He was historical adviser to the BBC television series on the British Empire.

RED YEAR

THE INDIAN REBELLION OF 1857

Michael Edwardes

Red the blood that flowed, red the fire that burned,
Red the sword, red the hand that held it,
And red the earth that year,
That year . . .
> Popular poem from Kumaon *c.* 1880

CARDINAL edition published in 1975
by Sphere Books Ltd
30/32 Gray's Inn Road, London WC1X 8JL

First published in Great Britain by
Hamish Hamilton Ltd 1973
Copyright © Michael Edwardes 1973

Set in Intertype Times Roman

Printed in Great Britain by
Hazell Watson & Viney Ltd
Aylesbury, Bucks

ISBN 0 351 15997 5

Contents

PART SIX

The Queen's Peace Over All

MAPS
drawn by Patrick Leeson

ILLUSTRATIONS

All the illustrations in this book are from contemporary sources, predominantly British. Those which pretend to narrate an event or which generalise about alleged incidents or experiences reflect British views of the time, and not necessarily the truth. The 'monstrousness' of Indian behaviour towards British women and children is heavily dramatised. British revenge is shown with special relish and panache. Illustrations depicting incidents which did not actually take place at all – such as the suicide of Captain Skene and his wife (no. 23) – were reproduced again and again, even after the truth had become known. Probable fictions – such as Miss Wheeler's dramatic defence of her virtue (no. 12) – which could neither be denied nor substantiated because no one survived to testify, both inspired and horrified the Victorian public. The effect of this essentially misleading propaganda was enormous and helped to darken the British view of India and of Indians for generations after the events themselves had become merely incidents in a history book.

British publishers were swift to supply their readers with details of what was happening in India. Illustrations 2, 3, 8, 10, 15 and 25 are taken from the *Narrative of the Indian Revolt from its outbreak to the capture of Lucknow by Sir Colin Campbell*, a work which was published in serial form in 1858. Slightly later in the field, and rather more solidly documented, was Charles Ball's *The History of the Indian Mutiny* (London 1859), from whose two substantial volumes illustrations nos. 1, 4, 5, 7, 9, 11, 12, 16, 18, 19, 20, 23 and 27 are drawn. Other illustrations are from the following sources:

6 John Nicholson. From an 1851 daguerrotype by Kilburn reproduced in Captain Lionel J. Trotter *The Life of John Nicholson, Soldier and Administrator* (London 3rd edn. 1898).

13 Brigadier-General James Neill. From *The History of the Indian Revolt* (Edinburgh 1858).

14 The Nana Sahib. From J. W. Shepherd *Personal Narrative of the Outbreak and Massacre at Cawnpore during the Sepoy Revolt of 1857*. Shepherd was the Eurasian clerk mentioned on p. 67 of the present work.

17 Courtyard of the Slaughter House, Cawnpore, during the Mutiny. Water colour, 1857, by Sir Richard Hieram Sankey of the Madras Engineers. India Office Library WD 132. *Foreign and Commonwealth Office*, London.

21 The Begum Hazrat Mahal. From the *Illustrated London News*, 1858.

22 The Rani of Jhansi, a posthumous portrait. No true portrait from life is known. Water colour on ivory, probably by a Lahore or Amritsar artist c. 1860–70. India Office Library Add. Or. 2607. *Foreign and Commonwealth Office*, London.

24 'Battle of the Bunass', 14 August 1858. Drawn by Lieutenant Frederick Prescott Forteath of the 12th Bombay Native Infantry. India Office Library WD 963. *Foreign and Commonwealth Office*, London.

26 Tantia Topi. Pencil sketch made by Captain C. R. Baugh at Sipri in April 1859, just before Tantia's execution. *Royal Services Museum*, Aldershot.

28 Head of Bahadur Shah II, pen-and-ink sketch made a few months after the recapture of Delhi. The artist was R. M. Edwards, Magistrate and Collector of the district of Muzaffarnagar, who commissioned and edited the Mubarak Shah narrative printed as Appendix 5 of the present work. India Office Library MSS Eur.B.138. *Foreign and Commonwealth Office*, London.

PREFACE

The Indian rebellion, better known perhaps as the Indian Mutiny, of 1857–59, occupies a special place in the history of British rule in India. More has been written about it than about any other episode in the long years of the British connection. Most British writers on the rebellion have seen it as an epic of British heroism, yet another triumph of the imperial race, this time over the mutinous Indian soldiers of the Bengal Army supported here and there by feudal elements whose privileges the British had rightly curtailed in the interest of the mass of the Indian people. Indian writers, on the other hand, during the period of agitation against British rule and after independence, have frequently treated the rebellion not as a military mutiny, but as a war of national liberation. The truth is that the rebellion was more than a mutiny, but a lot less than a war of independence.

On the surface, the rebellion may appear as a conflict of religions, a battle between rival gods. In fact, it was a bloody and violent clash between the old and the new, tradition and modernity, nostalgia for the past and fear of the future – the scenario, in effect, of what today is known as the 'development process'. As such, it is not without parallel in our own times. I have, however, made no attempt to underline that parallel, but have drawn from selected areas of the rebellion a picture of the physical and mental reactions of men and women, British and Indian, to a series of moral, social, and economic crises. From this I hope will appear a view not only of the modernising process itself in a mid-nineteenth-century colonial context, but of the fears, hopes and ambitions of men and women caught up in a process that is as uneven as it is irresistible, and almost always as brutal as it is inexorable.

The sources on which the present work is based include British state papers, personal memoirs, letters, and extracts from contemporary newspapers. Indian sources include memoirs, anecdotes, and popular ballads and stories of the time and later. Documentation on the British side is voluminous, almost overwhelmingly so, but on the Indian it is sparse. Apart from unpublished material, I have used some modern studies published by Indian historians in Hindi, Urdu, Bengali and Marathi. In Appendix 5 I have reproduced for the first time in print one of the very few continuous narratives of events – in this case, inside Delhi – available from Indian sources.

11

PART ONE

A cloud in the Indian sky

I know not what course events may take. I hope they may not reach the extremity of war. I wish for a peaceful time of office, but I cannot forget that, in our Indian Empire, that greatest of all blessings depends upon a greater variety of chances and a more precarious tenure than in any other quarter of the globe. We must not forget that in the sky of India, serene as it is, a small cloud may arise, at first no bigger than a man's hand, but which growing bigger and bigger, may at last threaten to overwhelm us with ruin.

Lord Canning. Speech at a banquet given in his honour by the Directors of the East India Company. London, 1 August 1855

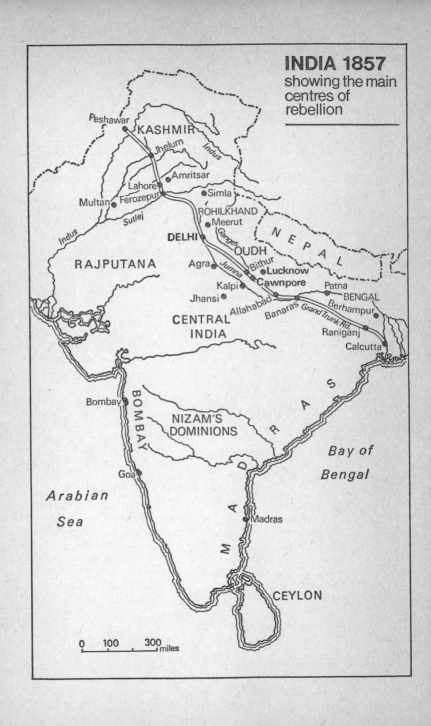

INDIA 1857
showing the main
centres of rebellion

Peshawar
KASHMIR
Jhelum
Indus
Amritsar
Lahore
Simla
Multan
Ferozepur
ROHILKHAND
Sutlej
Meerut
Ganges
Indus
DELHI
NEPAL
RAJPUTANA
OUDH
Agra
Bithur
Lucknow
Jumna
Cawnpore
Kalpi
Patna
BENGAL
Jhansi
Berhampur
Allahabad
CENTRAL
Banaras Grand Trunk Rd.
INDIA
Raniganj
Calcutta

Bombay
BOMBAY
NIZAM'S
DOMINIONS
M
A
D
R
A
S
Bay of
Bengal
Arabian
Sea
Goa
Madras
CEYLON

0 100 300 miles

CHAPTER ONE

SEEDS OF DISCONTENT

Fifteen years before Lord Canning made his tragically prophetic speech after taking the oath of office as governor-general of India, a shrewd Swedish statesman, ambassador at the Court of St James's, had asked himself a question – and partially answered it.

'But who, then, is the conqueror, who the sovereign of this immense empire over which the sun extends so gloriously his glittering rays, that has arisen on the continent of Asia as if by enchantment, and now rivals in extent that of Alexander, Tamerlane or Nadir Shah?

'Why, on a small island in another quarter of the globe, in a narrow street, where the rays of the sun are seldom able to penetrate the thick smoke, a company of peaceable merchants meet; these are the conquerors of India; these are the absolute sovereigns of this splendid empire.'[1]

The 'company of peaceable merchants' had first been given a charter to trade between the Cape of Good Hope and the Straits of Magellan by Queen Elizabeth I in the last year of the sixteenth century. There had been no dreams of colonial dominion then, but only of profit – in spices, in gems, in the luxuries of the gorgeous East. But dominion had come just the same; and so had the profits. Land had first been leased from Indian rulers in 1640, at Madras. In 1668 Charles II gave the Company Bombay, which he had received as a wedding gift with his Portuguese wife, Catherine. In 1690 Calcutta was established on a malarial swamp. But it was the eighteenth century which was to change the Company's future. In the first fifty years, trade expanded, but the profits went into private pockets rather than the Company's coffers.

In the crumbling world of eighteenth-century India, a world in which the once-great empire of the Moghuls was rapidly coming apart, wars between England and France in Europe became wars between those countries' trading companies in India. With them came visions of a wider dominion than the paltry acres of a trading post. To fight their wars – against each other and against the Indian rulers who became their allies and puppets – each acquired an army of mercenaries, Indian soldiers trained in the European manner and officered by Europeans, With these men, and with those no less effective weapons, corruption and intrigue, the English East India Company acquired Bengal after 1757, becoming in 1765 by a grant from the then fugitive Moghul emperor an *Indian* ruler and legally a feudatory of the empire.

From Bengal came immense profits, but again not for the Company. By 1772 its Directors were forced to confess that only an immediate loan of £1 million from the British government could stave off bankruptcy. From that moment they were no longer the 'absolute sovereigns' of a growing empire, for though they got their loan they also had to take 'an Act for establishing certain regulations for the better management of the affairs of the East India Company, as well in India as in Europe'. This Act opened the door to more coherent interference in the administration of the Company's Indian territories. Through it, in 1784, came legislation which, though it left to the Directors of the Company the lucrative and influential gift of patronage, placed the Company under the direct supervision of the British government. A Board of Control was established with a President at its head. The Board could overrule the Directors, and the head of the Company's administration in India could not be appointed without its approval.

This inefficient system of double government, with few modifications, lasted until 1858. During that time the Company lost its old trade monopoly, in India in 1813 and in China twenty years later. In 1853, the Directors were even forced to give up the power of patronage, the profitable appointments in the Company's civil service being thrown open to competitive examination. By then the Company had long ceased to be a trading concern and acted in effect only as an agent for the civil and military government of India. These changes coincided not only with the vast expansion of the Company's dominions in India but with an ideological offensive against the foundations of Indian life.

The offensive was slow to start. For some fifty years after the real foundation of their rule in India, the British had not really been sure of the permanence of their position. Their government was an oriental government with European overtones. They borrowed techniques from earlier rulers and modified them to suit their own ideas. But they tried to avoid interfering directly in the life of the people they ruled. Considering themselves heirs of the old Moghul empire, they adopted much of that empire's system, essentially one of non-interference in traditional religious and social values and behaviour. But before the end of the eighteenth century, influential men in England had demanded a revolution in Indian life. Charles Grant, who had served in India and become the chairman of the Court of Directors of the East India Company, proclaimed their aim. 'In considering the affairs of the world as under the control of the Supreme Disposer, and those distant territories [i.e. India] providentially put into our hands . . . is it not necessary to conclude that they were given to us, not merely that we might draw an annual profit from them, but that we might diffuse among their inhabitants, long sunk in darkness, vice and misery, the light and benign influence of the truth, the blessings of a well-regulated society, the improvements and comfort of active industry?'[2]

Grant and others like him thought that the conversion of Indians to the 'truth' – Western Christian truth – would not only raise their moral standards but inspire them to greater output and consumer demand. 'In every progressive step of this work, we shall also serve

16

the original design with which we visited India, that design still so important to this country [i.e. Britain] – the extension of our commerce.'[3] This view, a kind of Christian capitalism, shared by such men as William Wilberforce, the anti-slavery reformer, was not approved of either by a majority of the Company's Directors or by the men who actually ruled British India. They knew that British rule depended upon the consent of the people of India, who did not care who governed them as long as their customs and religion were not interfered with. Christian missionaries were, therefore, not only unwelcome in India but were actually prohibited from working there. The government of India, following the tradition of its predecessor, was neutral in religious matters. As an *Indian* government, it administered temple funds, controlled religious endowments, organised the pilgrim traffic. But those who wanted to keep India untouched were fighting a losing battle. As the government in London ruled the Company, it could not resist for long the pressures of men who could, and did, influence the government.

In 1813 the Company was forced to open its territories to Christian missionaries. It had also to make available a sum of money for education, because those who believed in Christianising India also believed that literacy – and through it access to the revealed words of the Bible – was essential to the success of the revolution they advocated with such single-minded enthusiasm. And there were others, less – at least, openly less – concerned with the souls of Indians who agreed with them but thought the process of conversion by education too slow, that what the evangelical Christians advocated was not a revolution at all. 'Ignorance,' thundered one of them, 'is the natural concomitant of poverty; a people wretchedly poor are always ignorant; but poverty is the effect of bad laws and bad government; and is never characteristic of any people who are governed well.'[4]

Both the evangelical Christians and the philosophers known as Utilitarians profoundly influenced the behaviour of the Company's government as well as that of individual members of the Company's army and civil service. After the end of the third war (1818) against the Marathas – the only native power that had ever seemed a challenge to the Company's ultimate conquest of the whole of India – an exhausted country was willing and anxious to be ruled by those who could guarantee peace and freedom from anarchy, who would protect, with power and sympathy, the living substance of Indian life. The British appeared to offer both. But those among them who wished to maintain the neutral attitude of government were against the trend of the times. That trend was towards change and innovation. With it came a distaste, amounting at times almost to hatred, of Indian religions and social practices, as well as an arrogant contempt for Indian civilisation in all its aspects. Such attitudes tainted even the most humanitarian of reforms.

Within twenty years the British had abolished widow burning, had suppressed female infanticide, and destroyed the criminal gangs known as the Thugs, all practices and activities which in the popular mind had the sanction of religion. Western education had been introduced, arousing scepticism among the young of the received beliefs of their fathers, a scepticism reinforced by such advocates of European learning as Lord Macaulay, who dismissed Indian culture as made up of 'medical doctrines that would disgrace an English farrier – Astronomy, which would move laughter in girls at an English boarding school – History, abounding with kings thirty feet high, and reigns thirty thousand years long – and Geography, made up of seas of treacle and seas of butter.' [5]

A minority – a very small minority – of Indians welcomed the Westernising tendencies of the British, but the masses saw government acceptance of change as patronage of change, a move from benevolent neutrality to support of innovation. Christian missionaries were viewed as agents of government and every piece of legislation which affected the daily life of ordinary people, or that of their traditional rulers, was seen as part of a conspiracy. And a conspiracy of the most insidious sort, an erosion rather than a sudden blow. Very soon those who felt themselves menaced believed that the British would use any kind of subterfuge or underground method to achieve their ends. Yet what could be done?

Without appearing to notice what was going on, the British continued to introduce change. In the matter of ownership of land in their newly acquired territories, they began to demand proof of title – in a country where written titles were virtually unknown. In one area alone, that heartland of the Marathas in the Deccan, some twenty thousand landlords lost their estates. In a country where the mass of the people were landless peasants, it might be assumed that an attack on the economic position and privileges of the landowning classes would receive popular support. But this too was seen as an attempt to destroy the traditional web of feudal relationships. The new proprietors felt they had no right, in traditional terms, to their newly acquired land, however much British law was on their side.

Under the rule of Lord Dalhousie (governor-general 1848–56) the tempo of change accelerated. This 'curious compound of despot and radical' [6] saw his task to be the rapid modernisation of India. With this, nothing was to be allowed to interfere. As the British had conquered India, they had left within their territories semi-independent states ruled by Indian princes, bound to the British by treaty. To Dalhousie these states were anachronisms, feudal remnants with no place in a modern, unitary state. No one, it seemed, however high in the traditional Indian élite, could escape. Dalhousie did not advocate annexation by conquest. In fact, after the second Sikh war of 1848–49, there was no great native state left in India. Dalhousie instead produced two excuses for annexation – the doctrine of lapse, and the charge of chronic misgovernment. Of these, the more controversial – for it struck at a long-held tradition – was the doctrine of lapse.

It had been the custom for Hindu rulers without a direct heir to adopt one, usually from another branch of the ruling family. This custom was not only of political but of religious importance. For any Hindu, it was necessary to have a son to carry out those essential religious rites after his death which only a son was fitted for. The soul's salvation depended on it. For a Hindu prince, a son also ensured the stability of his dynasty. However, it was also the custom that a prince should have the approval of his feudal lord for the adoption. This sovereign position had been inherited by the British. Dalhousie refused to recognise adoption. In the course of eight years, in consequence, he seized a number of states, including Satara, Nagpur and Jhansi. He also annexed, on grounds of misgovernment, the great Muslim state of Oudh, and gave notice that the Moghul king of Delhi, a powerless pensioner of the British, would be the last to hold that title.

Dalhousie's attention was not confined to the rationalisation of the map of India. A modern state must have a modern economy, and a modern economy depended on communications. Roads were built, the first railway lines laid, and thousands of miles of wire for the electric telegraph hung on posts and trees across the country. Educational reforms were pushed ahead, reforms which included the planning of three Western-style universities. A law was passed to permit the remarriage of Hindu widows. All these, in the minds of the people, were connected together as an attack upon their religion. The office of the inspector of schools at Patna in Bihar became the *Sheitanka dufter khana* – 'the devil's counting house'.[7] The telegraph wires were some magical weapon, the missionaries in the market place and the school were shock troops of a forced conversion. The connection between the railway, the telegraph, and missionary activities, made instinctively by Indians and frequently denied by the government of India, was overtly stated by a certain Mr Edmond in a circular letter to government officials in Bengal. 'The time appears to have come,' he wrote, 'when earnest consideration should be given to the subject, whether or not all men should embrace the same system of Religion. Railways, Steam Vessels and the Electric Telegraph are rapidly uniting all the nations of the earth; the more they are brought together, the more certain does the conclusion come, that all have the same wants . . . the same hopes . . . and therefore the same nature and the same origins.'[8]

This was what many Indians feared, but because their unease was generalised, the tensions hidden beneath a surface seldom penetrated by the foreigners who ruled India, no one noticed that the calm was superficial. A few more percipient men warned of the dangers of rapid modernisation and change. As early as October 1854, John Peter Grant, lieutenant-governor of Bengal, saw that the immediate danger lay in the continuing offence to the religious feelings of the Indian people. 'I am firmly persuaded,' he wrote, 'that unless in practice . . . all breach, and all appearance of breach, of religious neutrality can be avoided, a blow will be struck at our power in India, which in the course of time may prove fatal.'[9]

But no one listened. In the armour of their cultural arrogance, the British felt secure. There was no native power left in India to challenge their will. At least, not while they retained the loyalty of their native army.

CHAPTER TWO

THE CHAPATI AND THE CARTRIDGES

The armed forces of the East India Company had steadily grown in size as the conquest of India progressed. By 1857 the Indian element had reached the enormous number of 233,000 men. Though the Company had some all-European regiments (about 15,000 men) as well as hired units of the Royal army, British troops were outnumbered by nearly seven to one. Originally, Indian recruits had been mainly low-caste Hindus and Afghan or Turkish mercenaries no longer employed by the native princes, but as the Company's territories expanded a deliberate policy of involving peasants and the sons of landowners altered the caste balance of the Company's Hindu soldiers. In Bengal, which like Madras and Bombay had a separate army command, new recruits came almost exclusively from the highest Hindu caste, the brahmin.

Over the years many concessions had been made to the religious prejudices of the Indian soldiers (sepoys), but frequently those prejudices had been absurdly ignored. In 1806, offended by the unmilitary appearance of caste marks painted on the forehead and the luxuriant beards of the sepoys, an order had been issued to the Madras army that the former must be removed and the latter trimmed. Furthermore, the old turban was to be replaced by one with a leather cockade. Leather from the cow was objectionable to Hindus, for whom the cow is a sacred animal; no Muslim would willingly wear anything made from the skin of that, to them, unclean animal, the pig. The attempt was taken as an attack on the sepoys' faith. At Vellore, the sepoys mutinied. The mutiny was suppressed, brutally, but the regulation was withdrawn.

Eighteen years later, a sepoy regiment ordered to Burma refused to move because it felt that a refusal by the military authorities to provide special transport to carry the cooking pots – which each man required by caste usage – was not only an attack on the men's religion but a breach of contract. They received a shower of grapeshot in reply. Next morning, six of the alleged ringleaders were publicly hanged and hundreds of others were sentenced to fourteen years' hard labour on the public roads. Five more sepoys were later hanged and their bodies hung in chains as an example to others. There were more mutinies or near-mutinies, including the refusal by a regiment in 1852 to cross the sea to Burma. The sepoys took the command to do so not only as another breach of contract but as an attempt to break their caste by making them cross the open water. This time the matter was more delicately handled, and the sepoys were merely marched away to another station.

But the memories remained with the sepoys, and in place of unquestioning loyalty came a lack of faith not only in the government that employed them but in their officers, Indian or British. As the seniority system operated for both, it meant that promotion was long in coming. For neither was there the temptation to show merit, because merit meant nothing. Every sepoy had an equal chance of rising to the rank of commissioned officer, but there was no incentive for exertion. 'They had no motive to earn the good opinion of their superiors . . . it was enough for them to drowse through a certain number of years of service, to slide quietly into a commission, and then end their military lives in senile somnolence and apathy.'[1] The same criticism applied to senior British officers. The system usually meant that Englishmen joining the Company's army at seventeen could hope for no more than to become a lieutenant at twenty-one, a captain at twenty-nine, a major at forty-four, and – with luck – a lieutenant-colonel ten years later.

With the advance of the Company's frontiers, the need for administrators outran the supply, and the more ambitious young officers were detached from military duties, leaving behind them the aged, the very young, and those who were not intelligent enough for civilian duties. Fortunately, not every regiment of the Company's army was denuded of talent, but on the whole the British officers of native regiments were frustrated men with little sympathy for those they commanded. 'Officers and men,' wrote one critic, 'have not been friends but strangers to one another . . . The sepoy is . . . sworn at. He is spoken of as a "nigger" . . . as a "pig". The old men are less guilty as they sober down. But the younger men seem to regard it as an excellent joke and as a praiseworthy sense of superiority over the sepoy to treat him as an inferior animal.'[2]

All this led to a breakdown in discipline. The British officers did not care what their men thought and warmed themselves with the illusion that the sepoy would remain forever 'true to his salt'. The sepoy, however, was not only building up a file of genuine complaints. He began to see the way he was treated as part of a general pattern, especially when an officer insisted on trying to convert him to Christianity – and there were many who did. Again, there were men who observing the demeanour of the sepoys warned that one day they would rise and turn upon their rulers. But the authorities were convinced that a mercenary army was, by definition, loyal to its paymasters. In this they were mistaken. Ironically, perhaps, it was a technical development in the weapons of war which was to reveal their error.

Until the middle of the nineteenth century, the infantry weapon of the Company's army was the unrifled musket known as 'Brown Bess'. In 1852 a new rifle, the Enfield, was developed and used with considerable success in the Crimean war. Late in 1856 it was introduced into India. With the new rifle came a new cartridge, a narrow cylinder of paper containing the ball and a charge of gunpowder, heavily greased to keep the powder dry. Before the ball and charge

22

could be pushed down the long barrel of the new gun, the end of the cartridge had to be bitten off.

Preparations were made for selected Indian regiments to learn the use of the new weapon. A quantity of cartridges had been brought from England, but further supplies were to be manufactured at government arsenals at Dum Dum, near Calcutta, and at Meerut, near Delhi. The issue of rifles and ammunition for training purposes took place without remark or incident, until one day a low-caste Hindu worker at Dum Dum asked for a drink from a brahmin sepoy's brass water pot. Angry at the brahmin's reply that the pot would be contaminated by the lips of such a low-caste person, the worker retorted that the sepoy would soon lose his caste altogether, as the government were manufacturing cartridges greased with the fat of cows or swine. 'It is difficult to convey . . . an adequate idea of the force of the shock beneath which the imagination of that brahmin must have reeled when he heard those words. It was all true, then, he must have felt. The government was really bent upon ruining him. They had devised an expedient which, under the specious pretext of putting a better weapon into his hands, was to destroy his caste, his honour, his social position, everything that made life worth having, and to pave the way for his perversion to Christianity . . . For him to be told that he was to touch with his lips the fat of the cow was as appalling as it would have been to a mediaeval Catholic to listen to the sentence of excommunication.'[3]

The news spread quickly, the horror with it. Even the British officers at Dum Dum heard the news. The officer commanding the Musketry Depot ordered a parade on 22 January 1857 and 'called for any complaints that the men might wish to prefer; at least two thirds of the detachment immediately stepped to the front, including all the native commissioned officers. In a manner perfectly respectful, they very distinctly stated their objection to the present method for preparing cartridges . . . the mixture employed for greasing . . . was opposed to their religious feeling, and as a remedy begged to suggest the employment of wax and oil in such proportion as in their opinion would answer the purpose required'.[4] For the moment at least there was only fear. Anger would come later.

The authorities did indeed take swift action, incredibly swift for the ponderous machine of the Company's government. General Sir John Hearsey, commanding at the great military station of Barrackpur, near Calcutta, suggested that the sepoys should be allowed to grease their own cartridges. The government agreed. But six days had passed since the men at Dum Dum had made known their feelings, six days in which rumour piled upon rumour. Not only about the grease on the cartridges, but that powdered bones had been mixed with the sepoys' flour, wells deliberately polluted. Menaced from what appeared to be every direction, the fear of the sepoys was honed to a knife edge. And the rumours were not confined to the environs of Calcutta. Mysterious fires in the sepoy lines at Raniganj,

23

a hundred miles away, showed that unrest was taking a positive form. But there was worse to come.

When the rumours reached the men of the 19th Native Infantry stationed at Berhampur, they decided to refuse the cartridges. They were reassured by their commander. However, when a detachment of the 34th Native Infantry arrived from Barrackpur, their belief in their officers' explanations melted away. On 27 February the men refused to take the cartridges. A new element had been added to increase their fear. The paper under the grease was in one of two different colours. There *was* a simple explanation – the cartridges were from two different batches – and the sepoys might have accepted it. But their commander, Colonel Mitchell, was not a man of tact. Summoning his native officers he swore at them and threatened. 'They must take the cartridges, otherwise they would be sent to China and Burma, where they would die.' [5]

Mitchell's violent language only confirmed the sepoys' fears. They broke open the arms stores and loaded their muskets. Mitchell, who had no European troops to call on, brought up his native cavalry and artillery. With unusual good sense he allowed himself to be persuaded by his Indian officers that the men's conduct was due to fear and not disloyalty. If the cavalry and artillery were withdrawn, everything would quieten down. By nightfall all was peaceful. But the sepoys' behaviour could not be overlooked. An army is an army only for as long as discipline is preserved. Punishment there had to be. It was decided that the regiment must be disbanded. But it was too risky to carry out the operation at Berhampur. The native cavalry and artillery had *appeared* loyal, but could they be counted on to fire upon their own comrades should the 19th offer resistance? The regiment must march to Barrackpur, there to be disarmed in the presence of European troops hurriedly brought by steamer from Rangoon. The regiment moved down country quietly, but an embroidery of their heroism and martyrdom preceded them.

February and March 1857 produced other tokens of unease. From across northern India reports came to the governor-general. Strange prophecies were in the air. There was one that the British would be overthrown on 23 June, the centenary of the battle of Plassey by which they had first taken power in Bengal. There was a growing impression that some terrible calamity was about to strike the country. Magical symbols, their meaning unknown even to the writers, appeared on walls; amulets to protect the wearer from disaster were having a wide sale in the bazaars. Most mysterious of all were the reports that small wheaten cakes known as chapatis were circulating from village to village in northern India.

'One morning towards the end of last month,' reported a newspaper in March, 'the officials at Fatehgarh were in commotion. From [police outpost] after [police outpost] there arrived chapatis about two inches in diameter. They were accompanied by all kinds of reports by puzzled [police officers] ... It appears that a few evenings previous a [watchman] in Cawnpore ordered a [watchman] in Fatehgarh to make and bake twelve chapatis . . . Two he was to retain. Two more were to be given to each of the five nearest [village watchmen]. The order was obeyed and all night long there was running and baking of chapatis . . . The five obeyed orders and distributed their message to twenty-five and so the affair went on, in geometrical ratio, the cakes sweeping over the district at a speed which no Indian post yet travels.'[6] No one knew the meaning of the chapatis, no one dared refuse the instruction to pass them on.

When British officials heard of this they made enquiries. What did the chapatis mean? Some argued that it was a method of carrying off disease. In one part of the country, in fact, cholera broke out after the chapatis had been circulated. One official believed that the message was a 'fiery cross', but the superior to whom he reported dismissed it as the work of someone trying to propitiate the gods. The British later linked the affair of the chapatis with the rebellion that was soon to break out, but no connection was ever proved and it is unlikely that there was one – though some remembered that a similar distribution of chapatis had preceded the outbreak at Vellore nearly fifty years before. For Indians, it was yet another symbol of terrors yet to come.

Circulating, too, was a saying: '*Sub lal hogea hai*' – 'Everything will become red'. This so amused a Calcutta journal that it ridiculed those who thought it might be a threat with what was presumably intended as a satirical poem. This ended:

> Beneath my feet I saw 'twas nought but blood,
> And shrieking wretches borne upon the stream
> Struggled and splashed amidst a sea of gore.
> I heard a giant voice again proclaim,
> 'Mid shouts of murder, mutiny and blood,
> SUB LAL HOGEA HAI, and I awoke.[7]

But others were not amused. They were nearer to reality. At the Musketry Depot at Ambala in the Punjab, Lieutenant Martineau, appalled at the reaction both of the sepoys and of the commander-in-chief, General Anson, wrote to one of Anson's staff officers then comfortably esconced with his chief in the hill station of Simla. 'Good God, here are all the elements of combustion at hand . . . men sullen and distrustful, fierce – if a flare-up from any cause takes place at one station it will spread and become universal and then what means have we of putting it down? You can view the position more coolly in the Himalayas than I do in the plains.'[8] A few miles away from the clever newspaper gentleman of Calcutta, General Hearsey was also aware that the situation was no matter for humour. In an official letter written early in February, he said: 'We have at Barrackpur been dwelling on a mine ready for explosion.'[9] When the explosion came it was muted, but the radiation was widely diffused.

At Barrackpur, news of the imminent arrival of the 19th Native Infantry had its effect on the sepoys stationed there. On 29 March a young soldier fired the first shot in the Great Mutiny. Convinced

25

that the British would turn against all sepoys, he put on his uniform and, seizing his musket, walked down to the quarter-guard, calling on his comrades to follow him. At the guard, the sepoy ordered the bugler to sound the call for assembly. The bugler would not, but the men on guard did nothing even when the sepoy fired at an English sergeant-major. The shot went wide.

The adjutant, Lieutenant Baugh, now appeared on the scene, having been alerted by a European corporal. He had loaded his pistols, buckled on his sword, mounted his horse, and ridden down to the guard room where, as he arrived, another shot was fired. It missed Baugh but brought down his horse. The situation now developed into a tragic farce. Baugh fired at the mutineer – and missed. He drew his sword and he and the sergeant-major rushed at the sepoy. The sepoy seems to have been a better swordsman than either of the Europeans, for he succeeded in wounding both. He might even have killed them if another sepoy had not restrained him. But the guards now turned on the two Europeans, striking them with the butts of their muskets. One even fired at close range – and missed.

The news of what was going on soon reached General Hearsey. With two of his sons he, too, made for the guard room. As he passed by the men who seemed unable to act against this one sepoy, someone called out to the general that the sepoy's musket was loaded. 'Damn his musket,' replied Hearsey. Revolver in hand, he ordered the quarter-guard to arrest the mutineer and the men moved forward slowly. As they came, the man raised his musket. 'Father,' called one of the general's sons, 'he is taking aim at you.'

'If I fall, John, rush upon him and put him to death,' replied Hearsey, and galloped forward. The mutineer raised his musket to fire – and then turned it upon himself. But he was only slightly wounded, and was soon taken away by the guard, now anxious to do its duty.[10] The mutineer's name was Mangal Pandy. Soon the cry 'Remember Mangal Pandy' was to become a signal of revolt, and to the British the rebels were always to be known as 'pandies'.

CHAPTER THREE

THE BREAKING OF THE STORM

In the early part of 1857 there were warnings enough, and yet no one – not even those who felt the danger to be real – would allow themselves to accept the urgency of the situation. The majority of officers in the sepoy regiments believed their men to be essentially steadfast and loyal, troubled perhaps, but with the troubles of frightened children, soon forgotten. The unease among the civilian population, though recognised, was not taken too seriously. India was never quiet. Indians were excitable, and wayward, frightened by shadows. A rebellion was quite literally unthinkable. No preparations to meet it were made. As the hot weather season approached, European troops were being moved out of the plains to cooler stations in the foothills of the great mountains. The commander-in-chief and his staff were immured at Simla, nearly a thousand miles away from Calcutta and the governor-general. The telegraph line reached no further than Ambala, sixty-six miles from the summer residence of the commander-in-chief.

After the troubles of March, the general impression was that things were calm. Lord Canning was even relieved that the commander-in-chief was so far away. 'I have had a *mauvais quart d'heure* since my last letter,' he wrote to a close friend in England, 'and a very long one – in the matter of the Mutiny; but it is all well over, so far as danger goes; although troubles enough will spring out of it. It has been a much more anxious matter than Persia, ten times over; for a false step might have set the Indian army in a blaze. As it is, I am rather pleased with the way in which it has been dealt with. Do not whisper it, but, to say the truth, I have been rather glad to have the Commander-in-Chief up in the far North-West. He has plenty of pluck and plenty of coolness; but I doubt his judgement as to when and what to yield.' [1]

Elsewhere, life – the comfortable life of the British, even in the plains – went on. At Delhi during April, the English community was upset by the behaviour of a peppery colonel who at the station ball, believing himself insulted by a civilian, ordered his regimental band out of the room and refused to allow it to return until the bandsmen had received an apology from the highest-ranking English official present. The local newspaper carried complaints that 'the bigwigs get the strawberries from the station garden while a new subscriber cannot get a sniff of the flowers', and readers were entertained by the news that: 'A wedding is talked of as likely to take place soon, but the names of the aspirants to hymeneal bliss I will refrain from mentioning just yet, lest anything should occur to lessen their affection for each other before the knot is tied.' [2] A correspondent writing on 5 May could only deplore the fact that 'as usual no news to give you. All quiet and dull'.[3]

At Sialkot in the Punjab the British were dedicating a new church, 'the most chaste and beautiful structure of Modern Gothic in India', and congratulating themselves with the thought that 'the strength of the many made subservient to the will of the few, not by crushing armies from foreign lands but by sowing the seeds of peace and order around – a land a few years ago bristling with bayonets, an enemy's country, now cheerfully acknowledging our rule, and avowing it to be a blessing – is a truth that has been sealed by the ceremony just concluded'.[4]

At Lucknow in May the main complaint seems to have been the bad state of the road from Cawnpore, and the traveller by carriage was advised that he would need plenty of soft blankets. But the journey would be worth the discomforts. 'We have large plates of strawberries every morning. Calcutta people might well pay Lucknow a visit. Our hospitality is famous.'[5]

At Jhansi, the little state in Bundelkhand, recently annexed, Captain Alexander Skene, the political agent, was enjoying such sport as the locality offered, unaware that his sepoys were waiting to strike in the name of the widow of the last ruler.

The routines of British life were much the same at other stations. At Cawnpore there was no apprehension of danger among the officers of the sepoy regiments though some minor precautions were taken. At Meerut, some forty miles from Delhi, there were no anxieties at all. And there were good reasons for believing that in case of trouble Meerut would be one of the safest places in the whole of India. Meerut was an important military station which, unlike most other stations, had a strong force of European soldiers, cavalry, infantry and artillery, garrisoned there. Whatever the rumours going around the sepoy lines and the bazaars of the town, if it came to a confrontation the British had ample power to crush a mutiny.

There were certainly agitators at work among the sepoys. One, the commissioner of Meerut reported, 'appeared . . . in April ostensibly as a fakir, riding on an elephant with followers, and having with him horses and native carriages. The frequent visits of the men of the Native regiments to him attracted attention, and he was ordered, through the police, to leave the place; he apparently complied but . . . stayed some time in the Lines of the 20th Native Infantry'.[6] There were the usual outbreaks of arson, the usual seditious letters intercepted. The restlessness among the Indian soldiers was recognised but it was believed to be confined to those who were Hindus. In this the authorities at Meerut were soon disillusioned.

Among the native regiments stationed at Meerut was the 3rd Cavalry. The troopers were predominantly Muslim. Their commander, Colonel Carmichael Smyth, a hard and unpopular officer, returned from leave on 23 April and ordered a parade of ninety men of the regiment for the next day. He would talk to them and they would understand that there was nothing in the cartridge rumour –

28

and in any case, the order had now been given that the paper wrapping need no longer be bitten off but could be torn off by hand. When one of the British officers of the regiment heard of the order for the parade, he immediately wrote to the adjutant: 'Go at once to Smyth and tell him that the men of my troop have requested in a body that the [parade] tomorrow morning may be countermanded, as there is a commotion throughout the native troops about the cartridges . . . This is a most serious matter and we may have the whole regiment in mutiny in half an hour if this be not attended to.'[7]

But Smyth would not listen. It would be an act of cowardice to cancel the parade because of threats. The parade would take place. Smyth did not even consider it necessary to inform the officer commanding the station of the situation. Next morning the ninety men appeared on parade. Smyth informed the troopers that the cartridge bore no grease of any sort; in fact they would be allowed to grease their own. But still, when the cartridges were offered, the men refused to take them. Furious, Smyth rode his horse along the line of men, stopping at each. 'Will you take the cartridges?' Eighty-five men again refused, saying: 'I shall get a bad name if I do so.' Again, Smyth addressed the men. If they took the cartridges, they would win the acclaim of the entire Bengal army. But there was only a sullen silence. Abruptly the colonel rode off and the parade was dismissed.

A court of enquiry was appointed. It reported that the troopers' conduct was due only to fear of public opinion and not from disloyalty either to the colonel or to the government. But matters could not be left there; a court martial had to assemble. When General Hewitt, the divisional commander, heard of the affair he exclaimed to Colonel Smyth: 'Oh, why did you have a parade? My division has kept quiet and if you had only waited another month or so, all would have blown over.' But the machinery of military justice had been set in motion, though it moved very slowly. A court martial could only be authorised by an order of the commander-in-chief. While that was awaited, the eighty-five troopers were dismissed to their Lines. During the week it took for the commander-in-chief's decision to reach Meerut, the feelings of the sepoys lit the sky every night as huts were set on fire and left to burn. Some of the officers tried as best they could to ease the tension among their men. But the majority of British officers preferred to discuss the problem among themselves and came to the conclusion that there was nothing to get upset about.

At last the order arrived for the setting up of a court martial. Fifteen native officers were appointed to sit, ten from regiments stationed at Meerut and five from Delhi; six were Muslims, nine Hindus. One British officer was present to advise on legal and other matters. The accused pleaded not guilty, a few witnesses were examined and with one dissenter the court martial found the case proved. All the accused were sentenced to ten years' hard labour. There was, however, a recommendation for 'favourable consideration on account of the good character which the prisoners had hitherto borne . . . and on account of their having been misled by vague reports regarding the cartridges.' [8]

General Hewitt would not accept the recommendation. The harm had been done in bringing the matter to a court martial at all. Now there was no margin for mercy. As for the fears of the sepoys, soldiers did not have such fears – and even if they did, it was no excuse. Some of the men, Hewitt wrote, 'even had the insolence to desire that firing parades might be deferred till the agitation about cartridges among the native troops had come to a close . . . Even now they attempt to justify so gross an outrage upon discipline, by alleging that they had doubts about the cartridges; there has been no acknowledgement of error, no expression of regret, no pleading for mercy . . .' [9] Eleven of the younger troopers were to have their sentences halved, but that was that, and everyone seemed agreed. The presiding officer of the court martial wrote: 'You will hear no more of mutinies.' [10]

A punishment parade was ordered for the next day, 9 May, when the guilty would be publicly humiliated before their comrades by being shackled with fetters. That night, a young officer of the 3rd Cavalry, Lieutenant Hugh Gough, sat in the darkness of his veranda listening to the sounds of the city and the military lines. He thought back over a day which was the most disturbing he had ever spent.

It had been dark and heavy, with low clouds, and a dry hot wind had blown across the parade ground. There had been some four thousand men there, drawn up to form three sides of a hollow square. What a sight they had been – the shining brass helmets and leather breeches of the Bengal Artillery officers; the black horsehair plumes of the Dragoon Guards; the olive green of the 60th Native Rifles; the silver grey of his own 3rd Cavalry; and, of course, the scarlet coats and white collars of the Native Infantry. To the casual eye it must have been just another of the ceremonial parades which the commander loved to mount. But no eye at that parade had been casual. All had been wary, some angry, many a mirror of fear. The Indian troops carried their arms, but everyone knew that their ammunition pouches were empty – by order. The British troops had their rifles, the new Enfield rifles, loaded, and they pointed them at their Indian comrades.

On the fourth, open side of the square stood the eighty-five sepoys. They were clad in their uniforms, but their feet were bare and they carried no weapons. Around them stood a guard of British soldiers, themselves wary and hard of face. A British officer read aloud from a paper, but the dry wind seemed to blow his words away like fallen leaves. An Indian officer, with no flicker of emotion, translated into Hindustani and the words appeared to touch all the sepoys present. Then there was silence – and afterwards soldiers ripped the buttons from the sepoys' uniforms and the coats from their backs. Armourers with tools and shackles came forward and slowly began to fit fetters on the condemned men.

Among the condemned were many who had served the British

government in harsh battles and strange places, and had never before wavered in their allegiance. As the fetters were placed upon them, they lifted up their hands and implored the general to have mercy on them, but seeing no hope there they turned to their comrades and reproached them for standing aside and allowing them to be disgraced. There was not a sepoy present who did not feel indignation rising in his throat. Many of them were in tears, but what could they have done in face of the loaded field guns and rifles, and the glittering sabres of the Dragoons? For a moment it had seemed to Lieutenant Gough as if the sepoys were about to attack the British with their bare hands; but the prisoners were marched off and the tension eased.

Gough had gone down to the temporary jail and had been deeply shocked by the grief of the men, who had begged him to save them. Now, in the dark of the veranda, he wondered what would happen next. His reflections were shattered by a rustle in the darkness. A figure approached silently, almost furtively; but it was no thief. A whisper identified it as a native officer of his own troop who had come, he said, to discuss the troop's accounts. Gough found this puzzling. It was Saturday, a night for leisure, not for routine business. Then suddenly the true reason for the visit came pouring out. The lieutenant-sahib should know that tomorrow, Sunday, the men would mutiny – all of them, even the cavalry, the sahib's own men. They would break open the jail and release their comrades. Murder was planned, murder and fire.

After the man left, Gough went to the Mess and informed Colonel Smyth. His story was greeted with laughter and contempt, and he was told that he should be ashamed of listening to such an idle tale. But Gough was convinced, and he made another attempt – he went to the brigadier commanding the station. The reception was no better there. If no one else was worried, why should Lieutenant Gough concern himself?

The next day was 10 May, and all Gough could see when he went out on his veranda was a sea of flame on the horizon. Galloping down to the cavalry lines, he found 'a thousand sepoys dancing and leaping frantically about, calling and yelling to each other', and blazing away with their muskets in all directions.

By nightfall Meerut was a city of horror. British officers had been cut down by their own men, women had been violated – not by men, but by sticks of burning tow and thatch thrust far into their bodies. Everywhere there was chaos and confusion. Senior officers seemed struck by paralysis. There were as many British as native troops in Meerut, and the British had artillery, yet nothing was organised. Some of the younger officers did what they could, but the mutineers broke open the jail and, unhindered, set off for Delhi, forty miles away to the south-west. No one pursued them.[11]

When news of the outbreak at Meerut reached Calcutta there was panic. The majority of the European inhabitants of the City of Palaces were non-officials – businessmen and the like. They were known by the more worldy soldiers and civil servants as 'ditchers', because most of them had rarely travelled outside Calcutta and seldom went even beyond the old defensive line known as the Maratha Ditch. They knew nothing about Indians, except those with whom they did business, who formed a growing middle class not so very different from themselves. Safe, as they thought, in their great houses, they relied upon the government for their protection. But suddenly the government's power was in doubt. At Barrackpur, only a night's march from the centre of the city, men whom they had once looked upon as the trusted guardians of life and property had turned into potential despoilers and murderers. There was, too, a fear 'dominant over all, that the vast and varied population of the Native suburbs and bazaars would rise against the white people, release the prisoners in the jails, and gorge themselves with the plunder of the great commercial capital of India'.[12]

The atmosphere of impending doom was such that 'men went about with revolvers in their carriages, and trained their [servants] to load quickly and fire low. The ships and steamers in the rivers have been crowded with families seeking refuge from the attack which was nightly expected, and everywhere a sense of insecurity prevailed.'[13]

No one was reassured by the proclamation Lord Canning issued on 16 May warning Indians not to be deceived by alarmist rumours. 'The Government of India,' one passage read, 'has invariably treated the religious feelings of all its subjects with careful respect. The Governor-General in Council has declared that it will never cease to do so. He now repeats that declaration, and he emphatically proclaims that the Government of India entertains no design to interfere with the Religion or Caste and nothing has been, or will be done by the Government to affect the free exercise of the observances of Religion or Caste by every class of people . . . The Government of India has never deceived its subjects, therefore the Governor-General in Council now calls upon them to refuse their belief to seditious lies.'[14]

The British in Calcutta wanted action, not exhortation. Above all, what they needed was precise and categoric denial of the many rumours that washed around the city. 'One of the last reports,' wrote Lord Canning on 20 May, 'is that I have ordered beef to be thrown into the tanks [artificial pools] to pollute the caste of all Hindus who bathe there, and that on the Queen's birthday all the grain shops are to be closed, in order to drive the people to eat unclean food. Men, who ought to have heads on their shoulders, are gravely asking that each fable should be contradicted by proclamation as it arises . . . I have already taken the only step I consider advisable, in the sense of refutation of these and like rumours, and patience, firmness, and I hope a speedy return of the deluded to commonsense, will do the rest.'[15]

The governor-general's determination to keep calm, to carry on as normal, was no satisfaction to the British. Lady Canning could take her evening drive with only a small escort – that was her own responsibility – but surely it was a mistake to pretend that nothing had happened? Canning did not agree. On 25 May he gave a ball at Government House to celebrate the Queen's birthday, even though rumours had been rife in the bazaar that, on that day, attempts would be made – what kind of attempts no one quite knew – to convert all Hindus to Christianity. The celebratory *feu de joie* for the Queen was not abandoned, but it was fired from muskets, not from the new rifles. Some Europeans, fearing that the gathering would be used as an opportunity to murder all the leading members of the community, stayed away. One young lady hired two English sailors to sit up in her house and protect her on the night of the ball, 'but they got tipsy, and frightened her more than imaginary enemies'.[16]

A few days later, the sudden sound of what was thought to be gunfire rolled over the city at two o'clock in the morning. 'Many thought the Alipur jail had been broken open. Many gentlemen armed themselves and got carriages ready for the ladies to fly to the Fort. On going into the veranda I was thankful to see a great display of fireworks going up, which was the cause of all the noise. It was the marriage of one of the Mysore princes.'[17]

Canning found it rather pathetic. 'All I can say,' he wrote to a member of the Board of Control in London, 'is that in my life I never came across such a set of old women – some of them with swords by their sides – as those who fetch and carry the news of this town among the clubs and gossiping "tiffin" rooms of their acquaintance. Men, soldiers, whose authority on matters relating to the Army and the Sepoys is readily credited, and whose words are caught up by Newspaper caterers, are spreading not reports only – but opinions as to the state of things present and future, which makes me ashamed for Englishmen – and it is not the shame only, there is mischief in it – the example will be catching. Hitherto the merchants (even the native merchants, greatly as they hate the Sepoys) and the non-official community have (most of them) shown sense and calmness. But how long this will last if our officers and officials crawl about with their tails between their legs frightening themselves and everybody else with their whinings I will not say.'[18]

It was probably for this reason that Canning refused offers from the Calcutta Masonic Lodge, the European trade associations, and the French and Armenian communities, to enlist a volunteer corps. It was not that he did not think the defence of Calcutta important, but only that there were other priorities. At Delhi the rebels had found something that might unite the people of India against the British, for it seemed that the long-dead Moghul dynasty was emerging like a phoenix from the fire. 'If the rebels at Delhi are crushed before the flame spreads,' he wrote to Sir John Lawrence in Lahore, 'all will go well.'[19] Lawrence agreed with him. Long before Canning's letter had reached him, he had been bombarding the commander-in-chief with letters and telegrams, beseeching him to retake what had once been, and now seemed to have become again, the Navel of the World.

PART TWO

The city and the ridge

Let not a single effort be made to succour or bring off the guards at the magazine or the treasury; giving up everything for lost ... let all this happen in Hindustan on the 2nd of June, instead of among the Afghan mountains on the 2nd of November, and does any sane man doubt that twenty-four hours would swell the hundreds of rebels into thousands; and that, if such conduct on our part lasted for a week, every ploughshare in the Delhi States would be turned into a sword?

Henry Lawrence: *Defence of Macnaghten.* 1843.

CHAPTER ONE

NAVEL OF THE WORLD

In Delhi, there lived a king without a kingdom, surrounded by the physical and psychological remains of a line of conquerors which had once ruled the whole of India, memories a little dimmed, a little tarnished, showing signs of the years of decay but real with the reality of dead youth, embalmed in longing and regret. The past had been magnificent and the present was a constant reminder of it. Shah Jahan, fifth emperor of the Moghul dynasty, a house which traced its ancestry to that great conqueror, Tamerlane, had moved his capital to Delhi in the middle of the seventeenth century. The ruins of six cities, tangible remains of other great kings, surrounded his new one, bright with red sandstone, the smooth luxury of marble, and the richness of gilded domes. Poets and painters, workers in precious stones, made Delhi the envy of lesser rulers, its buildings, like those of Shah Jahan's near contemporary, Louis XIV, at Versailles, a subject for the flattery of imitation. The 'navel of the world'.

But within a century and a half of its founding the brightness of imperial Delhi had been sadly dimmed, the great empire of which it had once been the proud centre tattered by conquerors and shorn by rebels. In 1739 the Persian, Nadir Shah, had sacked the city, taking with him when he left the famous Peacock Throne, heavy with pearls and gems. Nearly fifty years later a petty chieftain had stripped the imperial city of its wealth, the silver roof of the great audience hall, the remaining treasures of the royal library all plundered, and the emperor himself blinded by needles thrust into his eyes.

Until 1803 that same emperor survived in his palace, the puppet of a Maratha prince. In that year another conqueror appeared in Delhi. On 16 September General Lord Lake, commander-in-chief of the army of the English East India Company, arrived at the palace for an audience with the emperor Shah Alam. The emperor's heir accompanied him on an elephant. As the commander-in-chief approached the audience hall, night had fallen. The hall was lit by flickering torches. And there was the emperor, 'the descendant of the great Akbar and the victorious Aurangzeb . . . an object of pity, blind and aged, stripped of authority, and reduced to poverty, seated under a tattered canopy, the fragment of regal state, and the mockery of human pride.'[1]

From this time onwards, the last Moghul emperor – and his decendants – remained in the palace of his ancestors, pensioners of the British. The then governor-general, Lord Wellesley, had wanted to remove Shah Alam and his heir from the imperial city, into exile in some other part of British India. But he had not been prepared to use force, and Shah Alam had no intention of leaving Delhi voluntarily

– that would have been tantamount to a denial of his imperial authority. The British paid his pension regularly, but they would sign no treaty with the fallen monarch, nor would they accept that their position in relation to him was anything other than that of overlord. Unlike previous conquerors, they did not treat the emperor as a puppet. Instead, they regarded him as an idol at whose shrine they did not worship themselves, but whom they thought it unwise to remove in case the faithful should be offended.

British policy was really a product of the particular British view of political reality. They regarded the emperor, whom they now called 'king of Delhi', as merely a pensioner, maintained out of sentiment and ignored out of policy. Such an attitude was, however, quite alien to the Indian political consciousness. As long as the king remained in his palace – pensioner or not, with or without real power – the dignity of his position somehow remained untarnished. However nominal his authority, the authority of his name could not be denied.

Because of what can best be described as an attack of romanticism, the British decided to act out what they thought was only a charade, a courteous and well-meaning exercise in make-believe designed to soften the blow that their victory had dealt to the Moghul dynasty. In certain circumstances, too, they believed that the Moghul name was politically valuable, especially that of Shah Alam. For thirty years after his death they continued to issue coinage bearing his name, as if it were a talisman. But it was no charade for the king and his family, nor for others who resented British power. The king, they said, was still king. Even the British admitted as much and acted in his name. It was a situation vibrant with danger, a danger which was compounded over the years. Until Shah Alam's death in 1806, there was some excuse for the British and the charade. Afterwards there was none, for with him died the last link with the empire's unconquered past. Within the walls of his palace, the king was permitted to exercise ruling powers. The inhabitants, servants, retainers, tradesmen, were his direct subjects, and members of the imperial family had immunity from British law. The ceremonial of the court was maintained. Officials still bore the high-sounding titles of their predecessors and the formal rituals of court etiquette were rigidly adhered to. When the British Resident – the real ruler – went to visit the king, he too followed traditional protocol, dismounting in an inner courtyard and standing respectfully in the royal presence.[2]

The deference to this shadow of a king was continued during the reign of Shah Alam's successor and into that of the next heir. Some British officials complained about, and frequently advocated the ending of, this peculiar and potentially dangerous position. But no action was taken until, in 1842, the then governor-general ordered the stoppage of nazars, or ceremonial gifts, normally offered to the king four times a year. On these occasions, the representatives of the dominant power had paid homage to the conquered, taking off their shoes in the imperial presence, offering a bag of gold coins, and humbly enquiring after his majesty's health and prosperity. 'For the first time,' wrote the last British official to make such a presentation, 'I myself became alive to the impropriety of an act which in reality made Queen Victoria, in Eastern estimation at least, hold her Indian possessions as a mere feudatory and vassal of the imperial house of Delhi.'[3]

The main conflicts between the king and the British were over the amount of his pension, an ostensibly substantial one of Rs. 100,000 a month, and the approval of an heir. Shah Alam's successor, Akbar Shah, wanted to disinherit his eldest son. The British would have none of it, irritated by intrigue and by the king's effrontery in addressing the governor-general as 'favoured son and servant'! But the affair did produce one of the few precise definitions of the king's position as seen by the British. 'We conceive,' wrote the Court of Directors of the Company in 1811, 'that our power in India is at this day of a character too substantial to require that we should resort to the hazardous expedient of endeavouring to add to its stability by borrowing from the king of Delhi any portion of authority which we are competent to exercise in our own name.'

This was all very well, but the actual problems of paying deference inside the palace while disregarding it outside were serious. The Resident, the senior British official in Delhi, did his best to ignore the king except on ceremonial occasions. But the outside world, the Indian world – so preoccupied with precedents and symbols – would not do the same. The king may indeed have been a shadow, but because the British did not choose to depose him the shadow had sharp edges. To those in India who feared and hated the British, the king of Delhi remained the symbol of ancient legitimacy.

In 1857 that symbol had occupied his powerless throne for twenty years. The prince, whose father had tried to bar him from the inheritance, had succeeded under the reign name of Bahadur Shah II, an ominous title, as the predecessor who had borne the name first had been the last of the Moghul rulers to exercise real power. On his accession, Bahadur Shah II had assumed the same titles as his father – Badshah (emperor), and Ghazi (holy warrior). These empty honorifics disguised, in 1857, a man in his early eighties who had none of the qualities of either an emperor or a warrior. He did have dignity, a phantom dignity suitable to a phantom court, a dignity compounded in the main of attention to protocol and precedent.

Bahadur Shah had one talent. He was a poet. While still heir apparent he addressed a great English official with a complimentary verse.

The glad tidings of your coming like the north wind, has made green the garden of my hope.
The bird of my heart endeavours to fly with the desire of seeing your resplendent garden, but (alas) he has not wings . . .
On the day of the Creation, Heaven threw to thee the lot of fortune which was to open the knot of my entangled affairs.[4]

During his reign he was constantly to find relaxation in poetry and published four volumes of it. This talented but superstitious man –

it was said that he was convinced that he could transform himself into a fly or gnat [5] – needed some relaxation, for he suffered from the demands of his family. He had asked the British for an increase in his pension, but this they would only grant if he would voluntarily agree to give up his palace and his title. This he would not do. Only one other subject seems to have interested him. He wanted the succession to go to a son, Jawan Bakht, by a favourite young wife, Zinat Mahal. There were several with better claims and the British would not agree to recognition, though Bahadur Shah never missed an opportunity to press his case.

The aim of the British remained the final extinction of everything at Delhi which maintained the fiction of continuity from the Moghul empire. When Dalhousie become governor-general, it seemed that at last there was someone who would achieve that end. Dalhousie neither understood nor accepted the veneration for tradition which was entrenched in Indian society. Politically, the king of Delhi was an anachronism. 'It is not expedient,' Dalhousie wrote in 1849, 'that there should be, even in name, a rival in the person of a Sovereign whose ancestors once held the paramountcy we now possess.' Dalhousie was convinced that the king could not really endanger the British position, even though 'the intrigues of which he might, and not unfrequently has been made the nucleus, might incommode and vex us.' [6]

The Court of Directors felt that the removal of the king would be too radical a change. It must wait for the death of Bahadur Shah. In 1849, when the recognised heir apparent died, the Resident came to an arrangement with his successor, Fakir-ud-din, that on his father's death he would retain the title of prince and give up the palace of the Red Fort. This agreement was secret, but not for long. Eight years later, Fakir-ud-din also died, possibly from poison, after eating a dish of curry. Again the old king pressed the claim of Jawan Bakht. Again it was rejected. On the eve of the rebellion, those in the palace knew with certainty that the days of the dynasty were numbered.

But the city itself remained, in its mixture of splendour and decay, curiously brilliant and alive. The approaches from the south had changed very little since that peregrinating bishop of Calcutta, Reginald Heber, had passed through them thirty years before. It was, he wrote, 'a very aweful scene of desolation, ruins after ruins, tombs after tombs. fragments of brickwork, freestone, granite, and marble, scattered everywhere over a soil naturally rocky and barren, without cultivation, except in one or two small spots, and without a single tree . . . The ruins really extended as far as the eye could see'.[7] But to the west and north, the landscape changed to suburbs with houses and walled gardens and groves of trees, with the river Jumna shining in the distance.

The city itself sat with its back to the river.* The walls were seven miles in circumference, of sandstone, twenty-four feet high, pierced by eleven gates. Once through the gates, the Western visitor would

* A map of Delhi appears in Appendix 5, page 184.

40

find all he required for an oriental romance. There were 'gardens full of shading trees, brilliant flowers, lovely fountains of white marble, which cast up their bright waters amongst the shining palaces, with sculptured mosques and minarets, like obelisks of pearl shooting into the sky whose colour would shame the brightest turquoise that ever graced a sultan's finger.' The streets were crowded, the shops of the bazaar stuffed with luxuries. The people themselves seemed to be of all races and professions, because 'even now the best dancing-women, the bird-tamers, the snake charmers, the Persian musicians, the jugglers, congregate from every part, not only of India, but of Asia.'[8]

But there were people of more consequence among Delhi's 200,000 inhabitants than these characters in an Arabian Nights' entertainment. Under the patronage of a poet king, Delhi was the last refuge of a traditional culture. There were painters and theologians, philosophers, even men who were interested in Western science. And in Ghalib, Delhi could boast the greatest Urdu poet of his time. In fact, during the reign of Bahadur Shah, Delhi had gone through a renaissance – but it was short-lived, like an exotic flower on a dying tree.

The romantic traveller had not noticed, or had at least not told his readers, that behind the façade of a bustling city lurked a terrible decay. The great palace which dominated the walled city with its even higher walls – nearly sixty feet of stone and marble – still seemed barely touched by the ravages of time and events. An occasional cannonball had chipped some of the sandstone and marble here and there, but nothing more. Inside, however, much of the glory had vanished. Little had been done to keep the vast number of palace buildings in any reasonable state of repair. In fact, it was beyond the king's resources to do so. The palace was really a city of streets and houses, some made of solid masonry, some only of mats of plaited straw. Inside the palace were about five thousand men and women. Some were servants, some were obscure relatives of the king. These distant relations, descendants of former emperors, lived in the most appalling conditions. At one time their ancestors had been confined to the palace to prevent them from becoming a focus of rebellion. When the British arrived, they refused to leave, as there was certainly no way in which they could earn a living outside the walls.

These people were known as *salatin*, were of the blood royal, and lived in a special quarter, in nakedness and near starvation. Relatives more closely connected to the king fared better, but there was never enough money to go round. Visitors always commented on the fact that large areas of the palace were neglected. Dirt and filth were everywhere, and it was generally assumed that the whole palace was some vast slum. It seems likely, however, that the private apartments of the king and the princes were not only in good repair but comparatively luxurious. None of the British was ever able to penetrate them to find out, so their impressions of the outer courts were taken as accurate descriptions of the entire palace.

On the whole, the British in Delhi and in Calcutta were prepared to dismiss the Moghul and his palace as rather a farce. Earlier, men

41

had been attracted by Delhi, but harder and more inflexibly Christian soldiers and civilians had followed them. For these, the palace was a 'great sty of pollution', full of lust and incest, torturings and sudden, terrible deaths. The pity was that they were not far wrong.

The British in Delhi – and there were very few – gossiped about the palace but tried to keep their own lives as similar as possible to that of their own class in Britain. There was Simon Fraser, the Resident and Commissioner, who lived in the nostalgically named Ludlow Castle outside the city walls. There was Sir Theophilus Metcalfe, the magistrate, member of a family which had been intimately and influentially connected with Delhi since the British arrived in 1803. There was Captain Douglas, the commander of the king's palace guard and supporter of the gallant title 'Keeper of the Fort'. Among the rest were a few English officers of the sepoy regiments who were stationed at the cantonments to the north-west of the city, and some non-commissioned officers. The Reverend Mr Jennings, a missionary accompanied by his daughter, had been in Delhi since 1852 and, despite opposition from Hindus and Muslims, had been practising his trade. He had also established a small school for English and Eurasian children.

Mr Jennings, on account of his cloth, was acceptable on the higher levels of British society in Delhi. So, too, was Mr George Beresford, manager of the Delhi and London Bank. But shopkeepers were not. Nor were the members of what was known as the uncovenanted civil service, men who had been appointed in India, not in London, and were often of mixed blood. Doctors certainly were accepted, the professors at the Delhi College, even the journalists who ran the two English-language papers, the *Gazette* and the *Sketch Book*. Without them, life would have been very difficult. The annual ball, on the Queen's birthday, would have echoed mournfully in the Assembly Rooms had it been confined to the top level of the social hierarchy.

Though relations with – and within – the palace were difficult for the British, there was considerable social contact between the British and the Indian aristocracy. The meeting of these two élites, that of the British and that of old Delhi, could best be seen when Sir Theophilus Metcalfe gave one of his regular afternoon receptions. These were held at Metcalfe House, which had been built by Sir Theophilus's father. It was a large house with a Classical colonnade and a veranda some twenty feet wide round all four sides. The interior was furnished in great luxury, with marble statues and elegant furniture. The library contained 25,000 volumes and the walls of the house were literally covered with fine engravings.

In the cold weather, Sir Theophilus would hold his reception in the magnificent gardens. On the river front of Metcalfe House there was a terraced pleasaunce. Gardeners had seen to it that there was not a leaf out of place or a blade of grass untrimmed. 'Long lines of English annuals in pots bordered the broad walks evenly, the scentless gardenia festooned the rows of cypress in disciplined freedom, the roses had not a fallen petal, though the palms swept their long fringes above them boldly, and strange perfumed creepers leapt to the branches of the forest trees. In one glade, beside an artificial lake, some ladies in gay dresses were competing for an archery prize. On a brick dais close to the house the band of a native regiment was playing national airs, and beside it stood a gorgeous marquee of Kashmir shawls with silver poles and Persian carpets; the whole – stock and block – having belonged to some potentate or another, dead, banished, or annexed. Here those who wished for it found rest in English chairs or oriental divans; and here, contrasting with their host and his friends, harmonising with the Kashmir shawl marquee, stood a group of guests from the palace.'

Among the guests were members of the royal family. 'Here was Mirza Moghul, the king's eldest son, and his two supporters, all with lynx eyes for a sign, a hint, of favour or disfavour. And here – a sulky sickly looking lad of eighteen – was [Jawan Bakht, the queen's] darling, dressed gorgeously and blazing with jewels which left no doubt as to who would be the heir apparent if she had her way. Prince [Abu Bakr], however, scented, effeminate, watched the proceedings with bright eyes; giving the ladies unabashed admiration and after a time actually strolling away to listen to the music. Finally, however, drifting to the stables to gamble with the grooms over a quail fight.

'Then there were lesser lights. [Ahsanullah Khan], the physician, his lean plausible face and white thin beard suiting his black gown and skull cap, discussed the system of Greek medicine with the Scotch surgeon, whose fluent, trenchant Hindustani had an Aberdonian twang . . . A few rich bankers curiously obsequious to the youngest ensign, and one or two pensioners owing their invitations to loyal service made up the company.'[10]

Though some British officials allowed themselves to think that Delhi might become the centre of a rebellion against their rule, nobody seems to have considered the possibility of a mutiny in the Company's army there. Though the largest ammunition store in upper India was located at Delhi, the only worry that crossed the minds of the authorities was that its position *inside* the city walls was dangerous – an accidental explosion was all that they feared. A large amount of powder and shot had been moved out in 1854 and centred at a new magazine three miles outside the city, but guns and ammunitions remained in the city store.

Both the city store and the magazine in the suburbs were guarded by sepoys. There were, in fact, no British troops in Delhi at all. Their presence might have upset the king and the people. In any case, forty miles away at Meerut were substantial numbers of European troops who could be brought to bear on Delhi in a matter of hours. Even when the state of unrest in the Bengal army became obvious to the most blinkered, nothing was done about Delhi.

There had been ample evidence of tension and rumour inside the city. Indian newspapers were full of vague prophecies. The Shah of Persia was coming with a great army, supported by the Russians. A proclamation of the Shah had been stuck up on a wall in the city but torn down by order of the magistrate. No one queried whether it was genuine, but many believed it. After a hundred years, British rule was about to end, no one knew how. The question of the greased cartridges was discussed in the bazaars and, undoubtedly, in the palace. In the sepoy lines, the same pattern as elsewhere was forming – a bungalow set on fire, an air of sullen, conditional obedience.

The morning of 11 May seemed little different from any other. Muslims hurried to eat their first meal before the sun rose, as it was still the fast of Ramadan and no food or drink was allowed the faithful between sunrise and sunset. Hindus were bathing in the Jumna, ready to worship the eternal wonder of the sun. The professors at the College were preparing another day in which the wonders of Western scholarship would be imparted to a few willing Indians. Simon Fraser, the commissioner, was still in bed. In the military lines, the first bugles had blown and the first of the Meerut mutineers were crossing the bridge of boats which spanned the Jumna.

The news of their arrival first reached a senior British official, John Hutchinson, and sent him running to the commissioner's house. Bahadur Shah, sitting in a room whose walls were of latticed marble, heard the sound of the horses' hooves on the bridge, and going out to an open turret which overlooked the bridge was seen and hailed by the sepoys. There was so much noise – so much menacing noise – that the old king withdrew and sent for Captain Douglas. When Douglas arrived and told the sepoys to move on, they did so. But only as far as the nearest city gate. This was closed, but another was soon opened from the inside. The news of the rising at Meerut had already reached the city, and the men of Meerut were welcomed almost as liberators.

The first to die in the city was an Indian Christian, Dr Chamanlal. Many others were to follow.

The sepoys made for the palace, ran through the gates, drove their horses over the flowerbeds and through the fountains. Where was the emperor? they called.

Bahadur Shah waited in an inner room. Douglas had not returned, for the very good reason that he was dead. So too were Simon Fraser and John Hutchinson, the Reverend Mr Jennings, his daughter, and her young woman friend. They had all been murdered at Douglas's quarters within the palace. In the city the mobs were already chasing the few British who remained. Mr Beresford at the bank, the journalists in their press room. But the news had not reached Bahadur Shah. When the mutineers called upon him to assume command, he temporised. Even when he heard about the murders, caution insisted that the British would surely have sent the European soldiers from Meerut in pursuit of the sepoys. But they did not come, nor did the troops stationed outside the city – or at least not to crush the mutineers. The 54th Native Infantry followed their commander as far as the Kashmir gate and then cut him down and shot the other officers. By nightfall the mutiny was complete.

Among all the noises of the city that day, two had stood out against the terrible murmur of the mobs as they chased their victims through the streets. The elegant church of St James, built by a Eurasian adventurer in imitation of St Paul's in London, had been attacked and ransacked. The bells had been given a peal before the ropes were cut and they went crashing to the ground. At least that symbol of the conquerors' faith had been treated as its believers had tried to treat the faith of Hindus and Muslims. Not far away, in the ammunition store, Lieutenant Willoughby and eight others were preparing for a last gesture. As the sepoys rushed forward to attack, a fuse was fired and with a tremendous blast the building exploded outwards. In the confusion six of the defenders managed to escape. But the gesture was only a gesture. The great magazine outside the city was handed over intact to the mutineers by its sepoy guard.

The British, even the Indian Christians, had been either murdered or driven from the city. But unlike Delhi, other places were to have some warning of the spread of rebellion. Two young Eurasian signallers in the telegraph office were able to contact Ambala, Lahore, Rawalpindi and Peshawar. 'The sepoys have come in from Meerut and are burning everything. Mr Todd the Telegraph Master is dead and we hear several Europeans – we must shut up.'

For the next few weeks Delhi was left alone. The British seemed to have disappeared from the face of India. In the palace the old king had been hailed as emperor of Hindustan. Age and temperament urged caution, his sons did not. Yet some form of discipline had to be reimposed on the chaotic city. On 12 May the king called a council of his advisors and to it invited some of the local nobles and important men of the city. Business was at a standstill, the streets were unsafe as criminals and others had taken the opportunity to loot, under the pretence of searching for Europeans and Christians. The sepoys had to be found places to camp and money to pay them, and the king's treasury was empty. The king appointed a governor for the city, his son Mirza Moghul became commander-in-chief, and other military titles were conferred on some of the princes. The king himself, with great reluctance, went out into the streets on an elephant in the hope of restoring confidence and order. 'From house to house the unwilling king was distracted by cries and petitions – now from the servants of the Europeans who had been murdered, now from the shopkeepers whose shops had been plundered . . . all looked to the king for immediate redress.'[10]

There was not much that Bahadur Shah could do. He was old, with no experience of the world outside his palace. No doubt the restoration of an empire never forgotten would have its appeal, but Bahadur Shah was not altogether a fool. Neither were his closest advisers. One at least – Ahsanullah Khan, the king's physician – got off a message to the lieutenant-governor of the North-Western Provinces, asking for aid. But the imperial family would not permit caution. A dream had apparently come true after all the years of waiting. The revived empire now had teeth, an army, well trained in the European fashion.

So European, in fact, that the new dispensation looked remarkably like the old. The sepoys, or at least those of them who saw more in their mutiny than a purely military rebellion, realised that some kind of order must be imposed. They had called upon Bahadur Shah to symbolise the legitimacy of a purely *Indian* dominion. It was, perhaps, a matter of sentiment being adapted to circumstance. But sentiment could not consolidate gain.

The army set up a court, or 'military and civil management committee' to 'do away with mismanagement and to remove disorder from the civil and military establishments'. The committee consisted of ten members, six of whom were elected from the army and given responsibility for purely military affairs. Four were given control of civil affairs. The titles were all from the enemy; the soldiers were not called by the high-sounding names of the Moghul empire, but by the English ones of colonel and brigadier; the civil administrators were called commissioner and collector. The president of the court was to be elected by the members, and he was responsible to the commander-in-chief who had to approve all decisions. In case of conflict between the commander-in- chief and the court, the matter was to be referred to the king, whose decision was absolute and must be accepted.[11]

The court was, in theory at least, an essentially democratic institution. But it achieved nothing, for no one accepted its authority. Many of the sepoys would not listen to its orders and continued their plunder of the city. Some insisted, vocally, that members of the royal family were in touch with the British. The queen, Zinat Mahal, was specifically charged on more than one occasion, and when guns on one of the bastions were found to have been tampered with Ahsanullah Khan was said to have sabotaged them. When the king had difficulty in raising money, the sepoys plundered rich men whom they alleged were friendly towards the British. In effect, anarchy and disorder prevailed.

But the court did have some concept of what the whole affair was about. It saw the conflict with the British as a clash of faiths, of one world of ideas against another. A proclamation issued with royal permission and, probably, approval, made that quite clear. It was addressed to *all* Indians:

'To all Hindoos and Mussulmans, Citizens and Servants of Hindostan, the Officers of the Army now at Delhi and Meerut send greeting:

'It is well known that in these days all the English have entertained these evil designs – first, to destroy the religion of the whole Hindostani army, and then to make the people by compulsion Christians. Therefore we, solely on account of our religion, have combined with the people, and have not spared alive one infidel, and have re-established the Delhi dynasty on these terms.'

The proclamation went on to offer inducements, double payment for supplies, and a reminder that officers must give a receipt for goods. It called upon all to 'unite in this struggle, and, following the instructions of some respectable people, keep themselves secure, so that good order may be maintained, the poorer classes kept contented,

46

and they themselves be exalted to rank and dignity.' There was an appeal to post the proclamation far and wide throughout India, 'in some conspicuous place (but prudently to avoid detection) that all true Hindoos and Mussulmans may be alive and watchful, and strike a blow with a sword before giving circulation to it.'[12]

It was a manifesto of – to use a modern term – a movement of liberation. There were to be others. But as in later times the gap between the ideologists and the rank and file was wide and deep. The slowness of the British to react to the fall of Delhi gave the rebels ample time to establish themselves, emotionally as well as physically. But the opportunity was not exploited. By 8 June it had been lost forever. On that day, watchers on the city walls saw flames rising from the old military lines. The British had returned to Delhi, and in an extravagant – and, as it proved, foolish – gesture, had set fire to the buildings that had once housed their Indian soldiers. It was a symbol of defiance to the imperial city.

CHAPTER TWO

THE MIND OF GENERAL NICHOLSON

The news from Delhi reached Peshawar in the Punjab on the evening of 11 May. Peshawar was the watchtower of the Indo-Afghan border, an area turbulent with old memories and present hates. The relations of the British with the Amir of Afghanistan were good, if only commercial. He had been dethroned by the British during their disastrous military adventure in his country nearly twenty years before, after which they had been compelled to allow him back. Peshawar had once belonged to Afghanistan, and the British were not quite sure that the Amir had really been reconciled to its loss. If the British were seen to be having problems with their army, he might consider making trouble in the border regions, peopled as they were with warlike tribes who would not hesitate if there was a prospect of loot.

The British had at Peshawar some 16,000 troops of all arms. But only 3,000 of these were European. There were also some remarkable men whose character and exploits had given to the conquest and administration of the Punjab an aura of holy war, muscular Christians who would not have felt out of place in Cromwell's New Army. They soon became heroes for the Victorians, whose thirst for symbols of greatness grew with the generations. Memoirs and biographies constantly gave the impression that these men worked almost exclusively for the Lord their God, and that the only law book they possessed was the Old Testament. This, however, was the propaganda of empire. It might have been better if it had not been so – for then their brutalities, their seeming indifference to the sufferings they caused, might be explained as individual megalomania rather than as the accepted norm of a highly efficient and carefully regulated system.

There had certainly been a time without system, a period which had ended less than ten years before. For four years before their final annexation of the Punjab in 1849, the British had operated in double government with the heirs of the last Sikh ruler of the country.

'What days those were! How Henry Lawrence would send us off to great distances: Edwardes to Bannu, Nicholson to Peshawar, Abbott to Hazara, Lumsden to somewhere else . . . giving us no more helpful directions than these, "Settle the country; make the people happy; and take care there are no rows".'[1]

Many still in the Punjab, still in places of authority, looked back on those times as a Golden Age. Some resented its passing. One such was Lieutenant-Colonel John Nicholson, in 1857 deputy to Colonel Herbert Edwardes, commissioner of Peshawar.

The Punjab system was not merely a technique of government but

48

an instrument for rapid modernisation. It thrust the framework of a civilised state upon a bewildered peasantry, with immense speed and energy. 'Order and firm rule established . . . disbandment of feudal troops, and the substitution of a strong and disciplined police; a simple, cheap and rapid system of Justice between man and man; a stern protection of life and property from violence and fraud . . . freedom of religion, freedom of trade, freedom of speech and writing, freedom of locomotion; the foundation of a system of national education; the lining out of roads, the construction of bridges . . . the establishment of Posts and Telegraphs; the encouragement of commerce and manufactures by the removal of every possible restriction.' It was no wonder the author of this rather breathless catalogue of achievement thought he should congratulate himself. 'When I think of all that has been done, when I recall the state of the country before the annexation, and the marvellous change that came over it in the course of so few years, I cannot but regret, that such men are not found for the other dark places of this globe.'[2]

With such definitions of purpose, and even of achievement, both Edwardes and Nicholson would have agreed. Edwardes had no doubts. He was cheerful in his sureness, and enormously self-confident. He was not only a convinced Christian but one who was never at a loss to explain the meaning of an obscure text or to reconcile apparent contradictions in sacred writ. In fact, he was a shallow but capable man, jovial, versatile, a well integrated if rather dull personality. Nicholson, on the other hand, had doubts despite his agreement.

Nicholson was quite unlike Edwardes. His was a complex and tortured personality. Modern apologists have tried to pretend that he was untypical of his fellows, but deeper investigation reveals the probability that he was more representative than the rest of the highly varnished figures in the pantheon of nineteenth-century British India. Nicholson was a homosexual, a repressed homosexual, disgusted by his own inclinations and one who translated his disgust into a violence manic in its manifestations.[3]

Nicholson approved of the modernising – he would have called it the 'civilising' process. Indeed, he was part of it. His functions as a military officer in civil employment were to be the law giver, the law enforcer, and the director of public works. These duties he carried out publicly, beating acceptance into his unwilling wards with the whip and the sword. Peace, or at least order, there must be. If the indigenous élite would not enforce it, then he would. A criminal would be pursued personally, his head cut off and displayed on Nicholson's desk as a reminder that change, even if brutal, was inevitable. Nicholson's support for his own religion was concealed. Subscriptions to missionary bodies were anonymous or given in his mother's name.

It was ironic that Nicholson's rigour, his violence, brought deification as well as sensible respect. In 1849, a Hindu devotee hailed him as an avatar of Brahma and began to preach the new gospel of

Nikalseyn. When converts descended upon their new god they were received with blows and threats, and accepted them as godlike. 'He is a just god,' they said, 'and punishes us for our own good' – and wisely went away. A young engineer working on an extension of the Grand Trunk Road from Lahore to Peshawar reported that one day he received a strange party of visitors. Sitting in his bungalow, he saw twenty men dressed rather oddly and with helmets on their heads, walking in single file. Seeing him, the men saluted courteously and then sat down in a row before him without speaking. There was a long silence during which the young man became increasingly uncomfortable. But at last one of the men spoke. 'We are Nikalseyn's fakirs. You are a white sahib. We are come to pay our respects to you as one of Nikalseyn's race.' A short conversation followed, in which the engineer learned for the first time of this new god. When it was over, the little line of men set off on their journey to worship the god in person.[4]

The violence with which Nicholson reacted to his religious devotees was an index of his doubts about his own god. Nineteenth-century empire-builders have been seen too frequently as the Victorian stereotype of the Christian hero, Bible in hand, doing God's work in a realistic manner. But if they existed at all in this simple, uncluttered, cardboard way, then they were very few in number. The majority of empire-builders formally accepted their God as an ally in their work, as a justifier of action and achievement, but a surprising number – in private correspondence – wondered whether, in effect, they had heard the Message aright, and expressed their uncertainty in the authentic tones of anguish.

Nicholson shared more with these men than his doubts and his suppressed sexuality. He shared, too, a dislike bordering on hatred for India and Indians. In 1843 he had written to his mother: 'I dislike India and its inhabitants more every day, and would rather go home on £200 a year than live like a prince here.' This attitude remained, but unlike other men he did not turn away from India into the little England of British society there. With his friends he was withdrawn and morose, with Indians rigid and violent. During the crisis of British power in India, men were to turn to this rock-like personality for reassurance and action. The inefficient and insecure were to see in him the apotheosis of their hopes and desires, a combination of faith and force, a warrior come 'to smite the Amalekites'. The dull but often shrewd Herbert Edwardes saw this clearly. 'You may rely upon this, my Lord,' he wrote to Canning early in 1857, 'if ever there is a desperate deed to be done in India, John Nicholson is the man to do it.'[5]

When news of the outbreak of the rebellion reached Peshawar, Edwardes, aided by Nicholson, took swift action. Sepoy regiments were hurriedly disarmed and their leaders executed. The method was simple and horrible. 'The first ten,' recorded an eye-witness, 'were picked out, their eyes were bandaged, and they were bound to the guns – their backs leaning against the muzzles, and their arms fastened to the wheels. The portfires were lighted, and at a signal from the artillery major, the guns were fired. It was a horrid sight that then met the eye; a regular shower of human fragments of heads, of arms, of legs, appeared in the air through the smoke; and when that cleared away, these fragments lying on the ground – fragments of Hindoos and fragments of Mussulmans, all mixed together – were all that remained of those ten mutineers.' Three times this scene was re-enacted, 'but so great is the disgust we all feel for the atrocities committed by the rebels, that we had no room in our hearts for any feeling of pity; perfect callousness was depicted on every European's face; a look of grim satisfaction could even be seen in the countenances of the gunners serving the guns'.[6] This affair certainly had a profound effect on the situation in the sensitive border area. 'As we rode to the disarming,' reported Edwardes, 'a very few chiefs and yeomen of the country attended us, and I remember judging from their faces that they came to see which way the tide would turn. As we rode back, friends were as thick as summer fires.'[7]

But what was happening at Delhi? Nothing, it seemed. Why did the commander-in-chief not move as rapidly as possible against the rebel city? Both Edwardes and Nicholson were constantly urging a swift stroke against Delhi, even while they both had their hands full on the frontier. Their anxieties were shared by many others. In a Lahore newspaper in the third week of May there appeared the following item.

'A COMMANDER-IN-CHIEF WANTED.

To the Editor of the *Lahore Chronicle*

Dear Sir, – Will you oblige the Indian public by giving a prominent place to the following in your next issue? The exigency of the times requires it, and, I trust, you will not hesitate.

Yours faithfully,

\- - - - - - - - - - - - -

Lost, strayed, or stolen, the Commander-in-Chief of H.M's and the Company's forces in India. Any information that can be afforded as to his whereabouts will be most gratefully received and handsomely acknowledged by the State.

The general supposition is that he has fallen into one of the trenches of the camp at Meerut, where, if a search is made, he will no doubt turn up.'[8]

In fact, General Anson, the commander-in-chief, had already marched, but only as far as Ambala where he died of cholera on 27 May, handing over his command to Sir Henry Barnard who, after winning a battle against the Delhi rebels at Badli-ke-serai on 8 June, moved on and occupied the military cantonments outside Delhi on what was known as the Ridge. There he sat and waited, fighting off attacks and making an occasional sortie, until he too succumbed to cholera on 5 July. Barnard was succeeded by General Reed who, himself an invalid, was 'fit for little more than lying on his bed all day'.[9] When the command became too much for him, General Archdale Wilson, who had shown chronic indecision at the time of the outbreak at Meerut, took over.

At least Wilson could organise the force on the Ridge, which had become virtually a rabble. Racked by the weather in their foolishly exposed position among the burnt-out ruins of the barracks fired by General Barnard, they suffered from the demoralisation of unchecked disease and the casualties engineered by incompetent officers. It was an army suffering badly and achieving nothing. Reinforcements had come in, but many more were needed. Above all, the few competent officers in the force needed someone of vigour and determination to lead them.

Nicholson had no doubt that he was the man. He was actively pursuing mutineers, but Delhi, and the punishment of those who had dared to raise their hands against the white race, were uppermost in his mind. His letters were full of suggestions for obscene punishments – flaying alive and impalement among them. Blowing from guns, it appeared, was too humane*. Nicholson had suggested the formation of a Movable Column, lightly equipped, which could be sent rapidly to any point of rebellion. The suggestion was accepted, and after the column's first commander had gone to Delhi to join the commander-in-chief's staff, Nicholson was appointed – greatly to the anger of many more senior officers – and given the rank of brigadier-general. But he remained *Mr* Nicholson to them, and in a sense they were right. He was officially a soldier, but he had spent most of his life detached on political duties. His experience of real war was very limited. His only, his overwhelming, qualification was his absolute sense of the righteousness and the immediacy of his cause.

Nicholson arrived at Delhi, ahead of his men, on 7 August. Very few in the camp knew him personally though his name was by no means unknown. One who had served with Nicholson was William Hodson, a man who might have been his mirror image. He had the same courage and almost reckless determination; his driving force, however, was not rectitude and virtue but a desire for loot. He knew that with Nicholson in camp the chances of capturing Delhi were increased, and so were the chances of plunder. With pleasure he noted in his diary: 'Nicholson has come on ahead; and is a host in himself.' [10] Others were also impressed, particularly by Nicholson's 'imperial air, which never left him, and which would have been thought arrogance in one of less imposing mien'.[11]

Everyone was waiting for the arrival of a siege train of heavy guns, sent on its way to Delhi by Sir John Lawrence in Lahore. With these guns, breaches could be made in the walls and an assault mounted. Nicholson was anxious for action and so were most of the younger officers. Wilson, however, was cautious, and sensibly so. A major defeat would mean a far greater disaster than the destruction of the force at Delhi. Now was a time for careful planning. Fortunately,

* See Appendix 2, p. 156.

the engineer officers were making their preparations. On 24 August Nicholson was to have action, when he sallied out and defeated a rebel force at Najafgarh. Meanwhile the engineers were erecting sites for batteries and anxiously wondering how long it would be before the siege train arrived.

The train arrived on the morning of 4 September, with enough explosives – it was said – to grind Delhi to powder. General Wilson at last decided that the risk of assault and the consequences of defeat should be taken. It was just as well, as Nicholson was at the centre of a conspiracy to replace him. But this proved to be unnecessary. 'The game is completely in our hands,' Nicholson wrote to John Lawrence on 11 September. 'We only want a player to move the pieces. Fortunately, after making all kinds of objections and obstructions, and even threatening more than once to withdraw the guns and abandon the attempt, Wilson has made everything over to the Engineers, and they and they alone, will deserve the credit of taking Delhi. Had Wilson carried out his threat of withdrawing the guns, I was quite prepared to appeal to the army to set him aside and elect a successor. I have seen lots of useless generals in my day; but such an ignorant, croaking obstructive as he is, I have never hitherto met with; and nothing will induce me to serve a day under his personal command after the fall of this place.' [12]

While the force on the Ridge waited for the final assault preparations to be made, Nicholson was tensely inspecting everywhere, riding around the outer trenches, querying this line and that, obviously conscious that he had been chosen by God to lead the first column against the city he saw quite clearly as the citadel of anti-Christ. But even at this late hour the doubts still tore at him. Sitting in the trenches with the engineer, Alex Taylor, he spoke bitterly of doctrines he had been brought up to believe. Was it possible that God had *not* created a world in which only Christians would be saved?

At 3 a.m. on the morning of 14 September the assault began. A few hours later, a young officer riding by observed a covered litter by the side of the road near the Kashmir gate, 'without bearers and with evidently a wounded man inside. I dismounted to see if I could be of any use to the occupant, when I found, to my grief and consternation, that it was John Nicholson, with death written on his face. He told me that the bearers had put the [litter] down and gone off to plunder; that he was in great pain, and wished to be taken to the hospital. He was lying on his back, no wound was visible, and but for the pallor of his face, always colourless, there was no sign of the agony he must have been enduring. On my expressing a hope that he was not seriously wounded, he said: "I am dying; there is no chance for me" '.[13]

Nicholson had been shot in a narrow alley by the Kashmir gate, rushing forward alone while wiser men sheltered from a shower of bullets. Cowards, Nicholson had thought them, and when he fell, exclaimed: 'The men who would not follow me shall not lift me from the ground.' He lived in great pain for another nine days, kept alive, it seemed, by the desire to hear that Delhi had been finally captured. When he heard a rumour of withdrawal, his anger against General Wilson made him cry out: 'Thank God I have still strength enough to shoot that man.' He died two days after a salute of guns from the king's palace announced that the city was in the hands of the British.

As the telegraph sent out the news, the legend of the 'so noble, so tender, so good, so stern to evil, so generous, so heroic, yet so modest' Hero of Delhi was born.[14] But the shade of the real, the violent, the arrogant Nicholson still hung over Delhi as other men carried out a terrifying vengeance on the city and its people.

A SIGNAL VENGEANCE

The disorganisation and lack of leadership on the Ridge, the anarchy of purposes, motives and emotions, had their parallel inside the city during the weeks before the British recaptured it.

Reinforcements for the mutineers brought new and more dynamic personalities to the scene, adding intensity to existing jealousies and a sharper focus for intrigue. On 1 and 2 July a large force of mutineers from Bareilly, in Rohilkhand, arrived at Delhi. In command was Bakht Khan, an Indian officer of artillery who had over forty years' military experience and had fought in the Afghan war. There is some uncertainty about his ancestry. One source claims him as being of the Delhi royal family *and* of that of Oudh. His former commanding officer described him as from a 'family of Hindu extraction, but converted [to Islam] under the temptation of territorial acquisition'.[1]

Bakht Khan was a giant of a man, not tall but immensely broad and fat, and because of this a bad rider. He was said to be very intelligent and fond of the company of Europeans. On his arrival in Delhi, Bakht Khan had a private audience with the king and emerged from it with the title of commander-in-chief, replacing Mirza Moghul, who naturally resented his supersession. But at least Bakht Khan was an experienced soldier. Furthermore, he had paid his men three months in advance, and brought with him a considerable amount of money looted from the Bareilly treasury. This in itself was a reinforcement of no small importance, for the financial position of the king and the rebels was desperate, and this had contributed to the disorder which continued to reign in the city. The king asked Bakht Khan to restore order and impose discipline on the rebel army.

The rebel army had suffered a defeat at the hands of the British on the Ridge on that most fateful of days, 23 June, the centenary of the battle of Plassey, a day which was to have seen the British hurled out of India. On their return, the shopkeepers of Delhi closed and boarded up their shops. The king had ordered the shops to be opened, by force if necessary, in order to avoid looting. The rebels, however, preferred looting to paying for their wants, and did not mind who suffered. Shopkeeper or poor man, it made no difference. The king was appealed to, and in turn appealed to the princes. They, however, were themselves enjoying the profits of plunder. An attack on the house of a member of the royal family by Mirza Abu Bakr was beaten off, and the king ordered that the prince be arrested. It had no effect. The princes and their men did what they liked and ignored the king. Even the countryside on which Delhi depended for its food was plundered, crops being stolen, and even agricultural tools 'requisitioned'.

To add to the tensions, there was a well justified fear that the British had spies in the city, some of them in very high places. The king's physician, Ahsanullah Khan, was frequently accused of being in correspondence with the British, and so was Zinat Mahal. The Raja of Balabgarh was said to be in touch with the army on the Ridge, which was true. The Nawab of Jhujhur was, too, and the house of one of his agents in the city was searched and plundered, though no evidence was found. Informers were everywhere, denunciations commonplace. Even Bakht Khan was accused of secret negotiations with the British.

A new danger was added towards the end of July, when Muslim fanatics declared that they would slaughter a cow in the courtyard of the Jama Masjid, the great imperial mosque, on the occasion of the festival of the Id. This would have caused trouble with the city's Hindu inhabitants. The king moved decisively. He issued a proclamation that 'no cows were to be killed within the city during the festival of the Id, and if any Muhammadan should do so he would be blown away from a gun; and whoever on behalf of a Mussalman helped kill a cow, would also be killed'.[2] The king himself sacrificed a sheep on the first day of the festival. The probability of conflict between Muslims and Hindus was averted and the British, who were well informed about what was going on, were disappointed that 'instead of fighting among themselves, they all joined together to make a vigorous attack to destroy us and utterly sweep us from the face of the earth'.[3] The only satisfaction for the British was that they were able to beat off the attack.

Soon afterwards, the rebels' suspicion of Hakim Ahsanullah Khan boiled over into action. An explosion took place in the magazine soon after the Hakim had visited it. His house was raided and revealing papers found. The king was forced to give in to demands for his friend's arrest. A traitor so near the king intensified the sepoys' fears that their leaders were about to sell them out.

No one seems to have suspected the king himself, though as early as June his agents had been in touch with the British. So, too, had Zinat Mahal, who now realised that if the rebels were successful her son Jawan Bakht would never win the throne. Her proposals were simple. If the British would restore the situation to what it had been before the arrival of the sepoys, maintaining the king's pension and privileges, the gates of the city would be opened simultaneously with the destruction of the bridge of boats across the Jumna. The British on the Ridge, now considerably strengthened, were not interested in negotiation. In any case, their spy reports did not convince them that the king's party could actually do what it promised. Their unwillingness to negotiate was reinforced on 20 August by an instruction from the governor-general that no concessions should be made to the Moghul family. But the rejection was polite. The king's influence, it was thought, could make the capture of the city an easier matter.

These top-level approaches remained, surprisingly, secret from the main sepoy leaders. Suspicions there were in plenty, but no proof. It was growing obvious to the rebels, however, that the tide was turning against them. They too had their spies, who listened and watched on the Ridge. They even managed some rather desultory sabotage. Among their reports was one that revealed that Indian tradesmen were returning to do business with the British camp, a sure sign of a change of wind. It also meant that the roads to the Ridge could no longer be controlled by the rebels and their friends. And if merchants travelled along them, so too could the siege train. When an attempt was made to intercept the siege train on 24 August it ended in disaster. For some reason, possibly a failure of nerve or rivalry between Bakht Khan and another rebel leader, no further effort was made to stop the siege train from reaching Delhi.

August had been a bad month for the king, too. Where previously he had negotiated loans with the merchants and bankers of the city, it now became necessary to force subscriptions to the treasury. Unfortunately for those known to be wealthy, there was more than one authority demanding payment. The king's agents, Bakht Khan's, the Mutiny Court – all made their demands. On 31 August, however, it was ordered that only the Mutiny Court could collect 'contributions' for military expenses. Credit reluctantly given by shopkeepers dried up, and when any attempt at coercion was made tradesmen just disappeared. The scavengers no longer cleaned the wide streets of the city. There were rumours that even the sepoys were deserting, though there is no concrete evidence for this.

The preparations on the Ridge were watched by those in the city with growing fear for the future. The rebels' lack of real military expertise became more obvious every day. Instead of preparing the fortifications, still immensely strong, for a siege, practically nothing was done. Parts of the wall were even left unmanned.

But when the British finally broke into the city it was strongly defended. The houses had been loopholed and fire from them was heavy. The rebels even had an ally, perhaps a fortuitous one, perhaps arranged. 'Strong drink,' wrote an eye-witness, 'is now, and has in all ages been, the bane of the British soldier.'[4] Bottles of beer and brandy, wine and arrack, seemed to the troops to be everywhere they looked. But not for long. The troops were soon dead drunk and unable to fight on. If the rebels *had* arranged for this to happen, they took no advantage of it.

General Wilson, fearing the complete demoralisation of his British troops, ordered that every remaining bottle of liquor should be destroyed. 'It was deplorable,' was one officer's comment, 'to see hundreds of bottles of wine and brandy which were sadly needed for our sick, shivered, and their contents sinking into the ground. Wine which had fallen to threepence a bottle, rose again to six shillings.'[5] But it was necessary. The city had not been cleared of rebels. On 21 September, however, the British flag flew over the palace, whose marble rooms were empty of all but the dead, and an evening meal was set

57

on camp tables in what had been the audience hall of the Moghul emperors.

There still remained the king. He had not been in the palace when it had fallen. Only a few retainers had stayed to fight to the death. He had left the palace with Zinat Mahal, her son, Jawan Bakht, and the three princes most active during the short-lived rebirth of the empire, Mirza Moghul, Mirza Khizr Sultan, and Mirza Abu Bakr. Bakht Khan, no longer commander-in-chief but still determined to fight on, tried to persuade the king to go with his troops to Oudh. But Zinat Mahal and others insisted on surrender. She was still convinced that a deal could be made with the British, if only for her son and her father. Zinat Mahal had been in touch with William Hodson and she knew that, for a price, he would save their lives, if nothing more.

The royal fugitives were at the tomb of Humayun, the second emperor of the Moghul Dynasty. It was Hodson, in control of the intelligence department, who received the news before anyone else. Through an agent, he had given Zinat Mahal a guarantee of safety for herself, the king, Jawan Bakht, and her father, even before they had evacuated the palace. Other members of the royal family were not mentioned, possibly because they were not able to make it worth Hodson's while, but more likely because Zinat Mahal insisted they be excluded. With the other heirs out of the way, perhaps even executed, her own son's claims could not be ignored. It was an incredibly obtuse reading of the situation, though she may have been encouraged in it by Hodson's agent.

The business details settled, Hodson now had to ensure that the royal family came to no harm. This was a difficult thing to achieve. Most of the British officers believed the king guilty of all the atrocities, real and imagined, which had inflamed their emotions while they waited on the Ridge. The most terrifying rumours about the torture and death of the British men and women captured inside the city had been accepted implicitly as absolute truth. Hodson himself had been as bellicose as the rest. 'If I get into the palace,' he had written on 30 August, 'the house of Timur [Tamerlane, i.e. of the Moghul family] will not be worth five minutes purchase.'[6] Hodson now went to General Wilson and after persistent argument persuaded him to allow Hodson to negotiate the king's surrender. When Wilson refused to send troops to the tomb, Hodson welcomed it and volunteered to go himself.

With fifty troopers Hodson made his way to the tomb of Humayun, which lay about five miles outside the city walls. There he took the old king, Zinat Mahal, and the two others who had been promised safe conduct and slowly returned, the king in a covered litter, to the palace.

There still remained the princes. Hodson asked Wilson's permission to go back and take them prisoner. Again, with reluctance, Wilson agreed. This time Hodson took a hundred heavily armed troopers, wild-looking men of his own, wearing a livery of scarlet turbans and dust-covered tunics bound by sashes of scarlet. At the tomb they found a crowd, apparently hostile, but overawed by Hodson's horsemen. The princes asked for a guarantee of their lives. Hodson refused to give it, but finally the three princes emerged riding in a small bullock cart. Again they asked Hodson to promise them their lives. 'Most certainly not,' he replied and, waving the crowd back, surrounded the cart with his own men. There was still the crowd to be dealt with. Raising his voice, Hodson demanded that the men throw down their weapons. A moment's hesitation, while the cart with the princes moved off towards the city, and Hodson repeated his demand. First one man threw down a sword, another a musket. In two hours, Hodson's men collected a thousand weapons.

Hodson himself rode off in an endeavour to catch up with the princes before they reached the city. Arriving in time, he asked his second-in-command: 'What shall we do with them? I think we had better shoot them here, we shall never get them in.' The princes were ordered out of the cart and told to strip off their top garments. Taking a carbine from one of his men, Hodson shot the three of them dead. The corpses he ordered taken away to be displayed outside the place where he believed, quite wrongly, that Englishmen had been killed.

Everyone in Delhi congratulated him. So did many elsewhere. Robert Montgomery, a leading advocate of Christian missions in India, wrote: 'All honour to you . . . for catching the king and slaying his sons. I hope you will bag many more.'[7] In the catalogue of terrors which formed the history of Delhi after its recapture, Hodson's act was only one entry among many. Worse were to follow.[8]

When the news reached Lord Canning that Delhi had been recaptured, he wrote to General Wilson: 'In the name of outraged humanity, in memory of innocent blood ruthlessly shed, and in acknowledgement of the first signal vengeance inflicted on the foulest treason, the Governor-General in Council records his gratitude to Major-General Wilson and the brave army of Delhi.'[9]

The signal vengeance was by no means over, nor was there any cessation in the amount of innocent blood ruthlessly shed, for the city of Delhi was put to the sword, looted and sacked with the ferocity of a Nazi extermination squad in occupied Poland.

After the capture of the palace, Colonel Bourchier had looked out from its walls over the devastated city. 'The demon of destruction,' he wrote in his diary, 'seemed to have enjoyed a perfect revel. The houses in the neighbourhood of the Mori and Kashmir bastions were a mass of ruins, the walls near the breaches cracked in every direction, while the church was completely riddled by shot and shell.'[10] Most of the city, however, was not badly damaged, at least until the soldiers got at it. Maddened by a heady mixture of fatigue, liquor and bloody rumour, they turned violently on the city and its inhabitants. 'All the people found within the walls when our troops entered were bayoneted on the spot, and the number was considerable as you may suppose, when I tell you that in some houses forty

59

and fifty persons were hiding. These were not mutineers, but residents of the city who trusted to our mild rule for pardon. I am glad to say they were disappointed.' [11] The writer exaggerated, for by no means all the inhabitants were murdered, but no one cared to compute the total.

The authorities were not much concerned with what happened to the male citizens, but they did think that women and children should be spared. General Wilson issued an order strictly forbidding violence against women and children, but few obeyed it, especially after a soldier observed, under the veil of a 'girl' he had caught, the beard of a rebel sepoy.

The fear of people who were as yet unmolested was such that men killed their women and then themselves. One writer reported that he had 'given up walking about the streets of Delhi, as yesterday an officer and myself had taken a party of twenty men out patrolling, and we found fourteen women with their throats cut from ear to ear by their own husbands, and laid out on shawls. We caught a man there who said he saw them killed, for fear they should fall into our hands; and showed us their husbands, who had done the best thing they could afterwards, and killed themselves.' [12]

When rough order had been imposed, old men, women (subject to some inspection) and children were on the whole left untouched. Sensibly, most of them chose to leave the city and were brutally encouraged to do so by the British. Frederick Roberts, the future Field Marshal, felt some regret. 'I have wished these last few days,' he wrote to his father on 26 September, 'that there were no such things as women where war was. Kicking men out of house and home matters little, but I cannot bear seeing unfortunate women suffering, and yet it can't be helped.' [13]

Perhaps the most revolting aspect of the violence was that the executioners seemed to enjoy what they were doing. Within a few days of the capture of the city, the provost marshal had officially hanged between four and five hundred, and it was said on good authority that the soldiers had bribed the executioners 'to keep them a long time hanging, as they liked to see the criminals dance a "Pandies" hornpipe, as they termed the dying struggles of the wretches.' [14] When a great multiple gallows was erected in a square in the city, 'English officers used to sit by it, puffing at their cigars, and look on at the convulsive struggles of the victims.' [14]

If there was much indiscriminate terrorising, there was also a kind of institutional violence. The magistrate, Sir Theophilus Metcalfe, reopened his court. In it prosecution was swift, and a decision of 'not guilty' so rare that few noticed it. Lesser princes of the royal family were charged with conspiring with the rebels, on evidence that was dubious to say the least. But they *were* members of the royal family and therefore, without question, guilty. They were 'all condemned, hanged, and carted off the same day'. [15] Metcalfe, for sound reasons, was held in dread by the citizens of Delhi. When a jeweller appeared to be asking too much for his wares, his British customer threatened: 'I shall send you to Metcalfe Sahib.' The man bolted in such a hurry that he left his treasures behind, and never again showed his face.[16] Certainly, there was little possibility of escaping alive from Metcalfe's justice. His victims usually ended up swinging from the beams of burnt-out Metcalfe House.

Life was cheap now in Delhi, but there was no squandering of property. Everyone except the most senior officers plundered whatever could be found before the official Prize Agents seized everything. Houses were attacked, their walls ripped down and their floors ripped up in the search for buried treasure. And there was a great deal to be found. 'The plunder being daily found in the city is more than enormous; it is almost incredible. I fancy every officer present at the siege might be able to retire at once.'[17] It was not only officers who benefited. One recalled later that when his regiment returned to England an unusually large number of men and non-commissioned officers bought their discharge from the army. They had succeeded in keeping their plunder from Delhi for nearly three years, and had then sold it. 'Many jewellers' shops in the town in which we were quartered exposed for sale in the windows, ornaments and trinkets of unmistakable Eastern workmanship.'[18]

When the Prize Agents took over they were no less rapacious, but much of the cream had gone. Even so, when the government of India decided not to divide the prize money but to give the captors of Delhi only the equivalent of six months' pay, there was such an outcry that the government surrendered. The sum involved was between half and three-quarters of a million sterling, at the then rate of exchange. It represented only a fraction of what had actually been taken from the city.

Between the private plunderers and the Prize Agents, Delhi had been very thoroughly ransacked. But although the Prize Agents had their methods, they were not as good as the Sikhs who had joined the British on the Ridge. In an attempt to fix their loyalty, before the city was captured, they had been reminded, deliberately, that there existed a prophecy which foretold the sacking of Delhi by men of their faith. 'Like hounds drawing a cover, they took street by street, and entering one deserted house after another, tapped each wall or panel with the delicate touch of an artist, poured water over the floors observing where it sank through fastest, and then, as though they had been gifted with the eye of the eagle, the ear of the Red Indian, or the nose of the bloodhound, cut their way straight through to the cranny or the cupboard, or the underground jars which contained the savings of a lifetime or of generations.'[19]

So Delhi suffered its reign of terror. The poet Ghalib mourned: 'Here is a vast ocean of blood before me, God alone knows what more I have to behold . . . Thousands of my friends are dead. Whom should I remember and to whom should I complain? Perhaps none is left even to shed tears upon my death . . . My pen dare not write more.'[20] Poet or Christian, trusted Indian assistant to a Prize Agent, it mattered nothing to the British. Professor Ramchandra of the

Delhi College, a Christian employed by the Prize Agents, was forced to leave his house. He was abused in the street and on at least one occasion attacked by an officer who did not care whether he was a Christian or not – for he 'was as black as jet'.[21]

It took many weeks before the truth about what was going on inside Delhi reached the ears of responsible authority outside. John Lawrence reacted strongly against indiscriminate vengeance, and so did Lord Canning. But they were crying against the strongest of winds. As late as 4 December, Lawrence was writing to Canning: 'I do not know what your Lordship has resolved to do with Delhi. But if it is to be preserved as a city, I do hope that your Lordship will put a stop to the operations of the Prize Agents. I also recommend that it be free from martial law. What Delhi requires is a soldier of energy, spirit and character to keep the troops in order, and a strong police and a magistrate to maintain the peace. Until there be some security for the lives and property of the natives, tranquillity will not be restored. I am a strong advocate for prompt and severe punishment when such has been deserved. But the systematic spoliation which I understand goes on at Delhi cannot fail to exasperate the natives, and render more wide and lasting the breach which has taken place between them and us.'[22]

It was not until John Lawrence arrived himself at Delhi towards the end of February 1858 that the reign of terror actually ceased.

Delhi had not suffered alone. Within a few days of its capture in September 1857, a large force had left again to take vengeance on another centre of rebellion, the town of Cawnpore. By the time they arrived there, it had already been taken, with the hysterical ruthlessness that now seemed almost commonplace.

PART THREE

The well and the wall

A corporal, who had travelled up from Bombay to join his regiment in the field, on his arrival at headquarters reported that in the course of the journey a mutiny had taken place among the bullock-drivers. On inquiry, it appeared that the hero of the affair was an honest fellow, who had disembarked with his head full of the Nana [Sahib] and the fatal well [at Cawnpore]. His story was simple: 'I seed two Moors talking in a cart. Presently I heard one of 'em say "Cawnpore". I knowed what that meant; so I fetched Tom Walker and he heard 'em say "Cawnpore", and he knowed what that meant. So we polished 'em both off.'

George Trevelyan: *The Competition Wallah*. London 1864.

1   Disarming the 11th Irregular Cavalry at Berhampur
2   Colonel Finnis shot by mutineers on the parade ground at Meerut

3 Massacre of the British in Delhi
4 British officers and their families take refuge in the jungle

5　The British assault on Delhi: capture of the Kashmir gate

6　John Nicholson, 'the hero of Delhi'　　7　Bahadur Shah II, king of Delhi

8 The slaughter inside Delhi after its recapture

9 William Hodson captures the king of Delhi

CHAPTER ONE

THE DREAM OF DHONDU PANT

The city of Cawnpore, about 260 miles east of Delhi, was an important military station and therefore a great centre of trade. The city itself was not old; it had grown up around the barracks which the British had established on land ceded to them by the ruler of Oudh towards the end of the eighteenth century. In 1857, Cawnpore stretched for about six miles along the south bank of the river Ganges, and was the headquarters of the military command for Oudh and an area known as the Doab.

Like all such stations, Cawnpore was divided into three parts. The native city was at the centre, a cluster of narrow streets and long bazaars. Approaching Cawnpore from the north-west, the visitor entered the civil lines, passing the administrative offices, the jail, and the treasury, the pleasant low bungalows of British officials, and the standard features – Assembly Rooms, church, theatre, and race course. To the west of the native city, the military lines were separated from it by a canal.

There were very few European troops stationed at Cawnpore, about three hundred in all. Indian troops consisted of three infantry regiments and a cavalry regiment, some three thousand men. In command was General Sir Hugh Wheeler, a veteran of over fifty years' service in India. He was considered a man not only of great experience but of sound common sense, and one of the best generals in the Company's army. He was reckoned to know the sepoy better than any other officer and had no racial prejudices, for he had married an Indian wife.

Cawnpore was a lively station. Apart from the military and civil officers and their families, there was a large European and Eurasian population, made up mainly of merchants and engineers working on preparations for the extension of the railway line from Calcutta.

But Cawnpore had another attraction. A few miles to the north-west, the town of Bithur had been the place of exile of the last titular leader of the Maratha confederacy, a power which had once challenged the British for the hegemony of India. In June 1818, Baji Rao, the last Peshwa, as he was called, had surrendered to the British on terms which included enforced exile and a substantial yearly pension of Rs. 800,000. The place chosen for the fallen prince was Bithur. The size of his pension was criticised at the time, but the government decided not to disown the agent who had made the promise. It comforted itself with the fact that Baji Rao came from a short-lived family and was not in good health at the time of his surrender. Baji Rao, however, survived until 1851. Apart from the continuing drain on the Company's exchequer, he caused the British no trouble during his exile, though he remained a cause for anxiety. His activities, and those of his household, were carefully watched in case he should become the figurehead of a revived Maratha nationalism. Though there were frequent rumours of intrigue, none seems to have had any foundation. The ex-Peshwa enjoyed his dancing girls and his pension. His only other concern appears to have been what would happen to the pension at his death.

Baji Rao had no legitimate male issue, and in 1827, following the normal practice of Hindu rulers, he adopted two sons. One was Dhondu Pant – known as the Nana Sahib – and the other Sadashiv Rao, called Dada Sahib. Later, another son was adopted, who took the name of Bala Sahib. In 1837 Baji Rao approached the governor-general with the request that at least part of the pension should be continued after his death, for the support of his family. He was told that the pension was personal and would die with him. The question was raised on two more occasions, but the reply was the same. It was pointed out that the ex-Peshwa must have accumulated reserves; not only did he have a large pension, but the income from a tax-free landholding. In 1841 Baji Rao made his will. Dhondu Pant was named as sole heir to his property, and to the '*gadi* [throne] of the Peshwa'.

At the time of his adoptive father's death, the Nana Sahib was in his mid-thirties. According to one Englishman he was 'a quiet, unostentatious young man . . . not at all given to extravagant habits'.[1] There were other views, but most seem to have agreed that the Nana was not a particularly impressive character. On one thing at least he was firm, however. The matter of his father's pension must not be allowed to rest. Shortly after Baji Rao's death, the Nana put in his first request. This went to the governor-general with a recommendation from the commissioner at Bithur that a portion of the pension should be paid, though subject to periodical reduction. Lord Dalhousie would have none of it. The pension had died with Baji Rao, and there was nothing to discuss.

This did not stop the Nana Sahib and the commissioner from repeating the claim. The ex-Peshwa had, indeed, left a considerable estate, but the calls upon it were also considerable. His followers numbered at least fifteen thousand, and many of them were supported directly. Even though the Nana had 'cut down on his establishments and considerably reduced his household expenses; still his monthly expenditure was very heavy and probably double his income'.[2]

For his pains, the commissioner was reprimanded by the governor-general. The ex-Peshwa during his exile had received, between his pension and the income from his tax-free lands, some £2·5 million. He had left a considerable fortune to his family. 'Those who remain,' wrote Dalhousie, 'have no claim whatever on the consideration of the British Government. They have no claim on its charity, because the income left to them is amply sufficient for them. If it were not ample the Peshwa out of his vast revenues ought to have made it so;

66

and the probability is that the property left is in reality much larger than it is avowed to be. Wherefore under any circumstances, the family have no claim upon the Government.'[3]

As it was obvious that the governor-general was immovable, the Nana Sahib decided to send a petition to the Court of Directors in London. The text was long and carefully reasoned. It quoted a number of precedents. The descendants of other conquered rulers had not been discriminated against. Above all, there was the case of the king of Delhi. The Company had 'delivered the dethroned emperor . . . from a dungeon, reinvested him with the insignia of sovereignty, and assigned him a munificent revenue' which his descendants still enjoyed. What made the Nana Sahib's case different?[4]

On the whole, the petition was a fine piece of special pleading, but it ignored the incontestable fact that the ex-Peshwa had known that the pension would die with him. He had also known that his adopted son would not be considered to have inherited his title or, indeed, anything at all which acknowledged that he himself had once been a ruling prince.

When the petition was received in London it was rejected. A second petition, changed only in some of the wording, was similarly rejected in 1853. This time, the Court of Directors made it clear that no further petitions would be considered. As far as they were concerned, the affair was closed. For the Nana there remained only one more recourse. He must send an agent to London to plead his case, not just before the Court – in fact, not before the Court at all – but before the British government and, if possible, that limited area of public opinion which carried influence. It had been done before, by the king of Delhi and, more recently, by the Rani of Jhansi. But who was to go? The Nana decided on one Azimullah Khan.

There is some confusion about Azimullah's background, especially as the only sources are British and date from after the rebellion, by which time he had been elevated to the rank of 'monster'. Mowbray Thomson, one of the few survivors of the débâcle at Cawnpore, claimed that Azimullah was 'originally a khitmutghar (waiter at table) in some Anglo-Indian family; profiting by the opportunity thus afforded him, he acquired a thorough acquaintance with the English and French languages, so as to be able to read and converse fluently, and write accurately in them both. He afterwards became a pupil, and subsequently a teacher, in the Cawnpore government schools, and from the last-named position he was selected to become the vakeel, or prime agent, of the Nana'.[5] But a Eurasian clerk who also survived gave a different story. According to him, Azimullah was 'a charity boy, having been picked up, together with his mother during the famine of 1837–38; they were both in a dying state from starvation. The mother being a staunch Muhammadan, would not consent to her son (then quite a boy) being christened. He was educated in the Cawnpore Free School under Mr Paton, schoolmaster, and received a subsistence of Rs. 3 per month. His mother earned her own livelihood by serving as ayah or maidservant. After ten years' study, Azimullah was raised to be a teacher in the same school, and two years after he was made over as a munshi to Brigadier Scott, who in his turn made him over to his successor (when leaving the station), Brigadier the Hon'ble Ashburnham, when Azimullah misbehaved himself and was turned out under an accusation of bribery and corruption'.[6]

Whatever his history, Azimullah was a handsome man of considerable intelligence. The Nana felt that his case would be in good hands. Azimullah arrived in London during the height of the season of 1854. His elegant manners and good looks, his command of English, and the veiled suggestion that he was himself really an Indian prince, opened a number of doors, some of them – it was later implied – leading to bedrooms. When the Nana's palace at Bithur was later sacked by the British, a number of letters were found, and their romantic contents offended at least one sensitive British officer.[7]

But successes in the boudoir were not repeated in the offices either of the Company or of the government. Azimullah left England in 1856, making his way back to India through the Crimea where the British were at war with the Russians. William Howard Russell of *The Times* was there, and remembered the 'handsome slim young man of dark-olive complexion dressed in an oriental costume . . . and covered with rings and finery' when he arrived in India to report the rebellion. Russell thought, with the advantage of hindsight, that Azimullah had seen the 'British army in a state of some depression, and he formed . . . a very unfavourable opinion of its *morale* and *physique*, in comparison with that of the French'.[8]

The news of Azimullah's failure to persuade either the Directors or the government to reopen the matter of the Nana's pension reached Bithur before he did. But there had been other indications that no real hope existed. During the life of the ex-Peshwa, a high British official had been stationed at Bithur. He had been removed by the middle of 1852. The ex-Peshwa had been allowed to retain the courtesy title of Maharaja. That too was abolished. The prince's land had been given extra-territoriality by the British; the inhabitants of it were not subject to British law. That privilege too was gone. There were many other minor irritants. For example, the usual free supply every year of a thousand rounds of blank ammunition for use at an important religious festival was cut off.

All these things, and the final failure of Azimullah Khan's 'embassy' rankled in the Nana's mind. Whenever a European visited him at Bithur, he would state his grievances and ask for help. In fact, the British at Cawnpore had much sympathy with the man whom, despite the attitude of the government, they still referred to as the 'Maharaja of Bithur'. The Nana was free with his hospitality, though some Europeans were prepared to make fun of it. His palace was full of European wares, deployed in such confusion that they were the cause of much innocent, and sometimes badly concealed, amusement. During the early period of his contact with Europeans, the same confusion reigned over his dinner table. A guest might be 'sat down to a table twenty foot long (it had originally been the mess table of a cavalry regiment), which was covered with a damask table-cloth of European manufacture, but instead of a dinner-napkin there was a bedroom towel. The soup . . . was served up in a trifle-dish which had formed part of a dessert service belonging to the 9th Lancers – at all events, the arms of that regiment were upon it; but the plate into which I ladled it with a broken teacup was of the old willow pattern. The pilao which followed the soup was served upon a huge plated dish, but the plate from which I ate was of the very commonest description. The knife was a bone-handled affair; the spoon and the fork were of silver, and of Calcutta make. The plated side-dishes, containing vegetables, were odd ones; one was round, the other oval. The pudding was brought in upon a soup-plate of blue and gold pattern, and the cheese was placed before me on a glass dish belonging to a dessert service. The cool claret I drank out of a richly-cut champagne glass, and the beer out of an American tumbler of the very worst quality'.[9]

When the Nana Sahib was not entertaining – even when he was, he only appeared for an hour or two to welcome his guests – he spent his time travelling (usually to places of Hindu pilgrimage such as Banaras, Allahabad, and Gaya). After the rebellion, in retrospect, his movements took on a sinister gloss and it was assumed – on the dubious evidence of informers, heightened by wishful thinking – that he had been engaged in fomenting a conspiracy against the British. For this there was no real evidence, though there may have been in his private papers, many of which were foolishly (or perhaps deliberately) destroyed by the British when they sacked the palace at Bithur. According to one informer, about three years before the uprising the Nana Sahib's *guru* had foretold that 'he would become as powerful as the Peshwa had been', and that it had been revealed in a dream that he would revive his father's lost dominion.[10] The same informer said that the Nana had been in correspondence with the Russians, who had promised him assistance once he had proved himself by capturing Delhi.

Only about the Nana's visit to Lucknow in the April before the mutiny are there any details, and these are mainly recollections committed to writing *after* the outbreak at Cawnpore. But he did leave rather unexpectedly, and Henry Lawrence thought that incident alone justified a warning to General Wheeler. The warning was ignored. There was some reason for Wheeler's attitude. He was personally friendly with the Nana, and it has been suggested that his wife – if not actually a relative of the Nana – was at least of the same sub-division of the same caste. In fact, Wheeler so trusted the Nana Sahib that he was prepared to ask for his assistance.

The news of the mutiny at Meerut seemed to have no immediate effect on the sepoys stationed at Cawnpore. Nevertheless, Wheeler made preparations to protect the European and Eurasian population in case of trouble. His main thought was to find a spot near the river which could be adequately fortified. From such a spot he could get the women and children on steamers, and down river to Allahabad or Calcutta. From about 20 May onwards it was obvious that there was unrest among the sepoys, and it seems, though the evidence is by no means conclusive, that Wheeler asked the Nana Sahib to supply some men to guard the treasury. In the meanwhile, Wheeler had decided upon a position. There had been two likely places. One was the magazine, some miles north of the military station. This was defensible and contained large stocks of weapons and ammunition, but it was rather hard to get to and lay some distance from the river – though this distance in fact disappeared when the river rose in the rainy season. The other possible site was two large barrack buildings, one of masonry and the other with a thatched roof, out in the open, and close to the road from Allahabad.

The latter site was the one chosen. The reason for the choice is not known, but it is possible that the Nana Sahib had assured Lady Wheeler that, should the sepoys mutiny, they would immediately make for Delhi and there would be no attack on the Europeans at Cawnpore. Whatever the reason, Wheeler ordered a parapet and gun emplacements to be erected around the barracks. Though there was plenty of water near by, insufficient supplies were moved in. The earthworks were built of loose earth only four feet high and were not bullet proof.[11]

Wheeler also sent a request for some European troops to Lawrence at Lucknow. Lawrence sent eighty-four men and two squadrons of native irregular cavalry. The officer commanding this little force found the chaos in Cawnpore almost beyond belief. 'Since I have been in India,' he wrote, 'I have never witnessed so frightful a scene of confusion, fright, and bad arrangement as the European barracks presented. Four guns were in position loaded, with European artillerymen in nightcaps and wide-awakes and side-arms on, hanging on to the guns in groups – looking like melodramatic buccaneers. People of all kinds, of every colour, sect and profession, were crowding into the barracks. While I was there buggies, palki-gharrees, vehicles of all sorts, drove up and discharged cargoes of writers [clerks], tradesmen, and a miscellaneous mob of every complexion, from white to tawny – all in terror of the imaginary foe; ladies sitting down at the rough mess-tables in the barracks, women suckling infants, ayahs and children in all directions, and – officers, too! ... I saw quite enough to convince me that if any insurrection took or takes place, we shall have no one to thank but ourselves, because we have now shown the natives how very easily we can become frightened, and when frightened utterly helpless.'[12]

There was an almost complete absence of proper organisation. Wheeler was perhaps reassured that the only real signs of tension could be found among the Europeans. Rumours there were, but Wheeler still thought the situation might hold. Even if it did not, he had based his strategy on what he thought to be two certainties – that if the sepoys mutinied they would, following the precedent at

Meerut, leave Cawnpore for Delhi; and that the Nana Sahib was loyal. He was wildly wrong on both counts. The sepoys remained where they were, and the Nana Sahib became their nominal leader.

The day before the awaited mutiny took place, Wheeler seemed to be more concerned with the fact that he had been passed over as successor to the late commander-in-chief, General Anson, than with ensuring that even the inadequate defensive position he had chosen was properly provisioned. Orders had been given – and that, apparently, he thought to be enough.

On the night of 4 June the sepoys mutinied, and next day helped the Nana's men to seize the treasury. Wheeler and the other Europeans were inside their low earthworks, convinced that all they needed to do was hold on and wait for reinforcements. It seemed as if Wheeler's belief that the sepoys would make for Delhi was confirmed, for they left the city by the Delhi road. A few miles away, however, they stopped and then returned. With them came the Nana Sahib.

Did the Nana join them voluntarily? Had he actually been part of a conspiracy long before the outbreak? The evidence is conflicting, and all of it tainted. After the rebellion, there were many who were prepared to shift the blame on to him. His own statements that he was forced to join the mutineers cannot be accepted on their own, and the only support comes from the deposition made by Tantia Topi just before his execution. On the whole, it seems most likely that the Nana was at no time a party to any conspiracy – if, indeed, there ever was one – but that when he recognised that the British were facing military rebellion he allowed himself to dream of taking power from them. No doubt there were men close to him who made out a good case. The sepoys may have made it clear that if he did not join them he would suffer. They needed a leader, any symbol that would help stretch the area of rebellion.

The first General Wheeler knew of the Nana's involvement with the mutineers was when he received a letter from his former friend, announcing that an attack would be made on the British position on 6 June. The attack took place, but it was confined to an artillery bombardment. Even a frontal assault, on the anniversary of the battle of Plassey, was driven off. But the position inside the entrenchment was impossible. There was neither adequate protection from shell and bullet, nor from the sun. Sixty years later it was discovered that underneath one of the barracks was a huge underground room which would have given shelter and protection. No one among the defenders seems to have known of its existence.

In the city, those suspected of associating with the British were killed. Bengali clerks employed by them were natural victims. Rich men were also in danger; a simple accusation, and their property disappeared. The Nana Sahib, now officially proclaimed Peshwa, issued orders that few obeyed. Proclamations outlining the organisation of the army and the state were published and ignored. But slowly some sort of administration was set up. Plans were drawn up stating the extent of the Peshwa's dominions; these were so vast that the whole document seems to inhabit a world of fantasy. Details were even given of the exact amount of tribute to be demanded from such monarchs as the king of Kabul and the emperor of China. The queen of England was down for Rs. 5 million.[13]

There was little hope for the new Peshwa's ambitions until the entrenchments were taken. The bombardment was kept up from a safe distance. The British, equipped only with weapons of small calibre, soon gave up replying to the enemy's fire. But without relief from outside it was only a matter of time. Lawrence at Lucknow, when appealed to for help, declined to send any men because he was himself in a dangerous position. On 24 June, when Wheeler had perhaps given up hope, he wrote to Lawrence that he was almost without ammunition and supplies, and that 'British spirit alone remains, but it cannot last forever! ... Surely we are not to die like rats in a cage?'[14]

The next day hopes revived. A woman was seen approaching the defences, and an officer, Mowbray Thomson, recognising her as the Eurasian wife of one of the city merchants, was just able to prevent a soldier from shooting her. The woman carried a letter from the Nana Sahib addressed to 'The Subjects of Her Most Gracious Majesty Queen Victoria'. Its contents were short and simple. 'All those who are in no way connected with the acts of Lord Dalhousie and are willing to lay down their arms, shall receive a safe passage to Allahabad.' The handwriting was identified as being that of Azimullah Khan.[15]

Was it a genuine offer? Wheeler, with the certainty of destroyed confidence, did not think so, but his younger officers pointed out the plight of the women and children, the lack of provisions, the absence of any news of reinforcements. Wheeler gave in, and later that evening, two emissaries, one of whom was Azimullah Khan, arrived at the entrenchment to discuss terms. The British asked for an honourable surrender which would allow them to march out, retaining their hand-arms, and embark on boats supplied by the Nana to carry them down the river. In the afternoon of 26 June, Wheeler was informed that the terms were acceptable, but the entrenchment must be evacuated that night. This was considered impossible, and though the Nana threatened to re-open the bombardment, he finally agreed to delay the departure until the following morning.

It was early when the convoy started off. The sick and the women were carried down in palanquins, the children, many of them, were carried by some of the sepoys who a day or two before had been trying to kill them. At 8 a.m. they were piling into the boats, large clumsy vessels with thatched roofs, 'looking at a distance rather like floating haystacks'. By nine o'clock, all were embarked and waiting to move off. What happened next was believed at the time, and later, to be 'so foul an act of treachery the world had never seen'. It is more likely that it was one of those ghastly accidents that spatter the pages of history and on which any interpretation, suitable to the needs of

72

the occasion, can be imposed. Probably a musket shot was heard, and the British, fearful of treachery and with nerves tattered by three weeks of constant siege, immediately opened fire. Soon, raked with grape-shot and ball, the little fleet was ablaze, and attempts to push the unwieldy vessels into midstream were unsuccessful. One boat did get away, and four of its occupants, after an adventurous journey which included swimming down river under fire, finally reached safety.[16]

The survivors of the massacre on the river were brought up on the bank. There the men, perhaps about sixty of them, were immediately shot, but the women and children were saved by some of the Nana's men and taken first to a nearby house. Afterwards they were lodged in a building known as the Bibighur – the 'ladies' house' which had once been used by a British officer to accommodate his Indian mistress. Some British fugitives from the countryside who arrived later in Cawnpore were sent to join them.

On 15 July, when news reached Cawnpore that the British under General Havelock were approaching the city, the women and children were murdered.

The fear created in Cawnpore by the news that avenging British troops were on the way came near to panic. The women and children had, possibly, been kept alive with some idea of using them as hostages, but as the British moved up country towards Cawnpore they instituted a reign of terror which seemed, as one contemporary put it, to leave 'their foe without inducement to show mercy, since he received none, and made even women valueless as hostages'.[17] They were coming like 'mad dogs', and some suggested that 'if it were not for the women and children in confinement the soldiers would not rush on with such impetuosity'. Why not kill the prisoners and let the British know of it, and then 'you will find the Europeans will be discouraged and go back'.[18]

Whatever the advice given to the Nana Sahib, the conclusion was that the prisoners had to be killed. There has been no evidence yet discovered which ties him directly with the massacre that was to follow. But it seems improbable that he could have been unaware that the decision had been taken. Later, he claimed not to have heard of the intention to murder the prisoners until after the affair had taken place, and it is possible that the decision could have been taken by others with the intention of binding the Nana to the rebel cause.

When it came to carrying out the decision, there was some difficulty. The sepoys ordered to fire into the room where the prisoners were kept would not obey, and apparently fired into the ceiling instead. Then a woman who acted as a kind of attendant to the British women and children called some Muhammadan butchers from the Cawnpore bazaar and, possibly, some members of the Nana's personal guard. They entered the house and attacked the prisoners with swords and cleavers. The following morning, the dying and the dead were taken out and thrown down a well in the garden of the house. Not all could have been disposed of in that way, and some bodies were probably thrown into the river; there must have been three hundred corpses to be removed from the house.

The Nana Sahib left Cawnpore either just before the massacre of the women and children, or immediately afterwards. He seems to have gone straight to his palace at Bithur, staging on the way a fake suicide in the river Ganges.

By 11 August, 4,000 rebel troops with guns were concentrated around the Nana's palace. Where he had been in the intervening period is not known for certain, but he seems to have visited Oudh. He was certainly with the troops that resisted Havelock's attack on Cawnpore, and he was also with those who unsuccessfully defended Bithur. Havelock did not stay to occupy Bithur. His purpose was to move as soon as possible to the relief of the besieged garrison in the Residency at Lucknow; the activities of the Nana and his allies prevented that until British reinforcements arrived from Allahabad. In fact, no real move was made against the rebels in the vicinity of Cawnpore until Sir Colin Campbell returned with the evacuated Lucknow garrison in November.

During the interval the Nana seems to have lost faith in both his dream and the future of the rebel cause. This, in spite of the fact that his most loyal supporter, Tantia Topi, now commanded a force of mutineers who had come in from the princely state of Gwalior. The Nana was convinced that the rebels needed European allies. With this in mind he sent two agents to the French possession of Chandernagar, near Calcutta. It is possible that he intended to go there himself. A letter was forwarded to Paris, but remained unanswered. The letter asked for the emperor Napoleon's 'protection over the people of Hindustan and above all to the Nana Sahib'.

Campbell's return to Cawnpore was not immediately followed by action against Tantia Topi, but on 6 December the rebel army was taken by surprise. Partly because at least 10,000 of Tantia's force were raw recruits, he was unable to hold his positions. This was really the end of any hope the Nana might have had of reviving the Maratha power. Within a few days of Tantia's defeat, the British were at Bithur. The Nana's palace was burned to the ground and so were a number of temples and mosques.

The Nana Sahib himself had fled, taking with him some of his treasure. But not all. A large quantity of it had been sunk in a well, and the British set about retrieving it. 'Four strong frames were erected on the top if it by the sappers, and large leathern buckets with strong iron frames, with ropes attached, were brought from Cawnpore; then a squad of twenty-five men was put on to each rope, and relieved every three hours, two buckets keeping the water down and two drawing up the treasure.' [19] It took nine days of hard work to clear the well. A number of heavy wooden beams had been thrown in on top of the treasure, but when they were removed 'a great quantity of silver plate – solid silver, be it understood – was brought to light, which, owing to the action of the water, came up jet black. Among these silver articles, the State howdah of the ex-Peshwa, in solid silver, was fished up, besides quantities of gold plate and other valuables. Below the plate, which was merely deposited loose in the water, as if in a hurry, the sappers came upon an immense number of ammunition boxes tightly packed with native rupees and gold mohurs (each gold coin being worth 16 rupees at least), the value of the coin alone being currently reported in camp on December 27 to be over £200,000, in addition to the value of the gold and silver plate and the ornamental jewellery'.[20]

The treasure was all claimed by the government, and none of the soldiers who had laboured so hard for its recovery received any part of it as prize money.

After Bithur, the Nana was on the run, though Tantia Topi had his seal and a number of proclamations were issued in the Nana's name. Tantia's former master remained in the area of Cawnpore for a while, and was reported to be with a small body of men who, early in February 1858, destroyed a police station not far from Bithur. The British heard rumour after rumour, acting on some and ignoring others, for 'wolf had been cried so often with regard to him'.[21] The pursuit was never given up – capturing the Nana had become one of the most important of the British war aims. The 'monster of Cawnpore' had to be brought to justice.

Chasing rumours did not lead to the reality, but towards the end of 1858 the Nana and his followers became entangled in Campbell's sweep in the direction of the Nepalese border. The Nana was always ahead of the pursuers. When emissaries caught up with him suggesting that he surrender, their terms were never acceptable. The Nana did not trust the British. Their attitude towards him was by now well known. He had become the 'beast of Bithur', a scapegoat for all the horror and fear the British had felt since May 1857. The Nana was not prepared to accept assurances from anyone but the queen of England herself.

Attempts at diplomacy did not prevent Campbell from moving steadily forward. On 30 December 1858 news was received that the Nana and 'some thousands of sepoys and desperadoes' were concentrated at a place called Banki, on the banks of the river Rapti and the frontier of Nepal. The going was hard for the British, for the terrain was a savage combination of forests of great sal-trees with marsh and jungle. But as William Howard Russell wrote in his diary: 'The mere chance of capturing the Nana Sahib, killing and dispersing some of the desperadoes around him before the old year closed, seemed to justify an undertaking which was esteemed hopeless by those most conversant with Indian warfare.'[22]

The British force moved with as much secrecy as it could and caught the rebels at Banki by surprise. The outcome of the battle was that many of the rebels, including the Nana Sahib and his brother, Bala Sahib, were forced across the river and into Nepal. There, the commander-in-chief decided not to pursue without the express sanction of the governor-general.

Just after the battle at Banki, a number of the more prominent rebel leaders gave themselves up. 'The scene,' wrote Russell, 'was extremely interesting, and the particular coolness and self-possession of these men, who had been fighting against us a few hours before, and who now sat perfectly at their ease in the Special Commissioner's tent, was very striking. The present aspect of the country would indicate that the storm is over. Those who have escaped its fury are, with an anxious eye, scanning the clouds, fearful to trust themselves to believe in the calm, and, for my part, I believe it will be long indeed ere the roll and swell of the great waves shall have passed away.' [23]

Unfortunately, the Nana Sahib was not among those who surrendered, and no orders came from the governor-general. Campbell set off back to Lucknow, leaving a force behind to watch the frontier passes.

The Nana Sahib had disappeared, and the British could get very little firm intelligence as to his movements or the real attitude of the Nepalese government towards him and his large entourage of family and followers. They still wanted him badly; a reward of Rs. 100,000 had been offered for his capture, dead or alive. When the Nana had heard of this, in June 1858, he had offered twice as much for the head of the governor-general. But now the reward was given an extra edge. An absolute and unconditional pardon was to be given to any Indian – even to one who had been guilty of the murder of Europeans – who brought about the Nana's capture.

The Nana was apparently met on his arrival in Nepal by an emissary of Jang Bahadur. The Nepalese leader's terms were simple. The women of the Nana's household were to be put under his protection, but no shelter would be given to the Nana. The Nana was apparently not informed that Jang Bahadur had agreed to allow British troops to cross the frontier in pursuit of him, but he was told that Nepalese forces would not try to arrest him. This was not entirely reassuring. The Nana and his brother decided to make an approach to the British for terms, and on 23 April 1859 a messenger was despatched with two documents, one a simple letter from Bala Sahib, the other an *ishtahar*, a kind of proclamation addressed to Queen Victoria, the British parliament, the Court of Directors of the East India Company, the governor-general, and a number of other named civil and military officers.

The proclamation denied that the Nana had any responsibility for what had taken place at Cawnpore. He had been forced by the sepoys to join the rebels, and had done everything he could to prevent the murder of the English. The women and children massacred in the Bibighur were, he had heard, 'killed by your [mutinous sepoys] and [criminals] at the time that my soldiers fled from Cawnpore and my brother was wounded.' The Nana referred to himself as an 'insignificant' person, who could not have given aid to the British against the mutineers, but he ended on a note of defiance. The British, he said, had been unable to catch him. 'It is strange that you, a great

76

and powerful nation, have been fighting me for two years and have not been able to do anything; the more so when it is considered that my troops do not obey me and I have not possession of my country.' As the proclamation reached its end, the note of bravado swelled. 'If I alone am worthy of being the enemy to so powerful a nation as the British, it is a great honour to me, and every wish of my heart is fulfilled: death will come to me one day, what then have I to fear ...'[24]

Bala Sahib's letter took quite a different line. He claimed that he had been coerced not only by the sepoys but by his brother, and that he too had done his best to save British lives.

The British officer who received these two communications replied quoting Queen Victoria's proclamation. Its terms applied to all, without exception. If the Nana was not guilty of murder then he had nothing to fear. But this was not enough for the Nana. 'I cannot surrender in this manner,' he wrote. He would only do so if he were sent a letter written by Queen Victoria and sealed with her seal, and brought to him by 'the Commanding Officer of the French or the Second in Command'. Placing reliance on these officers, he would 'accept the terms without hesitation'. He knew how the British had taken bloody vengeance even on the innocent, and he could not trust their unsupported word. If the British were not prepared to give him guarantees of this kind, it must be war and blood between them still, 'as long as I have life . . . whatever I do will be done with the sword only.'[25]

The governor-general, who had not been consulted, did not approve of the reply that had been given to the Nana. He should merely have been referred to the Queen's Proclamation, and no further comment should have been added. On 13 May, as nothing further had been heard from the Nana or his brother, the government instructed its agents that the terms of the Queen's Proclamation no longer applied. The Nana was to be told, if he again offered to surrender, that what he would get was a fair trial – nothing more.

There was little the Nana could do but accept Jang Bahadur's terms for refuge in Nepal. The women of his family were given a house in the Nepalese capital. The Nana, his brother, and a few followers moved to the district of Butwal. In October 1859, Jang Bahadur informed the British Resident in Katmandu that the Nana was dead. So, too, were Bala Sahib and Azimullah Khan. They had all died of 'fever', no doubt malaria, as this jungly area was particularly malarial during the rainy season.

Was the information true? Some of the British thought so, but there was no way of proving it. The rumours began to circulate again. No one could be found who had actually seen the Nana Sahib's corpse. In 1860, the *Friend of India* reported that a man had been kidnapped by the Nana's supporters; after his escape he claimed to have seen the Nana in person in what according to his description must have been Tibet. The man's statement was so circumstantial that the government of India ordered the Resident in Katmandu to investigate.

In Tibet, the Nana was said to have had with him a large force of sepoys and several guns. Other rumours saw him alone, visiting the holy place of Muktinath in Nepal. A pilgrim reported a 'person dressed as a fakir, with long hair plaited round his head,' who passed him 'on an elephant attended by from fifteen to twenty followers, all very dirtily dressed and looking like fakirs. The latter spoke to me and asked me who I was and where I was going? Their master shortly afterwards, when on his way back, turned his elephant round and came towards me, and asked me if it were true that I was going to [Muktinath]. I said "yes". Upon this he immediately took out ten Company rupees and gave them to me'.[26] The pilgrim was told that the man was a 'great Maratha raja, who was continually engaged in religious ceremonies . . . and was very charitable'.[27] When enquiries were made by the British Resident in Katmandu, the pilgrim was reluctant to say more, as he alleged that the Nepalese government had ordered people who talked about the 'fakir' to leave the city.

This story was soon reinforced by similar reports, and Jang Bahadur suggested that the British might like to send an investigation team to Nepal. But he made a strange condition. If the team failed to catch the Nana Sahib, then they must cede some territory to Nepal. As the Resident put it, 'Jang Bahadur could not lose' since 'he could with the utmost facility keep the Nana or any other party out of the way of any cavalcade of persons'.[28] Jang Bahadur even admitted that the evidence for the Nana's death might be open to doubt. He seems to have hinted that the Nana was actually back in India.[29]

So far, the rumours of the Nana's return to India had been scarce. Now they became more precise and more frequent. In August 1863, *The Times* published a Reuter despatch saying that the Nana Sahib had been captured in Ajmir. The same report even claimed that Tantia Topi, who had by then been hanged by the British, was still alive and commanding a large force of sepoys. The story was based on an actual incident. A member of the Secret Service had reported to the deputy commissioner of Ajmir that he had actually located the Nana Sahib. The deputy commissioner had taken a force and surrounded a temple where the alleged refugee was staying, and arrested a person said to be the former rebel leader. A close enquiry was made into his identity, photographs were taken, handwriting was compared, and on the whole the deputy commissioner was convinced. The Nana Sahib had at last been captured. But the government of India was decidedly sceptical, and those who had actually met the Nana agreed. When the prisoner was brought to Cawnpore there was considerable excitement, but the general opinion was that he was not the Nana – though he knew Cawnpore. In November the man was released.

There was still to be another Nana, this time in Mewar. On this occasion, the press was so annoyed that *The Englishman* of Calcutta advised the government to 'hang pretenders on the strength of their

78

assertions'.[30] That was the only way to scotch the rumours that the Nana was still alive. In October 1874 another Nana was arrested in Gwalior and handed over to the British. The same exhaustive investigation was begun. Mowbray Thomson, one of the survivors of the massacre of Cawnpore, was sent to see the prisoner. He did not think it was the Nana Sahib but he was not sure, and when changes were made in the man's dress and hair he found the 'likeness extraordinary'. The then viceroy, Lord Northbrook, did not think Thomson's testimony had any value at all. 'I saw Colonel Mowbray Thomson yesterday,' he wrote, 'who inclines to think the prisoner is the Nana; but his evidence is worth very little, for he had only the kind of acquaintance with the Nana that a subaltern has with a Raja near cantonments.'[31] The final conclusion of a laborious enquiry was that the man was not the Nana.

But some of the British who had fought in the rebellion remained convinced that the Nana was still alive; so too did many Indians. In 1877 it was said that the Nana was about to invade India at the head of a Russian army, and would revive the Maratha empire with the aid of the Tsar.

Suspects continued to be arrested and released until the government of India became tired of the whole affair. What did it matter? Even if the Nana were still alive, it would be foolish to put him on trial if he could be caught. In 1894 the then viceroy rehearsed the possibilities and came to the conclusion that it was time to forget. 'An identification, whether it failed or succeeded, would stir passions which it is the primary object of every one of us concerned in the Government of India . . . to allay.'[32]

Officially, that was the end of the Nana. It no longer mattered if he had been seen in Istanbul or Mecca, or that he was said to have acquired a young English girl for his harem. In the changed India of the late nineteenth century, when others were about to challenge British rule, it was better to silence any echoes from the past. Not that the Nana could be disposed of quite so simply. Fantasy had subsumed reality. A subject people looking for heroes found, in him, a leader of the first Indian 'national war of independence'.[33]

THE MADNESS OF COLONEL NEILL

On 26 May 1857, the governor-general wrote to General Wheeler at Cawnpore to assure him that help was on its way. 'A steady stream of reinforcements is now being poured into Banaras. Every horse and bullock that can be bought on the road is engaged and the mail cart establishments have been increased to the utmost.'[1] Men who travelled by post-horse could, the governor-general said, reach Banaras in five days, those by bullock cart in ten. Those who went up river by steamer took sixteen days to make the journey. This must have been reassuring for Wheeler, and in fact dictated some of his strategy. Unfortunately, the letter was one of hope rather than reality.

The system for moving troops was aggressively slow. Three years earlier the government, in an excess of economy, had disbanded the Military Transport Establishment and was now entirely dependent for transport on the services of Indian contractors. The railway from Calcutta only went a hundred miles, to the town of Raniganj, and even that seemed incapable of carrying more than twenty-four men and their officers at a time. But the problems really started after Raniganj. White troops could only march short distances in the gruelling heat of an Indian summer. The best estimate those responsible for moving troops could make was that by 12 June 266 men would have reached Banaras by horse carriage and 400 by bullock cart.

On 23 May, 900 men of the 1st Madras European Fusiliers arrived at Calcutta from the south. In command was Colonel James Neill. Neill, a Scotsman aged forty-seven with thirty years of military service behind him, had hoped he would be called to take part in the suppression of the rebellion. From the quiet of Madras, he had looked upon the behaviour of the northern sepoys with horror and had 'thought that God might call him to take his part in its suppression'.[2] This was not unreasonable. Neill's god was the 'god of battles', the harsh, unbending Jehovah of the Old Testament. Neill himself was a stern figure, inordinately proud of his faith and of his physique, but said to be 'tender as a woman in his domestic relationships, chivalrous and self-denying in all the actions of his life, and so careful, as a commander, of all under his charge, that he would have yielded his tent or given up his meals to anyone more needing them than himself.'[3] His tenderness, however, was not extended to anyone, black or white, whom he considered an enemy. 'He knew, when he embarked for Bengal, that there was stern work before him; and he brooded over the future so intently, that the earnestness and resolution within him spoke out ever from his countenance, and it was plain to those around him that, once in front of the enemy, he would smite them with an unsparing hand, and never cease from his work until he should witness its full completion, or be arrested by the stroke of death.' [4]

Certainly, Neill was not a man to be hindered in carrying out his 'holy work'. He showed this when he was instructed to embark a number of his men on the railway to Raniganj. Arriving at the Calcutta terminus with some seven hundred of them – the rest were to go by steamer – he found apathy and indifference among the station staff. The terminus was on the river, and the troops were to be moved directly to the station, on flats, from the ship which had brought them from Madras. The flats were slow-moving, and the railway authorities refused to delay the departure of the scheduled train to suit the troops' convenience. Neill protested, but was shouted at by a number of officials. 'One said that the Colonel might command his regiment but he did not command the railway.' [5] At this, Neill put the stationmaster, the engineer, and the stoker of the train under arrest, and they remained so until the first batch of men had entrained. With some justification, Neill called the railway officials traitors and rebels, and loudly regretted that it was not in his power to hang them.

When the news of Neill's forcefulness leaked out, everyone from the governor-general downwards approved. At last, here was someone who knew what he was doing. The British of the sadly shaken capital of the empire began to look upon Neill as a possible saviour. They had been calling for stern and ruthless action, now they had a foretaste of it.

Neill arrived at Banaras on 3 June, expecting to pass through quickly and on to Allahabad. But at Banaras he found a situation he saw as dangerous, and one that only he could resolve.

Banaras was causing the government considerable anxiety. It was, of course, the most sacred city of the Hindus and, as such, a kind of ideological powerhouse of the rebellion. More important still, it had for many years been a repository for state prisoners, both Muslim and Hindu. There were, among others, members of the Moghul family there, and it was feared that some attempt might be made by the rebels to use them. Banaras also lay on the lines of communication with the north-west. It was essential that the town should remain completely in the hands of the British.

The civil authorities, though not men of great decision, had taken a line which seemed to display confidence. The magistrate rode through the city unarmed, accompanied by his daughter, on the principle that, as 'the Lord is my rock and my fortress . . . in Him will I trust', any attempt to prepare for action would be a 'betrayal of want of faith in the Almighty.' If and when the worst happened, he would go out to meet the enemy 'with a Bible in his hand as David had gone out to meet Goliath with a pebble and a sling.' [6] When it was pointed out to him that David had at least had a weapon, the magistrate had reluctantly agreed that arms and ammunition should be given to the European residents. In the circumstances – and there were no European troops at Banaras – the magistrate's attitude was undoubtedly more likely to keep the peace than to destroy it. Reinforcements were on the way. When they arrived it would be time to consider more positive action. On the whole, Banaras remained quiet until early in June when there began the familiar outbreaks of arson which had already preceded so many other risings. It was also said that some of the state prisoners were in touch with the sepoys. The military authorities in the city had not approved of the magistrate's display of nonchalance. In fact, they themselves evacuated the city and retired into the fort of Chunar.

Such was the situation when Neill arrived. Next day, it was heard that there had been a mutiny at Azamgarh, and it was immediately thought that the sepoys at Banaras would also mutiny. Neill pressed for the immediate disarming of the 37th Native Infantry. A Sikh regiment, and another of Irregular Cavalry, were assumed to be untainted and could be used in the disarming. The 37th was ordered to place its weapons and ammunition in the arms store, and six companies did so without resistance. But at this point European soldiers arrived on the parade ground and the sepoys assumed that, like so many of their comrades elsewhere, they would be attacked after they were disarmed. Their commander failed to reassure them, and it is possible that some of the remaining sepoys reached for their arms. At this point, the Europeans opened fire. The Sikhs and Cavalry, then approaching the parade ground, heard the firing, and fearing that they too would be attacked opened fire themselves. At this, the artillery officer turned his guns on the Sikhs and Cavalry as well. If these men had been loyal, and there seems little doubt that they had, the guns drove them into rebellion.

It is not clear from the evidence whether Neill had, at this point, assumed command at Banaras. It seems likely that he had, perhaps on his own authority. He was certainly responsible for the hasty decision to disarm the 37th, an affair so inefficiently handled that the Sikhs and Cavalry were 'drawn into resistance'.[7] Neill did not view it like this. He had done God's work and smitten the enemy.

Satisfied, he left Banaras on 9 June for Allahabad. Even the magistrate of Banaras had to admit that it was 'quite a miracle to me how the city and the station remain perfectly quiet . . . I do believe there is a special Divine influence at work on men's minds.' He thought it was all due to the prayers which had been offered up, 'and I fully believe that they are accepted at the Throne of Grace and that this is the cause of the quiet we enjoy.'[8]

It was not quiet in the surrounding districts. But Colonel Neill had not been idle in encouraging the more bloodthirsty among the civilians at Banaras to ensure that the 'hand of the Lord' fell heavily on anyone who appeared to be, by the remotest definition, a rebel. Within a couple of days of disarming, military courts or civil commissions were at work feeding the gallows set up near the Mint. No one was spared. 'On one occasion, some young boys, who, perhaps, in mere sport had flaunted rebel colours and gone about beating tom-

toms, were tried and sentenced to death. One of the officers composing the court, a man unsparing before an enemy under arms, but compassionate, as all brave men are, towards the weak and helpless, went with tears in his eyes to the commanding officer, imploring him to remit the sentence passed against these juvenile offenders, but with little effect on the side of mercy.' [9]

The 'official' commissions, which now – though they were not yet aware of it – had the full support of a legislative act of the governor-general,[10] also had amateur support. 'Volunteer hanging parties went out into the districts, and amateur executioners were not wanting to the occasion. One gentleman boasted of the numbers he had finished off quite "in an artistic manner", with mango-trees for gibbets and elephants for drops, the victims of this wild justice being strung up, as though for pastime, in "the form of a figure of eight".' [11] As the jail was full, 'the Gibbet disposed of the higher class of malefactors, and the Lash scored the backs of the lower ,and sent them afloat again on the waves of tumult and disorder.' [12] The executions were known as 'Colonel Neill's hangings'. The magistrate preferred to believe that 'no civilian is likely to order a man to be executed without really good cause.' [13] He was tragically mistaken.

Colonel Neill had, however, departed. It was now to be the turn of Allahabad. Neill's reputation had preceded him. The sepoys there, who had shown themselves loyal and had even volunteered to go to Delhi to help the British on the Ridge, were so frightened that they mutinied before he arrived, and were joined by many of the inhabitants of the city. Those of the British who were not caught unawares – and there were many – managed to get to the Fort, protected by a body of Sikhs under the command of a former gardener, Lieutenant Brasyer, who had acquired a highly personal but solid dominance over his men.

In the town, a former Muslim schoolmaster, Maulvi Liaquat Ali, had declared himself governor on behalf of the king of Delhi and was trying to restore order, though without much success. Among the main targets of the rebels were the telegraph wires and the embankments which had been prepared to take the railway.

Neill and his men arrived on 11 June to be received by a sentry on the Fort with the cry of: 'Thank God, sir, you'll save us yet!'

Neill was exhausted by his rapid journey in the great heat, and could not stand up for long. His bodily weakness exasperated him, but was not allowed to interfere with his determination to crush the rebels. 'I could only sit up for a few minutes at a time,' he wrote to his wife, 'and when our attacks were going on, I was obliged to sit down in the batteries and give my orders and directions . . . For several days I drank champagne and water to keep me up.' [14] Neill complained that the Sikhs were constantly breaking discipline and going out to loot. As they brought back large quantities of the finest French champagne and sold them at sixpence a bottle, his complaint was somewhat churlish. But they were also selling it to British soldiers, and that could mean, not therapy, but 'a reign of intoxica-

83

tion'. Neill ordered the commissariat to buy from the Sikhs all the liquor possible and lock it away in the store rooms.

By 17 June, Neill had managed to clear Allahabad of rebels. He should have moved on immediately in the direction of Cawnpore, where Wheeler's position was serious, but he did not. There was an excuse in the fact that a large number of bullocks had been lost to rebels, but Neill seems in reality to have decided that he ought to stay and institute a regime of fear in the area. The town of Allahabad was indiscriminately bombarded and set on fire. As the inhabitants tried to escape, they were mown down with grapeshot from a steamer on the river. The surrounding districts were next to feel the weight of repression. Villages were attacked and set on fire, while troops ringed them to see that no one escaped. No attempt was made to discover whether anyone was guilty of anything. 'Old men who had done us no harm, helpless women with sucking infants at their breasts, felt the weight of our vengeance.' [15]

Neill, tortured with sickness, comforted himself that 'it was a duty I had never contemplated to perform. God grant I may have acted with justice. I know I have with severity, but under the circumstances I trust for forgiveness'.[15] He was convinced that all the rumours he had heard of the bestial treatment of women by the mutineers were true. The three cases he noted in his journal were not. But about his own direct acts and those to which he gave his approval, there is no doubt. 'It mattered little,' wrote a contemporary Indian, 'whom the redcoats killed, the innocent and the guilty, the loyal and the disloyal, the well-wisher and the traitor, were confounded in one promiscuous vengeance. To "bag the nigger" had become a favourite phrase of the military sportsmen of that day. "Pea-fowls, partridges, and Pandies rose together, but the latter gave the best sport. Lancers ran a tilt at a wretch who had taken to the open for his covert." In those bloody assizes, the bench, bar, and jury were none of them in a bland humour, but were bent on paying off scores by rudely administering justice with the rifle, sword and halter, making up for one life by twenty. The first spring of the British Lion was terrible, its claws were indiscriminating.' [17]

It was thought that six thousand perished in one way or another, 'their corpses hanging by twos and threes from branch and sign-post all over the town . . . For three months did eight dead-carts daily go their rounds from sunrise to sunset, to take down corpses which hung at the cross-roads and the market-places, poisoning the air of the city, and to throw their loathsome burdens into the Ganges'.[18]

Colonel Neill was no longer at Allahabad, but it was agreed that his actions had 'speedily contributed to frighten down the country into submission and tranquillity'. Unfortunately, they had also led to the massacre of his countrywomen at Cawnpore.

On 27 June Wheeler had marched out of his entrenchment to death at the riverside. Three days later, Neill at last ordered a detachment to leave Allahabad to go to Wheeler's assistance. The departure had been delayed by an epidemic of cholera among the British troops, but the real cause had been the difficulty of obtaining supplies and transport from people too frightened to come forward and offer them. The detachment was under the command of Major Renaud, and he carried with him precise instructions from Neill. His first object was to be the relief of General Wheeler, but he was to expose his troops as little as possible to the heat of the day. He was told to 'attack and destroy all places en route to the road occupied by the enemy, but touch no others; encourage the inhabitants to return, and instil confidence into all of the restoration of British authority'.[19] One village, Mubgaon, was specifically marked down for destruction, with its surrounding neighbourhood, and all the men caught in the area were to be killed, without exception. When Renaud reached the town of Fatehpur, he was to hang any sepoys found there. 'If the deputy collector is taken, hang him and have his head cut off and stuck up on one of the principal Muhammadan buildings of the town.'[20]

Renaud took his instructions literally, leaving a trail of bodies and burning villages behind him. William Howard Russell was told by an officer who had been attached to Renaud's column that 'the executions of natives in the line of march were indiscriminate to the last degree. The officer in command [Renaud] was emulous of Neill, and thought he could show equal vigour. In two days forty-two men were hanged on the roadside, and a batch of twelve were executed because their faces were "turned the wrong way" when they were met on the march. All the villages in his front were burned when he halted. 'These severities,' Russell commented, 'could not have been justified by the Cawnpore massacre, because they took place before that diabolical act. The officer in question remonstrated with Renaud, on the ground that if he persisted in this course he would empty the villages and render it impossible to supply the army with provisions'.[21]

Renaud first heard of the disaster on the river bank at Cawnpore on 4 July. The news had reached Allahabad on the evening of 30 June after he and his column had left. Neill had not believed it but General Havelock, who had arrived that day to take over command, did. Neill was scathing. In his journal he wrote that Havelock and his staff had lost their nerve and wanted to recall Renaud. Havelock did, in fact, send an order to Renaud to halt where he was and wait for Havelock to arrive. 'Burn no more villages,' the message went on, 'unless actually occupied by insurgents.'[22] Havelock, though as rigid a Christian as Neill, could not accept that the work of his God was assisted by unnecessary violence. Neill disliked Havelock intensely.

Havelock did not waste time in Allahabad. He overtook Renaud on 12 July, having passed through a countryside which showed all the painful evidence of Renaud's zeal, with burnt villages, and dead bodies swinging from trees, the lower parts eaten away by predators. After a series of hard-fought battles in which the enemy had a powerful ally in the sun, Havelock entered Cawnpore on 17 July.

As his advance troops marched into the city, they found it deserted except for a man with a kettledrum who put himself at the head of the column and began crying out that the rule of the British was restored. Another detachment was met by a 'haggard looking almost naked East Indian [Eurasian], a clerk in some office'.[23] This was William Shepherd, who had escaped from the Nana's prison. He took the soldiers to the Bibiguhr.

'Eager and maddened,' wrote one of them later, 'we sped round the dreary house of martyrdom where their blood was outpoured like water; the clotted gore lay ankle deep on the polluted floor.'[24]

When the troops had settled in to Cawnpore, regular parties were taken round the scene of the massacre. 'Most of the men of my company,' wrote Sergeant Forbes-Mitchell of the 93rd Highlanders, 'visited the slaughterhouse and well, and what we saw there was enough to fill our hearts with feelings which I need not here dwell on; it was long before those feelings could be controlled. On the date of my visit a great part of the house had not been cleaned out; the floors of the rooms were still covered with congealed blood, littered with trampled, torn dresses of women and children, shoes, slippers, and locks of long hair, many of which had evidently been severed from the living scalps by sword-cuts. But among the traces of barbarous torture and cruelty which excited horror and a desire for revenge, one stood out prominently beyond all others. It was an iron hook fixed into the wall of one of the rooms of the house, about six feet from the floor. I could not possibly say for what purpose this hook had originally been fixed in the wall. I examined it carefully, and it appeared to have been an old fixture, which had been seized on as a diabolical and convenient instrument of torture by the inhuman wretches engaged in murdering the women and children. This hook was covered with dried blood, and from the marks on the whitewashed wall, it was evident that a little child had been hung on to it by the neck with its face to the wall, where the poor thing must have struggled for long, perhaps in the sight of its helpless mother, because the wall all round the hook on a level with it was covered with the hand-prints, and below the hook with the foot prints, in blood, of a little child.'

At the time of Forbes-Mitchell's visit, the well was 'only about half filled in, and the bodies of the victims only partially covered with earth. A gallows, with three or four ropes ready attached, stood facing the slaughter-house, half-way between it and the well; and during my stay three wretches were hanged, after having been flogged, and each made to clean about a square foot of the blood from the floor of the house. Our guide told us that these men had only been captured the day before, tried that morning, and found guilty as having assisted at the massacre'.[25]

By this time, Havelock had left Cawnpore for Lucknow. Neill, raised to the rank of Brigadier-General, had taken over. His mark was already on the city. Havelock had ordered his provost-marshal to control the emotionalism of the British troops, and had given 'special instructions to hang up their uniform, all British soldiers that plunder'.[26] But Neill had other punishments and other victims in mind. The day before he arrived in Cawnpore, he had received a letter from Havelock asking him to move as fast as he could. 'Have a note from General Havelock,' he wrote in his journal, '. . . anxiously awaiting my arrival; immediately I do, he will strike a blow that will resound through India. God in his infinite mercy grant we may.'[27] Havelock meant a blow at the guilty, Neill was to direct it at the innocent.

Neill did not like being left behind in Cawnpore while Havelock set off across the river in an attempt to reach Lucknow. Havelock had decided to leave him there for purely military reasons. 'I have not another officer whom I could entrust with the duty for an hour.'[28] But Neill was irritated. He confided in his journal: 'There is a farce in two Generals being with a handful of men and one of them allowed to do nothing.'[29] He informed the commander-in-chief, however, that he was not idle, but 're-establishing police and authority in bazaar and city'.[30]

While Havelock remained in Cawnpore, he would not allow Neill to issue any order whatsoever, but when he had gone Neill had a free hand. He used it, with a vengeance. He believed that 'severity at the first is mercy in the end', and issued an order which, 'however objectionable to the Brahminised infatuated elderly gentlemen' in Calcutta and elsewhere, was 'suited to the occasion'.[31]

The order was issued on 25 July. 'The well in which are the remains of the poor women and children so brutally murdered by this miscreant, the Nana, will be filled up, and neatly and decently covered over to form their grave: a party of European soldiers will do so this evening, under the superintendence of an officer. The house in which they were butchered, and which is stained with their blood, will not be washed or cleaned by their countrymen; but Brigadier-General Neill has determined that every stain of that innocent blood shall be cleared up and wiped out, previous to their execution, by such miscreants as may be hereafter apprehended, who took an active part in the mutiny, to be selected according to their rank, caste, and degree of guilt. Each miscreant, after sentence of death is pronounced upon him, will be taken down to the house in question, under a guard, and will be forced into cleaning up a small portion of the blood-stains; the task will be made as revolting to his feelings as possible, and the Provost-Marshal will use the lash in forcing any one objecting to complete his task. After properly cleaning up his portion, the culprit is to be immediately hanged, and for this purpose a gallows will be erected close at hand.'[32]

The police, Untouchables – whose very presence was considered pollution by caste Hindus – were detailed for supervision of this revolting task, adding another element of cruelty. After sentencing, a prisoner was taken by the police to the Bibighur and 'there made to crouch down, and with their mouths lick clean a square foot of the blood-soaked floor before being taken to the gallows and hanged. This order was carried out in my presence as regards the three wretches who were hanged that morning. The dried blood on the floor was first moistened with water, and the lash of the warder was

87

applied till the wretches kneeled down and cleaned their square foot of flooring'.[33]

Neill recorded the treatment of two captives in a letter which ended: 'No doubt this is strange law, but it suits the occasion well, and I hope I shall not be interfered with until the room is thoroughly cleansed in this way . . . I will hold my own, with the blessing and help of God. I cannot help seeing that His finger is in all this – we have been false to ourselves so often.'[34] Neill was not interfered with, and Forbes-Mitchell states that the 'order remained in force till the arrival of Sir Colin Campbell in Cawnpore on the 3rd of November, 1857, when he promptly put a stop to it as unworthy of the English name and a Christian government'.[35] Another source alleges that the order was virtually ignored; but there were certainly a large number of executions in Cawnpore during Neill's stay there. The same source considered that Neill was an exhibitionist. 'He could not but suppose that whatever position he was in, something marked would be expected of him. Hence some of his orders.'[36] There might have been an excuse for the executions if the men hanged had been among those responsible for the massacre, but it is unlikely that they were. 'If these people had been really guilty of the massacre it would have been disgusting enough, but Neill himself does not say that they were guilty of the murders . . . The really guilty . . . were not likely to trust themselves in Cawnpore at the time.'[37]

There were few contemporary critics of Neill's severities. For the British, Cawnpore was a horror that had to be exorcised in blood. As each new draft of soldiers arrived in the city, they were taken to visit the room and the well. The room was no longer in quite the same condition as it had been when the first relief column had arrived. Then, there had been no writing on the walls. When the writing appeared, no one is sure, but it seems probable that it was added in Neill's time. Perhaps someone thought that the mute evidence of tragedy was not enough to inflame the British soldier, to give him an incentive to fight. Most of the writings were obvious forgeries, for they contained the date of the massacre. 'Countrymen and women,' ran one inscription. 'Remember the 15th of July 1857. Your wives and families are here in misery, and at the disposal of savages who had ravished both young and old and then killed, oh! oh! my child, my child. Countrymen avenge it!' Most of the writings called for retribution and seemed designed to appeal to the semi-literate.[38] But they were soon repeated in the newspapers of Britain, Europe and the United States, helping to darken a whole generation's view of India and the Indians.

On Neill's mind there was nothing to worry him except the continuing belief that Havelock was weak and sentimental, and a bad soldier as well. When Havelock was forced to give up the attempt to reach Lucknow because he had not the men to resist the growing attacks of the enemy, he received an angry letter from Neill. 'I deeply regret you have fallen back one foot. The effect on our prestige is very bad indeed . . . In fact the belief amongst all is that you have been defeated and forced back . . . The effect of your retrograde movement will be very injurious to our cause everywhere . . . You ought not to remain where you are . . . you ought to advance again and not halt until you have rescued, if possible, the garrison of Lucknow. Return here sharp, for there is much to be done between this [place] and Agra and Delhi.'[39]

This was too much for Havelock. 'There must be an end to these proceedings at once,' he responded. 'You send me . . . a letter of censure, of my measures, reproof and advice for the future. I do not want and will not receive any of them from an officer under my command, be his experience what it may.' Only the needs of the time prevented him from putting Neill under arrest. 'You now stand warned. Attempt no further dictation. I have my own reasons which I will not communicate to anyone, and I alone am responsible for the course which I have pursued.'[40]

It was not until the arrival of reinforcements under General Outram on 15 September that both Havelock and Neill were able to leave for Lucknow. Neill entered the beleaguered city a corpse, accompanied by a case of arrowroot, wine and other provisions which this strange man had specially packed for distribution to some of the ladies of the garrison. Neill was shot in the head when a column which had lost its way in the complex city streets of Lucknow was ambushed. He might have reached the Residency alive if he had not insisted on remaining on his horse, an easy target for enemy snipers. So died the 'idol of the British Army'.[41] He had shown no signs of any particular military talent – on the contrary, during the attack on Lucknow he was timid and unwilling to take a decision without higher authority – but the White Terror he had helped so conspicuously to institutionalise in life was enriched, almost sanctified, by his death.

The queen awarded Neill a posthumous knighthood, and almost a quarter of a century later the author of one of the standard histories of the 1857 rebellion was still able to write, without much fear of contradiction, that 'every one of Neill's acts was marked by judgement, by a keen appreciation of the end to be attained'. Though many years had 'elapsed since he fell, the memory of him still lives, fresh and green, in the hearts of those who knew him – and who knowing, loved and respected him – alike in India and in England'.[42] Indians had, and retained, a very different memory.

PART FOUR

The siege and the symbol

Paradoxical as it may appear I think it more important to establish our power in the centre and capital of Oudh, which has scarcely been two years in our hands, than to recover our old possessions. Every eye in India is upon Oudh . . . and our dealings with it have been in every native's mind for the last two years.

Lord Canning to Sir Colin
Campbell, 29 December 1857

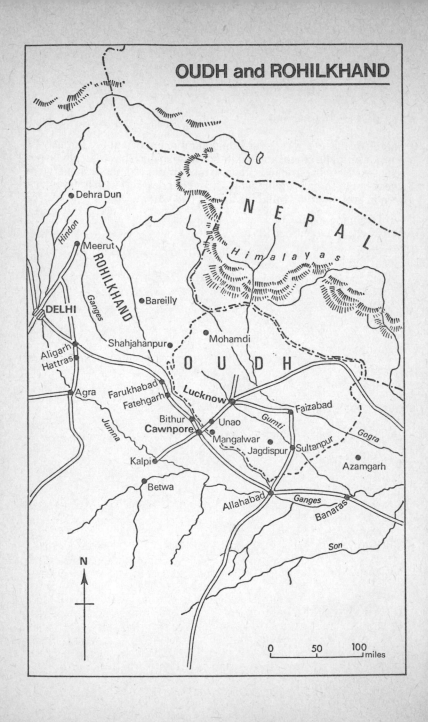

OUDH and ROHILKHAND

N E P A L

Himalayas

Dehra Dun

Meerut

ROHILKHAND

Hindon

Ganges

DELHI

Bareilly

Aligarh
Hattras

Shahjahanpur

Mohamdi

O U D H

Agra

Farukhabad

Fatehgarh

Lucknow

Faizabad

Jumna

Bithur

Cawnpore

Unao

Gumti

Kalpi

Mangalwar

Jagdispur

Sultanpur

Gogra

Azamgarh

Betwa

Allahabad

Ganges

Banaras

Son

N

0   50   100
                  miles

CHAPTER ONE

GREAT NURSERY OF SEPOYS

The territory of the former kingdom of Oudh was about the size of Scotland, roughly triangular in shape, lying between Nepal and the river Ganges, and with a population of about three millions. The capital, Lucknow, was in the middle of the nineteenth century the second city of India, full of elegant palaces in a variety of architectural styles, and of great pleasure gardens, but having an air of slightly worn luxury. Away from the city, Oudh was a vast plain sloping to the great river; to the north ranged the pine-clad hills that hid the Himalayas. From east to west ran a broad belt of forest. Oudh was a land of narrow fields and wide rivers, of open barren tracts, single great trees and dense mango groves, of patches of jungle and shallow reedy lakes, dry river beds and ravines cut deep into the rock by the floods of the monsoon rains.

For those who lived in the mud-walled, reed-thatched huts, who scraped the soil and herded cattle on bare grazing, life was poverty-stricken – the hunger-line often crossed. The hands of the revenue collector and the village moneylender grasped for their meagre earnings.

Above the peasant was a kind of peasant aristocracy, a class of yeomen consisting mainly of high-caste Hindus, but also of Muslims, most of whom were converts. The yeoman worked his own holding of land, seldom of more than twenty-five or thirty acres. Generally speaking, he was a tough, turbulent, but conservative type, quick to fight for his few rights but unwilling to cooperate with his fellows in the process. Above, again, were the talukdars, the great landowners. Almost all of these were Hindus of Rajput descent. Before the annexation of Oudh by the British, many had been officials of the king of Oudh's government, tax farmers, thinly disguised robber barons.

The kingdom had had a brief history of thirty-eight years, during which five rulers had held the throne. Before that it had been a province of the Moghul empire, its governor one of the great officers of state. When the empire began to come apart at the seams, the governor had made himself an independent ruler. His descendants, however, soon found themselves owing allegiance to a new empire, that of the English East India Company. The Company guaranteed the dynasty and protected its possessions from any rapacity other than the Company's own. When money was needed, Oudh was milked. When Oudh had no money a piece of territory was taken instead. In 1819, partly in recompense, and partly to diminish the stature of the king in Delhi, the ruler of Oudh was granted the title of king.

What was actually happening inside Oudh worried the British

93

occasionally, but not for long. The kings of Oudh degenerated into a succession of royal imbeciles, sunk in debauchery, and subject to the whims of fiddlers, eunuchs and poetasters. The country was dominated by the private pleasure and personal profit of favourites and panders, while the army, unpaid, dissolute, and mutinous, roamed round the country terrorising a populace already squeezed by ruthless tax collectors and petty tyrants.

But with the arrival of Lord Dalhousie, anxious to tidy up India and bring the blessings of rational administration to all, things began to move – if not at any great speed. In the years 1849–50 the then British Resident at the court of Oudh made an extensive tour of the country, and his reports made alarming reading. Colonel Sleeman did not, however, advocate annexation. In fact, he was strongly against it. His advice was: 'Assume the administration but do not grasp the revenues of the country.' [1] The advantages of indirect rule he thought significant. Native states with their misrule and absence of security made valuable propaganda contrasts with the peace and quiet prevailing in the Company's dominions. They also offered a safety valve for the ambitions of Indians who could find no place in British India.

Sleeman's report was in the hands of the governor-general in 1851, but the governor-general took no action, although in private correspondence he wrote that the outcome was inevitable. The Company would have to take over the administration. There was still no mention of annexation, perhaps because other problems to a large extent occupied Dalhousie's time. In 1854, however, Sleeman was replaced at Lucknow by James Outram. Outram's instructions were contained in a Minute from the governor-general. He was to 'make an inquiry into the present state of that country; with a view to determine whether its affairs still continue in that state in which Colonel Sleeman from time to time described them to be'. He was also to determine whether any changes in the existing system would 'in truth any longer admit of our honestly indulging the reluctance we have felt to have recourse to those extreme measures which alone can be of real efficacy in remedying the evils from which the state of Oudh has suffered so long'.[2]

In March 1855, Outram submitted a voluminous report covering everything from the court to roads and public works. Outram had considerable difficulty in compiling accurate statistics. Naturally, the king's officials were uncooperative. The total revenues for 1853 and 1854 appear to have amounted to about £1·2 million, a third of which actually reached the treasury, the remainder disappearing into the pockets of the officials.

Courts of justice existed only in the capital, and 'such as were there maintained were worthless, being presided over by men of no character, who treated their position simply as a means for extortion'. The army consisted of a total of sixty thousand men. Four regiments were commanded by European officers and were fairly efficient. The rest were an undisciplined rabble paid three or four rupees a month, well in arrears; they were permitted to compensate themselves by living on the peasants. Roads and public works hardly existed. The only metalled road – and that a bad one – was between Cawnpore and Lucknow. Two permanent bridges spanned the river Gumti at the capital, and six more in the rest of the country. In Outram's words, 'with the exception of a few government forts, there are literally no other public works in Oudh'.

At the end of his report, Outram felt himself bound to declare – though with some reluctance because he believed, like Sleeman, that native states were valuable breakwaters – that 'the lamentable condition of this kingdom has been caused by the very culpable apathy and gross misrule of the Sovereign and his Durbar'; that no improvements had taken place; and that it was his opinion that the British government should no longer refrain from 'those extreme measures which could alone be of any real efficacy'. In other words, the governor-general should take over the administration of Oudh. [3]

From Outram's report Dalhousie composed a vast minute to the Court of Directors in London, outlining possible courses of action. On 2 January 1856 their reply was received in Calcutta. The Directors agreed that misgovernment in Oudh must end. If Dalhousie thought the king might accept a kind of Vatican authority, he was to offer it. If not, Oudh should be annexed.

The governor-general immediately called a meeting of his council and the terms of a treaty were thrashed out. The king was to be offered jurisdiction over the palace of Lucknow and his favourite parks, the right to retain the title of king, and an allowance of £150,000 a year for him and his successors. For the rest, 'the sole and exclusive administration of civil and military government of the territories of Oudh shall henceforth be vested, for ever, in the Honourable East India Company together with the full and exclusive right to the revenue thereof'.

Outram, who was in Calcutta, was given the treaty and two draft Proclamations, the first to be used if the king consented to sign the treaty, the second in case of refusal. Both promised justice and protection to the people, rare commodities in Oudh. The Resident arrived back in Lucknow on 30 January and immediately informed the prime minister of the British government's intentions. He also announced that a column of Company's troops was advancing on the capital. The minister expressed surprise and distress, and 'attempted to contrast the reign of the present king with those of his predecessors and to point out the manifest reforms which were to be seen on both sides'. The Resident replied that the decision of the government was final.

Now that it was brought home to the king, his family, and his ministers that this time the British were determined to take over Oudh in one way or another, all attempted to stave off the inevitable. Promises of reform were made – and rejected. The king threatened to go to Britain and throw himself at the foot of the throne. He would not sign the treaty. Outram therefore assumed the government of Oudh in the name of the Company.

All went smoothly. British troops moved in, the king departed to exile in a comfortable house at Garden Reach, Calcutta. 'Everything,' wrote Outram a few days later to the governor-general, 'has been going most satisfactorily. The populace of the capital appear to have already forgotten they ever had a king, and display the same civility to Europeans they were previously noted for. Even the higher classes and nobles of the court appear already reconciled to the change. In the districts our Proclamations have been heartily welcomed, I am informed, by the middling and lower classes, and even the highest display no dissatisfaction; while the more powerful talukdars and chieftains in the provinces are turning their allegiance with alacrity.' [4]

But the calm was a calm induced by shock, and very soon wore off. Outram, a man of at least some sympathy, was compelled to give up his appointment as the first Chief Commissioner of Oudh because of ill health. The question of a successor could not have been more important. Sir Henry Lawrence, brother of John, a man over-praised after his death but, in spite of his faults, a rare character who knew that it was wise to tread warily on the sentiments of others, offered to stand in for Outram while he was on sick leave. But the offer came too late.

Coverley Jackson, an authority on revenue administration, would have been a reasonable appointment if he had not had a choleric temper and if his second-in-command Martin Gubbins – the new Financial Commissioner – had not had exactly the same fault. The administration of Oudh degenerated into displays of temper, irritation and resentment. Had Coverley Jackson expended as much energy on the administration as he did in attacking his subordinates it is possible that the state of Oudh might have been improved. But surrounded by clouds of charges and counter-charges, the commissioner unconsciously cultivated the seeds of rebellion.

And there were many. In Lucknow itself, nothing had been done to ease the change from one form of government to another. In fact, the conditions there were appalling. An extravagant court had disappeared almost overnight, but left behind were hundreds of court functionaries, tradesmen and pensioners. These men were ruined by the annexation. While Jackson and his associates wrangled over precedence, they and their families starved. Other changes pressed heavily on the people. New laws, new taxes, increased popular discontent. A tax on opium raised the price to such a level that many addicts were said to have committed suicide. The British, delighted to clean up an Augean Stables, tried to do so in one great cataract of reform.

Away from the capital, the countryside also suffered. The British were rightly convinced that the position of the peasant under the old regime had been that of a serf under a feudal lord. The big landowners, the talukdars, maintained their own private armies, with which they kept the peasant in a state of servility. Most of the talukdars had no title to their land other than that of the sword – a perfectly respectable title in Indian terms. But the British viewed annexation as an act of liberation. They transferred rights to village communities and resident cultivators in half the lands formerly held by the talukdars. Naturally, there was resentment. Among those who had lost only part of their holdings, the resentment remained submerged, though not very far below the surface. For those who lost all, there was banditry and terror.

To these amateur groups were added the slightly more professional talents of the state army. A quarter of the force, some fifteen thousand men, retained its employment under the new administration. The rest were given small pensions and gratuities and dismissed, to add another element to the growing unrest. Even those soldiers lucky enough to be retained under the colours were dangerous, for as Henry Lawrence was later to report: 'The Irregulars are bodies of men who last year served the king and have been taken in . . . as regiments with all their old associations . . . It is quite a mistake to suppose that these regiments like our service better than the king's. The small extra pay [about 5p a month] does not cover the extra bother – the pipe-clay and discipline and duty. Besides, the officers and men have lost their consideration and opportunities of plunder.'[5]

Conditions in Oudh also had repercussions outside the state. William Sleeman had warned Dalhousie that the annexation of Oudh would lead to a mutiny in the Bengal army, for the state was 'the great nursery of the sepoys'. This was true, for the larger portion – nearly two-thirds, in fact – of the army were high-caste Hindus from the king's territories. Every village had at least one soldier in the Company's forces. Before annexation a sepoy derived great advantages from service, for every man was, so to speak, represented at the court of Lucknow by the British Resident. The sepoy's commanding officer was authorised to frank any petition to the Resident, and in a state such as Oudh the sepoy was one of the few citizens with an advocate powerful enough to ensure justice from the king and his ministers. In Oudh, they formed a privileged class and took advantage of the fact. With annexation, all this was lost. 'I used to be a great man when I went home,' an Oudh cavalryman told Henry Lawrence. 'The rest of the village rose as I approached; now the lowest puff their pipes in my face.'[6]

Stories of what was going on in Oudh – and there was no need for exaggeration – were assiduously circulated among members of the Bengal army in the first months of 1857. Some were traced to the exiled court at Garden Reach. In June, the king and his closest advisors were taken into protective custody and lodged in Fort William. Whether he was guilty or not (and not guilty seems the more likely), it did not really matter. The damage had been done.

Henry Lawrence, who had taken over in Lucknow in March 1857, was soon convinced that he was sitting on a mine of explosive material. Others did not seem to agree. When the first rumours of the greased cartridges reached Lucknow in April, Lawrence knew that the situation was serious. The danger lay in the fact that the number of European troops in Oudh was ridiculously small and widely scattered; they were outnumbered by nearly ten to one. Lawrence did his best, using a mixture of firmness and conciliation. He was temporarily successful in reminding the sepoys of their loyalty, but the emotions that had been roused were not to be calmed by reason or crushed by inadequate strength.

As early as April, therefore, Lawrence began to make preparations. He decided to make them discreetly, so that neither the sepoys nor the general population would think he anticipated danger. If they did, he believed they might take the initiative before he was ready. He began to fortify the Residency and its surroundings.

Lucknow covered an area of twelve square miles. On the right bank of the river Gumti, running approximately from the north-west, there was a line of palaces and public buildings, the central ones of the Chuttur Munzil – or 'old palace' – nearer the river, and the Kaisarbagh, a much larger and more modern one, further away from it. To the north lay the Residency and its subsidiary buildings, on a raised plateau near the river, and further up an old fort, the Machchi Bhawan, which with the Residency shared the only commanding position in the city. To the south and west lay the city proper, bounded on the south, south-east and south-west by a canal. Across the river were other buildings forming a kind of subordinate town. This north bank of the river was connected with the south bank by a stone bridge near the Machchi Bhawan, an iron bridge a little up stream from the Residency, and a bridge of boats beyond the Chuttur Munzil. The buildings of the city were closely packed around the Residency. From a military point of view, the Residency area was almost indefensible.

But it had to be defended. On 14 May news of the rising at Meerut reached Lucknow. Lawrence had already been forced to disarm a unit of Oudh Irregulars, and there was trouble in the sepoy lines. A few days later, preparations were speeded up and the old fort of the Machchi Bhawan was put into some state of repair. By the end of May, the revolt had begun in earnest. Fortunately, the European force in Lucknow prevented a massacre, and the mutineers were chased into the countryside. But the countryside, too, was in revolt.

By early June, British rule in Oudh had ceased. 'Every outpost, I fear, has fallen,' wrote Lawrence on 12 June, 'and we daily expect to be besieged by the confederated mutineers and their allies.' [7]

THE MAULVI AND THE DANCING GIRL

During June, the fortification of the Residency continued, though without any marked efficiency, for on Sir Henry Lawrence's express order no attempt was made to demolish the houses which pressed upon its perimeter so closely. Towards the end of the month, news of the surrender of the garrison at Cawnpore reached the British, though in rather less detail than it did those Indians in the city who were waiting for a signal to rise. That signal was given by Lawrence himself. Yielding to the pressure of some of his more hysterical subordinates, he decided to attack a body of mutineers rumoured to be approaching the city. If this were not done, said one Englishman, 'we shall be branded at the bar of history as cowards'.[1]

On 29 June, news came that the mutineers' advance guard was now at Chinhat, about ten miles from Lucknow. The report stated that there were about 500 foot, 50 cavalry, and one small gun. Lawrence regarded the report as untrustworthy, and believed the numbers to be greater. Nevertheless, arrangements were made for an expedition against them. A force was assembled which amounted to 300 men of the 32nd Foot, 170 Native Infantry, 36 Volunteer Horse, and 84 Oudh Irregular Cavalry. They had ten guns and a howitzer drawn by an elephant. Lawrence, who was ill with overwork and strain, nevertheless decided to command the troops himself. His military experience was limited, and there were others more competent to command.

It was decided that the force should move off at dawn on 30 June, but because of inefficient organisation the sun was already hot when the march began. The men had had no breakfast. After covering three miles, the force reached the bridge over the river Gumti at Kokrail. Here a halt was called, and the 32nd were ordered to have breakfast. But for some reason unknown, rations were not distributed.

Lawrence reconnoitred forward and saw no enemy; he gave the order to return to Lucknow, the wisest course to follow. Then he made his second error (the first had been to order the expedition at all). While the command was being given to countermarch, he received news from some 'native travellers' that there was no rebel force at Chinhat at all. Lawrence changed his mind and ordered an advance.

Everything went wrong. The heat of the day was overpowering, and the water-carriers seem to have deserted. The troops had had no food, and there was some doubt about the loyalty of the native gunners. No proper forward reconnaissance took place – someone who was there recorded that, suddenly, 'a turn in the road showed us the enemy drawn up with their centre on the road and their left

99

resting on a lake'.[2] The Lucknow force never had a chance, for the enemy's numbers were later estimated at about 5,500 foot, 800 horse and twelve or sixteen pieces of good artillery. In command was one Barhat Ahmad, who was obviously a much better soldier than Lawrence.

As the British force moved forward, roundshot smashed into them. A party of the 32nd, who had occupied the small village of Ismailganj, was thrown out of it by a detachment of the enemy. On the other side, the mutineers attacked a party of loyal sepoys. At this stage, Lawrence's native gunners and cavalry deserted. The 32nd tried to retake Ismailganj but, weakened by the heat and lack of food, failed to do so. Lawrence's column was now in danger of being encircled. The enemy's horse artillery was on its flanks, and the cavalry had moved in and taken the bridge at Kokrail, cutting the British off from Lucknow.

A force of volunteer cavalry charged the enemy at the bridge and succeeded in breaking through. They were followed by the rest of the force, now pretty much of a rabble. Lawrence, rather too late, handed over command of the column to a professional soldier and rode back to the Residency at full speed, realising that this defeat would mean an immediate attack upon the fortifications. Behind him, he left almost half the 32nd dead or wounded and some of the best of the garrison's commissioned and non-commissioned officers.

To the Europeans who had remained in Lucknow, the return of the defeated force brought fear and anxiety. Mrs Inglis, watching from the Residency, wrote in her journal: 'You may imagine our feelings of anxiety and consternation. I posted myself and watched the poor men coming in; a melancholy spectacle indeed – no order, one after the other; some riding; some wounded, supported by their comrades; some on guns; some fell down and died from exhaustion not half a mile from our position. The enemy followed them to the bridge close to the Residency . . . I could see the smoke of the musketry and plainly discerned the enemy on the opposite bank of the river.'[3]

The blow to prestige was almost worse. The siege of the Residency was precipitated when more work on the fortifications was still necessary. All of Lawrence's careful preparations were jeopardised by his own bad leadership and inept organisation. That night, inside the Residency, he wrote: 'This morning we went out to Chinhat to meet the enemy, and we were defeated, and lost five guns through the misconduct of our native artillery, many of whom deserted. The enemy have followed us up, and we have now been besieged for four hours, and shall probably tonight be surrounded. The enemy are very bold, some Europeans very low. I look on our position now as ten times as bad as it was yesterday; indeed it is very critical. We shall have to abandon much supplies and to blow up much powder. Unless we are relieved quickly, say in fifteen or twenty days, we shall hardly be able to maintain our position. We lost three officers killed this morning and several wounded.'[4]

Five days later, Lawrence himself was dead, mortally wounded by a shell. But the garrison was able to maintain its position for a great deal longer than he had expected.[5]

The news of the defeat at Chinhat, of course, delighted the rebels in the city. There was extra cause in the fact that the victorious force had not consisted entirely of mutinous sepoys from the Company's army. It seems that some of the disbanded state troops were there too. More significantly, three talukdars with their own men were present at the battle. By no means all the talukdars rose immediately; some remained, not loyal but at least passive, for the whole of the rebellion; some even helped the British. Few were as chivalrous as Raja Lal Hanumant Singh of Dharapur, who escorted Captain Barrow, the deputy commissioner of Salone, to the safety first of his own fort and then through hostile country to the banks of the Ganges opposite Allahabad. When Barrow said he hoped the raja would support the British, the raja replied: 'Sahib, your countrymen came into this country and drove out our king. You sent your officers round the districts to examine the titles to the estates. At one blow you took from me lands which from time immemorial had been in my family. I submitted. Suddenly misfortune fell upon you. The people of the land rose against you. You came to me whom you despoiled. I have saved you. But now – I march with my retainers to Lucknow to try and drive you from the country.'[6] The fact that at least some of the traditional élite and their feudal serfs had risen in revolt gave to the rebellion in Oudh a 'national' character which was to be regarded as significant by later Indian historians.[7] But the dispossessed had reasons other than patriotism, and the revival of feudal relationships was assisted more by the known and feared threat to religion than by any desire to return to the old order of economic dependency.

Nevertheless, to certain – though not all – classes the sepoys did make a direct appeal for unity. A proclamation issued by the mutineers at Azamgarh in Bihar, in June 1857, was soon circulating through Oudh; the sepoys saw to that, for after mutinying at Azamgarh they left with bands playing and colours flying for Faizabad, in Oudh. In their proclamation, the sepoys called upon the upper classes to sink their differences in the fight against the hated foreigners. To the land-owners – even the new ones created by the British – they said: 'It is very well known that the British assess lands very highly.' Besides, when a landowner was 'sued by a mean labourer or a male or female servant', he was 'summoned without investigation to attend at Court and . . . thus dishonoured and degraded'. Furthermore, when a landowner had to prosecute 'a case in their Court' he was 'put to the expense of doing so on stamp paper', and had to pay court fees, 'which are ruinous'. Besides which every landowner had 'to pay a percentage for roads and schools'. Those in business were reminded: 'You are well aware that the faithless British have appropriated to themselves the monopoly of lucrative trade such as indigo, opium, cloth etc and left the less lucrative merchandise to you . . . Moreover they realise money from the public in the shape of postage

101

and school funds and you, like the [landowners], are degraded by being summoned to their Courts and imprisoned or fined on the assertion of mean and low people.' Those of the official class, said the proclamation, must certainly be aware that 'in the Civil and Military Departments all the less lucrative and dignified positions are given to the natives, and the well-paid and honourable ones to Europeans'. Craftsmen were told that 'the Europeans import every sort of article from Europe leaving but a small trade in your hands'. And the religious, especially priests and scholars, Hindu or Muslim, were advised to remember that the 'British are opposed to your religion'.[8]

In fact, the emphasis on religion in danger and the need for a defensive holy war had been the message carried throughout Oudh from village to village, and from town to town, during the months prior to the outbreak of formal rebellion. Much of this propaganda had been directed towards the Muslim peasantry by wandering Muslim preachers. To Hindus, holy men and fakirs brought warning and fear.

Among the Muslim leaders, the most important still remains essentially a mystery man. There is no certainty even about his name, though it seems most likely that this was Ahmadullah Shah. He was best known to the British as simply the 'Moulavie' (*Maulvi*: literally, 'a learned Muslim') of Faizabad. The Maulvi had appeared in Faizabad in February 1857. No one knew where he had come from or who he was. It was said that he came from the town of Arcot in the Madras Presidency, and it has been suggested that he was responsible for a proclamation posted up in Madras city in January 1857 calling for a bloody war.[9] What is reasonably certain is that the Maulvi did travel about the country accompanied by a small band of armed followers and that he did make seditious speeches calling for a holy war against the infidel. So loudly did he shout that even the British heard him. At Faizabad he was arrested and his followers were forcibly disarmed. When the sepoys at Faizabad mutinied, he was quickly released and made for Lucknow, where apparently he had already made contact with members of the royal family and others unreconciled to the imposition of British rule.

There were many to listen to this dynamic orator. Even his presence was exciting. He was a 'tall, lean, muscular man, with thin jaws, long thin lips, high aquiline nose; deep-set large dark eyes, beetle brows, long beard, and coarse black hair, falling in masses over his shoulders'.[10] He seemed to personify the spirit of rebellion and among the rebel leaders in Lucknow he stood out as one of the few who not only knew what he was doing but why he was doing it.

Lucknow, once the British had been driven inside the walls of the Residency, was in anarchy. There were plenty of armed men, though there was a shortage of heavy ammunition, of shot and shell for the artillery. There was no leadership. Instead the rebels were a collection of private armies. There were the sepoys who, in an excessive reaction against authority, had like their fellows in Delhi turned to a form of democratic election for their leadership. But, as so often in democratic processes, it was not the most honest or the most competent who were elected. Even those who *were* chosen found their tenure unsure. Their actions, or lack of them, were subject to open criticism, and they themselves to summary demotion. It was hardly the way to run an army. Those who found it irksome either left the town or formed themselves into loose associations whose loyalty was more traditional than egalitarian. This might or might not lead to greater military efficiency, but it did not encourage general unity. The talukdars' men were little more than a badly armed rabble.

Even so, it would have been easy for the rebels to overrun the Residency. But they tried seriously only four times, and in each case were beaten off, though not without difficulty. This lack of success on the part of a besieging force estimated by the British as fluctuating between 50,000 and 100,000 men, attacking a virtually indefensible perimeter guarded by a few hundred, was easily rationalised after the rebellion in terms of racial superiority. On the surface, it seemed at least an explanation, for the attacks *were* genuine and there is no doubt that the standard of military expertise on the British side was of a very low order. What other reason could there be than 'the spirit of the race'?

It is, however, possible that the rebels saw the Residency for exactly what it was. Militarily speaking, it was without meaning. The rebels found its existence offensive, especially the tattered Union Jack, constantly repaired and replaced, which flew provocatively on the topmost tower, but they had more important work elsewhere. What they did not realise was that the defence of the Residency, and the inevitable suffering for women and children that went with it, became a symbol for the British, one of those symbols that in time of war concentrate the mind, excite the emotions, and make all issues seem of great simplicity. In fact, the rebels knew as little about the psychology of the British as the British knew about theirs.

But there were some among the rebels who realised that a leader, even if only a figurehead, was needed to give some kind of focus to the conflicting purposes of the various styles of rebel. The ex-king of Oudh was under restraint in Fort William in Calcutta, but perhaps some other member of the royal family could serve the purpose. The ex-king had had a number of male children by various members of his harem, though this in fact only complicated matters, as it meant that factions within the rebel camp could claim a candidate with equal legitimacy, if not equal precedence. As early as 7 July, however, it seems that agreement had been reached. Birjis Qadr, a young son by a minor wife, Hazrat Mahal, was selected. Barhat Ahmad, who had triumphed over Henry Lawrence at Chinhat and appears to have been in command of the rebel sepoys in Lucknow, had another prince in mind, but he seems to have been relieved of his command soon after the selection of Birjis Qadr. The Maulvi, who called himself the *khalifat-ullah* (or 'deputy of God'), supported the latter prince, then ten years of age. Perhaps in deference to his father, or

103

even to the king of Delhi who had once been Oudh's overlord, Birjis Qadr did not take either the title of king or the earlier one of nawab. Proclamations in his name used only the title 'Wali', which means ruler or governor.

Whatever the new ruler's title, real power rested in the hands of his mother and her advisors. Little is known of Hazrat Mahal's early life; even her age at the time of the rebellion is unrecorded. The last king's palace diary, the *Mahal Khana Shahi*, says that she was a courtesan by profession, who had been sold by her parents to the royal agents. The diary also noted that, as she wanted to live an honourable family life, the king gave her shelter in his harem as a dancing girl, with the name of Mahak Pari. Progression in the royal harem followed a precise pattern. A girl usually entered as a *khawasin*, or attendant. If the king liked her, she was promoted to *pari*, or dancing girl. If she were taken into concubinage, she became a *begum*. Ultimately, if fortunate enough to have a child by the king, her name was changed and the word *mahal* added to it. This particular dancing girl achieved all the promotions possible.

Once a formal head of state had been agreed, a council was appointed, carefully designed to balance both the conflicting ambitions and the differing religions of the parties involved. A number of ministers from the ex-king's former government, were among the chosen. A Muslim became chief minister, while the portfolio of finance went to a Hindu. The man who was thought to be Hazrat Mahal's lover was given the post of Chief Justice, while a Hindu became minister of war. Only Barhat Ahmad was left out. Unfortunately, those to whom military authority was delegated had no experience of the army or of war. Too careful balancing of interests frequently means that the general interest of the cause itself is neglected. This was certainly the case in Oudh.

The installation of Birjis Qadr took place in Lucknow on 6 August. There was a great deal of noise and the firing of a salute of guns led the defenders in the Residency to believe, for a moment, that relief had come.

In fact, General Havelock had made an attempt to reach Lucknow but had had to fall back on Cawnpore to await reinforcements. When these arrived, he was able to move forward very slowly, meeting the opposition of sepoys, talukdars and villagers on his way. With great difficulty, he broke through the rebel-infested streets of the city of Lucknow to reach the Residency on 25 September – but his force was too weak to break out again. A reserve force had been left at one of the royal parks, the Alambagh, a few miles outside the city, but the rebels were able to prevent the British from opening up communications between there and the Residency. Even after Havelock's arrival, the rebels still made only half-hearted attempts to assault the Residency, relying on trying to blow the defenders up with the aid of mines tunnelled towards the defences.

The British failure to relieve the Residency in force, may have convinced the rebels that they still had little to fear. Their intelligence was good, far better than that of the British, but their evaluation of it was faulty. Even the news of the fall of Delhi did not alter their view that the British had been effectively defeated. This was mainly a product of the rebels' ignorance of the larger world outside India. The British were still thought of as being without resources. They had conquered India with Indians; without Indians, they must lose it. Very few Indians had travelled to Britain, and even fewer of those were on the rebel side. The rebels' view was the traditional Indian view. For centuries, new rulers had emerged – and just as certainly disappeared when their armies and revenues had gone. The rebels knew that British manufactures – cotton cloths and other products – had destroyed Indian crafts, but they had no conception of the industrial and financial power that underpinned this assault on the traditional economy. Some Indians even believed that the entire population of Britain had deserted Britain for India.

The slowness with which the British moved to the relief of the Residency only encouraged the rebels in their beliefs. As the weeks went by without any further move from the British to attack Lucknow, it looked as if Havelock's sortie had been no more than an isolated gesture. It was not until the end of October that the new commander-in-chief in India, Sir Colin Campbell, felt able to take an initiative. At Cawnpore, the British were once again threatened, this time by a force commanded by Tantia Topi, but Campbell decided to ignore it and press on to Lucknow. He, at least, knew the value of symbols – as long as they were kept bright. The British had looked upon the defence of the Residency as an epic of racial heroism, but the effect on the morale of the troops if nothing were done quickly to bring out the women and children beleagured there would have been disastrous.

Campbell reached the Alambagh on 14 November. The enlarged garrison in the Residency had been able to extend the perimeter, and three days later he reached the Residency. His decision was to evacuate the garrison and leave the recapture of the city until later. On 22 November, the tattered flag was pulled down in the night and the Residency was abandoned. A substantial force under the command of James Outram was left in the Alambagh to await Campbell's eventual return, in force.

Campbell and the refugees from Lucknow reached Cawnpore just in time to prevent the city from falling into rebel hands for a second time.

The decision to abandon the Lucknow Residency had been a sensible one in military terms, but wars are more than tactics. Campbell, after securing the lines of communication with Agra and Delhi to the west, and towards Calcutta in the east, wanted to leave Lucknow alone and concentrate for the time being on Rohilkhand. Lord Canning thought otherwise, even after Campbell had sent in his recommendations and prefaced them with gentle reminder that he knew more about war than the governor-general. 'It is very possible,' wrote Campbell on 22 December, 'that many of the points may have

occurred to your Lordship: but some of them are so purely professional, that it is likely they would escape one not bred in the army.'
Canning, however, was convinced that 'so long as Oudh is not dealt
with there will be no real quiet on this side of India',[11] and he made
his views quite clear to Campbell. Just as the capture of Delhi had
had its effect on the morale of British troops and on the rest of the
country, as yet untouched by rebellion, so everyone was now waiting
to see what the British would do about Lucknow. 'I believe,' Canning
wrote on 7 January, 'it to be impossible to foresee the consequences
of leaving that city unsubdued.'

His professional objections overruled, Campbell began to make
preparations to conquer Oudh. New troops were arriving from
Britain every day, and a powerful ally, Jang Bahadur of Nepal, who
had been assisting the British since July 1857, offered his personal
aid in the reoccupation of Oudh.

It was not until March 1858, however, that Campbell began the
last campaign against Lucknow. As he moved into Oudh, his forces
were constantly harassed by sepoys and by bodies of men raised by
some of the talukdars. In the Alambagh, Outram also made his
preparations. He had spent the winter under frequent attack. On one
occasion, the enemy force was accompanied by Hazrat Mahal
mounted on a war elephant. Another attack was said to have been
commanded by the Maulvi in person. But Outram had managed to
withstand everything and to keep his communications with Cawnpore
open. His spies now reported that in and around the city there were
some 100,000 rebels.

News of Campbell's movements made the rebels look to their own
defences. They had begun to construct a defensive wall at the time
of the first relief. This was now completed, and three further lines
of earthworks and other defences were built inside the city. But no
attempt was made to fortify the north bank of the river Gumti. This
was to be a fatal error for the rebels. Messages bearing the seal of
Birjis Qadr had been sent out to all the loyal chiefs, calling on them
for aid. Diplomacy was brought into play, and Jang Bahadur was
offered a large tract of territory if he would desert the British side.
But Jang Bahadur had made his choice; the British, not the rebels,
were going to win.

Campbell's campaign was much criticised at the time, and later,
for its slowness. His preparations were so meticulous that he
altogether missed the cold weather season, the best for fighting and
especially so for his European troops. Even when he did move, his
handling of the attack on Lucknow was particularly inept. He did
not use his cavalry to their full advantage, and he gave to General
Outram one of the most surprising orders ever given by a commander
in a war. While Campbell moved with his main force along the north
bank of the river to take the city on its undefended side, Outram
asked for permission to move from the south. Campbell's reply was
that 'he was not to do so if he thought he would lose a single man'.[12]
More surprising still, Outram accepted the order without question,

did not move, and so failed to cut off the rebels who were later able to escape from the city comparatively unscathed. Outram was assisted in this débâcle by the almost wilful stupidity of the officer commanding the cavalry.

The rebels put up very strong opposition to Campbell's force, but even their own incompetence could not prevent the British from winning. A large force of rebels – possibly accompanied by Hazrat Mahal, who was extremely active at this time – held out in one of the royal parks until 19 March, but were finally driven out by heavy gunfire into what should have been the arms of the cavalry. But for some unaccountable reason the cavalry was not there. Officially, it had lost its way, but an officer who was there condemned its commander in no uncertain terms. 'His error appears to have partaken of wilfulness. He moved his force in utter disregard of the statement of his guides, in opposition to the protestations and explanations of all to whose information and advice he was bound to listen.' [13]

The Maulvi, like Hazrat Mahal, had been active in defence of the city. After the failure of his attempt to capture the Alambagh in January, there had been a conspiracy among the supporters of Hazrat Mahal to reduce his influence with the rebels. He was apparently imprisoned, probably at some distance from Lucknow, but escaped, and with his powerful personality was able to regain his position. According to British intelligence reports, there had actually been armed conflict between elements supporting the Maulvi and those supporting Hazrat Mahal. All this, if not forgotten, was put aside at the approach of Campbell's force. The Maulvi had fortified a house in the heart of the city. A determined assault broke the defence on 21 March, however, and the rebels retreated. This time the cavalry was there to receive them, but the Maulvi escaped.

Next day the city was in Campbell's hands. It had been a victory with very few casualties on the British side, and Campbell was congratulated for it. But it was not really a *military* victory at all. The majority of the rebel forces escaped, as did their leaders, to fight again and again. The propaganda effect, however, was all Canning had hoped for. Outside Oudh, at least. The effect inside was somewhat spoiled by an ill-timed proclamation from the governor-general. Instead of offering an immediate amnesty to the civil rebels, the proclamation announced the confiscation of the possessions of all landowners except six specifically mentioned by name in the proclamation. There was a clause inserted on the insistence of James Outram, offering 'indulgence' to those who surrendered, but the indulgence amounted only to a guarantee of 'lives and honour'. Anything more depended on the 'justice and mercy of the British Government'.[14]

The proclamation was not well received, either by the landowners of Oudh or the British in Lucknow. William Howard Russell of *The Times*, who was there, reported on 22 March that he had obtained a copy of the proclamation 'which I sent to London, where no doubt it will excite as much disapprobation as it does here. I have not heard one voice raised in its defence; and even those who are habitually silent, now open their mouths to condemn the policy which must perpetuate the rebellion in Oudh'.[15] The proclamation was, indeed, bitterly attacked in London and its terms were repudiated by the government. But the damage had been done.

Through a mixture of threats and cajolery, the people of Lucknow were persuaded to return to their shattered city. Shattered not so much by the fighting, though that had been fierce in parts, as by the plundering of the victorious army. Russell, who lost the chance of an armlet of enormous pearls and other stones because he did not have a hundred rupees in cash to give to the soldier who had 'liberated' it, found the scene of plunder 'indescribable. The soldiers had broken up several of the store-rooms, and pitched the contents into the court, which was lumbered with cases, with embroidered clothes, gold and silver brocade, silver vessels, arms, banners, drums, shawls, scarfs, musical instruments, mirrors, pictures, books, accounts, medicine bottles, gorgeous standards, shields, spears, and a heap of things, the enumeration of which would make this sheet of paper like a catalogue of a broker's sale. Through these moved the men, wild with excitement, "drunk with plunder". I had often heard the phrase, but never saw the thing itself before. They smashed to pieces the fowling-pieces and pistols to get at the gold mountings and the stones set in the stocks. They burned in a fire, which they made in the centre of the court, brocades and embroidered shawls for the sake of the gold and silver. China, glass, and jade they dashed to pieces in pure wantonness; pictures they ripped up, or tossed on the flames; furniture shared the same fate'.[16]

No one was absolutely sure what happened to all the official loot, estimated by the Prize Agents at over £1·5 million in value. According to Sergeant Forbes-Mitchell of the 93rd Highlanders, 'it was shrewdly suspected by the troops that certain small caskets in battered cases, which contained the redemption of mortgaged estates in Scotland, England, and Ireland, and snug fishing and shooting-boxes in every game-haunted and salmon-frequented angle of the world, found their way inside the uniform cases of even the prize agents. I could myself name one deeply-encumbered estate which was cleared of mortgage to the tune of £180,000 within two years of the plunder of Lucknow'. All Forbes-Mitchell was certain of was that 'each private soldier who served through the relief and capture of Lucknow got prize-money to the value of Rs. 17·8'.[17]

The rebels did not take long to start up the campaign again; in fact it never really stopped. There were few pitched battles; the rebels had taken to heart the advice given by one of their own number. 'Do not attempt to meet the regular columns of the infidels, because they are superior to you in discipline and bunderbust [organisation], and have big guns; but watch their movements, guard all the ghauts [landing places] on the rivers, intercept their communications, stop their supplies, cut up their daks [relays] and posts, and keep constantly hanging about their camps; give them no rest.'[18]

The Maulvi was active near Lucknow only a few days after his retreat from the city but was forced once again to retire, this time into Rohilkhand. There he descended on the weakly-held British outpost at Shahjahanpur and was able to seize the fort, turning his guns on the British who had taken refuge in and around the jail. The Maulvi was quick to execute those who had given aid to the British, but he was unable to capture the British themselves, who held out for eight days before a large force commanded by Brigadier Jones arrived. By this time the Maulvi had himself been reinforced by two bodies of troops, one commanded by Hazrat Mahal and the other by one of the Moghul princes, Firuz Shah, who had not been in India at the time the rebellion broke out and had thus escaped the fate of the rest of his family at Delhi. Active in Central India, he had made his way to Lucknow, arriving only just in time to be caught up in the British attack.

But even with reinforcements and his natural flair for leadership, the Maulvi could not stand up against Jones's force. Retiring from Shahjahanpur, he fell upon Mohamdi, destroying the fort and much of the town. On 5 June he suddenly reappeared at Powain, a few miles from Shahjahanpur. The raja hurriedly closed the gates of his fort, and refused to open them for the Maulvi. A parley took place, but the raja insisted he would not give up his fort.

The Maulvi, who was riding a war elephant, ordered its driver to smash down the gate. The animal's head hit the gate with a loud crash, and it was already shaking on its hinges when one of the defenders – the raja's brother, it was said – shot the Maulvi dead. The defenders then rushed out and cut off the Maulvi's head. Seeing their leader killed, the Maulvi's men broke and ran.

Wrapping the severed head in a cloth, the raja set off almost immediately for Shahjahanpur, riding his own elephant, and surrounded by an escort. When he arrived, he found the magistrate and some British friends sitting down to their evening meal. Without hesitating, the raja marched into the dining-room and produced a spectacular entrée. Opening the cloth, he rolled the bloody head of the Maulvi on the floor. Next day, it was set up on a pike over the police station. The raja received a reward of Rs. 50,000 which had been offered by the governor-general for the death or capture of this remarkable rebel.

No better epitaph could be found for the Maulvi than the words of an enemy. 'If a patriot is a man who plots and fights for the independence, wrongly destroyed, of his native country, then most certainly the Maulvi was a true patriot. He had not stained his sword by assassination, he had connived at no murders: he had fought manfully, honourably, and stubbornly in the field against the strangers who had seized his country, and his memory is entitled to the respect of the brave and the true-hearted of all nations.' [19]

Hazrat Mahal and her son survived the rebellion. When Campbell was able to turn his attention once again to Oudh, his strategy was to push the remaining rebels towards the Nepalese frontier. There he hoped either to crush them or leave them to die in the jungly forests of the Terai. The Oudh rebels, however, persisted in thinking that they would be able to persuade Jang Bahadur to come to their aid. Letters had been sent to him on more than one occasion, in the name of Birjis Qadr, but these overtures had all been rejected. The British continued to push the rebels towards the foothills. Yet even at this late stage, Hazrat Mahal remained undaunted. She issued a counter-proclamation to that of Queen Victoria, though what effect it had is not known.* But it did not influence the course of events. On the last day of 1858, the rebel leaders crossed the frontier into Nepal.

Hazrat Mahal still hoped for assistance from Jang Bahadur, but on 15 January 1859 he wrote to her: 'Be it known, that an intimate friendship exists between the British Government and the Nepal State, and both of them are bound by Treaty to apprehend and surrender to the other the enemies of either. I therefore write to you, that if you should remain or seek an asylum within my Territory and Frontier, the Gurkha troops will most certainly, in pursuance of the treaty agreed upon by both the high states, attack and make war on you . . . And be it also known, that the Nepal State will neither assist, show mercy to, nor permit to remain in its territories or within its frontier those who have been so faithless and ungrateful as to do mischief, and raise animosity and insurrection, against their masters, of whose salt they have partaken; to whom they owe their change for the better; and by whom they have been fostered.' [20]

Jang Bahadur, however, does not appear to have pressed too hard upon Hazrat Mahal and her son, and they were allowed, with their small retinue, to remain in peace. Hazrat Mahal could have taken advantage of the amnesty offered by the British, but she made no attempt to negotiate terms. With the failure of an attempt by the British Resident at Katmandu to persuade her to return to India, Hazrat Mahal passes out of history – a dancing girl who became a queen, and behaved like a queen to the end. In this she was not alone, for in Central India another queen had been forced into rebellion to defend her rights.

* See Appendix 3, p. 168.

PART FIVE

The fortress and the pyre

Whatever her faults in British eyes may have been, her countrymen
will ever remember that she was driven by ill-treatment into rebellion,
and that she lived and died for her country.

Colonel Malleson on the Rani of Jhansi, in
History of the Indian Mutiny, vol. iii.
London 1878

Our very remarkable friend, Tantia Topi, is too troublesome and
clever an enemy to be admired ... He has sacked stations, plundered
treasuries, emptied arsenals, collected armies ... Up mountains,
over rivers, through ravines and valleys, amid swamps, on he goes,
backwards and forwards, and sideways and zigzag ways – now falling
upon a postcart and carrying off the Bombay mails – now looting a
village ... yet evasive as Proteus.

William Howard Russell, 17 January 1859

THE JEZEBEL OF INDIA

Captain Alexander Skene, political officer in the small Maratha state of Jhansi, some 140 miles south-west of Agra, was not particularly perturbed when the news of the outbreak at Meerut reached him. Though he had only a small force of Indian soldiers and no Europeans, he felt reasonably secure. 'The troops here,' he wrote on 18 May, 'I am glad to say, continue staunch and express their unbounded abhorrence of the atrocities committed at Meerut and Delhi. I am going on the principle of showing perfect confidence, and I am quite sure I am right.'[1] Twelve days later, he reported a certain amount of unease in the town, especially among the merchants and bankers, but he felt that 'all will settle down here, I am perfectly certain, on the receipt of intelligence of success'.[2]

Skene had few fears about the sepoys, and even fewer about the inhabitants of the city. He did not consider that there might be men there who were anxiously waiting to see what the British would do. Jhansi had not long been part of the Company's India, just over three years, in fact. In the days before Baji Rao had become a pensioner of the British at Bithur, Jhansi had been the seat of a Maratha governor. But British expansion had detached Jhansi from the Maratha confederation before its collapse. The governor had signed a treaty with the Company, and found himself an independent ruling prince – independent, at least, of the Peshwa. That had been in 1804. Thirteen years later, another treaty had guaranteed the state to the ruler and his heirs in perpetuity. In 1835, the then ruler had been invested with the grandiloquent title of Maharajadhiraj Fidvi Badshah Jamjah Inglistan – 'Devoted Servant of the Glorious King of England'.

The bearer of this title had died without a direct heir and his widow had adopted a son of her sister's. The Company did not approve, and another heir was appointed to suceed to the throne. Here, the British were following Hindu tradition, for there was no sanction for adopting as an heir someone from outside the royal family. When the man chosen to succeed turned out to be dissolute and incapable of ruling the state, the British stepped in and took over the administration. They did not depose the raja, but when he died there was once again a dispute over the succession as he had left no legitimate heir. The Company decided on one of his natural sons, Ganghadar Rao, who was allowed to succeed in 1843.

The new raja was a man of considerable taste and some scholarship. He collected a fine library of Sanskrit manuscripts and considerably enriched the architecture of the town of Jhansi. But he, too, was unable to supply the state with an heir. The day before he died in November 1853, he adopted with all the necessary Hindu rites and in the presence of the British political agent at his court, a boy from another branch of his own family. He then handed over for transmission to the governor-general a letter, in which he asked for the protection of the British government for his wife and child. In the letter, the dying raja asked that, as an acknowledgement of the loyalty of his dynasty, the British 'should treat this child with kindness'. He further requested that 'the government of the state should be given to my widow during the length of her life, as the ruler of this principality and the mother of my adopted child'.[3]

The governor-general, Lord Dalhousie, ever anxious to bring the boons of progress to what he considered as reactionary outposts of feudalism, would not accept the dead raja's pleas. Dalhousie argued that Jhansi, unlike other states in which such an adoption had been endorsed by the British, had never been an independent entity. First it had been a dependency of the Maratha Peshwa, then of the Company. The promises of the treaty of 1817, and the subsequent actions by the Company in matters of the succession, were dismissed as irrelevant, and Jhansi was annexed in March 1854.

The widow of the last raja, the Rani Lakshmi Bai, had submitted memoranda to the governor-general rehearsing the precedents of her case, but these had been ignored. An appeal to the Court of Directors in London was rejected. In essence, the British – putting aside the doubtful legality of their action – had not been ungenerous. A life pension of Rs. 60,000 had been settled on the Rani, and though she had to evacuate the fort she was permitted to live in the city palace. She and her retinue were not to be subject to the jurisdiction of British courts, and the adopted heir was allowed to inherit the personal estate of the raja. This, amounting to some Rs. 600,000, was however held in trust by the Company until the boy came of age. It seems likely that the Rani would have accepted the situation in time, though when the Company's decision to annex Jhansi had been communicated to her she had cried out; 'I shall not surrender my Jhansi.'

But neither she nor the people of Jhansi actually resisted the take-over. The Rani moved into the city palace. The state army was disbanded and all seemed quiet. Nevertheless, both the Rani and the people deeply resented the action of the British. Loyal they had been, and how had their loyalty been repaid? With, apparently, indifference to the feelings of Indians. Villages which had been assigned to the great Mahalakshmi temple, the shrine of the royal family, were detached, and the revenue was diverted into the Company's treasury. This so angered the Rani that she at first refused to accept the pension that had been granted to her. When she did, it was to discover that the last raja's debts would have to be paid out of it. When she asked for Rs. 100,000 out of the estate to pay for the ceremony of the sacred thread – the Hindu coming of age – for her adopted son, the government refused unless she could produce four sureties for the repayment of the amount, should the boy demand it when he came of age – which would, according to the Company's European reckoning, be several years later. As for the people, not only did they resent the way their former rulers were being treated; they also resented the way in which their religion was being ignored. The British formally permitted the killing of cows in Jhansi.

In 1857, the Rani was in her early thirties, though her exact date of birth is unknown. She was the daughter of a retainer of Chimnaji Appa, the brother of Baji Rao, and had been born in Banaras, where Chimnaji had settled after his brother's surrender to the British. On Chimnaji's death in 1832, the girl's father had taken his family to Bithur and the court of the exiled Peshwa. After the rebellion, it was alleged that the Rani had been a playmate of the Nana Sahib and Tantia Topi, but both were much older than she, and the story is undoubtedly a fiction. Nevertheless, it was Baji Rao who suggested to the raja of Jhansi that she would make a suitable wife for him.

John Lang, an English lawyer who met her soon after the annexation of Jhansi, described the Rani as being 'rather stout but not too stout'. Her face 'must have been very handsome when she was younger, and even now it had many charms – though, according to my idea of beauty, it was too round. The expression also was very good, and very intelligent. The eyes were particularly fine, and the nose very delicately shaped. She was not very fair, though she was far from black. She had no ornaments, strange to say, upon her person, except a pair of gold ear-rings. Her dress was a plain white muslin, so fine in texture, and drawn about her in such a way, and so tightly, that the outline of her figure was plainly discernible – and a remarkably fine figure she had'.[4] On her husband's death, Lakshmi Bai gave up purdah, the traditional concealment of women, and went out into the streets with her face uncovered. Only when visited by British officials did she remain behind a screen, thereby increasing the formality of the occasion. There was no doubt in anyone's mind that she was a highly capable woman. Between the death of her husband and the official takeover of the state by the British, she supervised the administration with a constant attention to detail. The governor-general's agent, Major Malcolm, reported that she was 'a woman highly respected and esteemed, and I believe fully capable of doing justice to such a charge [i.e. governing the state]'.[5]

When news of the outbreak at Meerut reached the Rani, she asked Captain Skene for permission to raise a body of armed men for her own protection. Skene approved, for he was convinced of the Rani's loyalty to those who had stolen her state. One Indian source alleges that, the day before the sepoys mutinied, Skene went to the Rani and asked her to 'take charge of the state'.[6] But there is no supporting evidence. Nor is there any real basis for the assertion that she was involved in conspiracy with the sepoys before they mutinied. Mutiny they did.

There had been warning. On 1 June, some of the bungalows belonging to British officers were set on fire. Captain Skene and the commander of the troops, Captain Dunlop, believed it was an accident and took no precautions. Two days later, some of the sepoys seized a small building known as the Star Fort, inside which were the

115

treasury and the magazine. The rest of the men seemed still to be loyal, but next day Captain Dunlop and two other British officers were murdered. The remaining British and Eurasians took refuge in the fort inside the city and prepared to defend it. They numbered only fifty-five, including women and children, and only four of the men were soldiers or had had military experience. Next day, it was seen that the sepoys had brought up two guns. At this stage, Skene – for some reason never discovered – decided that he could not hold out and asked the sepoys for a safe conduct. It is possible that, as Skene had had no fear of mutiny, he had not sent ammunition or provisions into the fort, and therefore decided he could not put up a defence.

On 8 June, Skene received the assurances he needed. Through an emissary, a doctor named Saleh Muhammad, the sepoys swore 'on the most sacred oaths' that the party in the fort would be allowed to leave without interference after laying down their arms. The party marched out and was immediately taken prisoner and moved to a garden known as the Jokhan Bagh. There, the whole party was massacred. Only one rather dark Eurasian woman, with her two children, managed to escape from the fort disguised as Indians. Four days after the massacre the sepoys left Jhansi, having extracted from the Rani a large sum of money. Their case had been simple. They had freed the state from the British and must be rewarded. Already, they had approached another member of the royal family and offered to make him raja, but this seems to have been designed only to bring pressure on the Rani. There was also more direct intimidation. The sepoys surrounded the palace and their leaders threatened to blow up the building, laying a trail of gunpowder to underline the threat.

With the departure of the sepoys, the Rani could do nothing but take over the administration. No other authority existed. The same day, the Rani sent a messenger to the commissioner of the Saugor division, Major Erskine. In her letter, she told what had happened. 'The troops stationed at Jhansi through their faithlessness, cruelty and violence, killed all the European civil and military officers, the clerks and all their families; and the Rani not being able to assist them for want of guns and soldiers, as she had only a hundred and fifty people guarding her house, she could render them no aid, which she very much regrets . . . Since her dependence was entirely on the British authorities who met with such a misfortune, the sepoys, knowing her to be quite helpless, sent her messages . . . to the effect that if she at all hesitated to comply with their requests they would blow up her palace with guns. Taking into consideration her position, she was obliged to consent to all the requests made and put up with a great deal of annoyance, and had to pay large sums in property, as well as in cash, to save her life and honour.

'Knowing that no British officers had been spared in the whole district, she was, in consideration of the welfare and protection of the people and the District, induced to address orders to all the government subordinate Agencies, such as Police, etc., to remain at their posts and perform their duties as usual. She is in continual fear for for her own life and those of the inhabitants.' [7]

Two days later, the Rani wrote another letter to Erskine. 'It is quite beyond her power,' she said, 'to make any arrangements for the safety of the district and the measure would require funds, which she does not possess, nor will the usurers in times like these lend her money. Up to the present time, after selling her own personal property and suffering much inconvenience, she has managed to save the town from being plundered and has kept up the form of the late government. She has recruited many people for the protection of the Town . . . but without competent Government Force and funds she foresees the impossibility of holding on any further.'

To these letters, which were carried in hollowed sticks through a countryside in a state of anarchy, Erskine replied on 2 July. He thanked the Rani for her actions and went on: 'Until a new Superintendent arrives at Jhansi I beg you will manage the District for the British Government.' He called upon all 'great and small' to obey her.[9]

Erskine's response was not altogether approved of in Calcutta, though no blame was attached to him. However, he was told that if the Rani's account of events in Jhansi turned out to be false, she could not hope for protection from the British government. The Rani was not told this officially, but it seems likely that she knew of the government's attitude through spies in Erskine's office. But she soon had troubles nearer home. The rival who had been offered the throne by the mutineers tried to assert his claim and had to be attacked. On the first occasion he escaped, and afterwards returned. This time he was caught and imprisoned in the Jhansi fort. This comparatively minor irritation was followed by a much more dangerous threat to the Rani's position. Jhansi was invaded by the troops of two neighbouring states, Orchha and Datia, who were ostensible allies of the British but in fact intended to divide Jhansi between them.

The Rani appealed to the British for help but received no answer. The British were now convinced that she had been responsible for the massacre of the British at Jhansi. She had become the 'Jezebel of India . . . the young rani upon whose head rested the blood of the slain'.[10] The Rani therefore appealed for help against the invaders to those who had once been feudatories of the state. They responded. The Rani set up a foundry to cast cannon and, after an initial setback, decisively crushed the invaders. But her position had changed. In order to defeat the invaders, she had become involved with the rebels. Among her forces were mutineers, and at least two rebel rajas had given her their support. Nevertheless, her intention was still to hold Jhansi on behalf of the British.

From the defeat of the invading forces in August 1857 until January 1858, Jhansi was at peace, though battles were being fought not far away. These implied that the British were gaining the upper hand. In January the Rani again tried to get the British to understand her situation. She even wrote to say that she had not received a pro-

117

clamation promised by Major Erskine and had therefore been forced to assume control of Jhansi in her own name. Intelligence reports reaching the British, though never very reliable, confirmed that she was unwilling to take any aggressive action against the British. But they also said that her advisors and officers were divided. Her army and most of her allies and feudatories wanted her to fight for the state, not to hand it over to the British when (and if) they finally came back. The British had tried to stabilise the position in Jhansi by announcing the imminent arrival of their troops, but the fact that these troops did not arrive only strengthened the arguments of those in Jhansi who advocated war.

The Rani's personal position was, in fact, precarious. She had the support of the people and of her allies, but only for as long as she appeared to rule. The rebellion had released ambitions, some of them long suppressed. The fate of the rebellion elsewhere meant very little. There were no tears shed in Jhansi for the fall of Delhi and very few for the tribulations of the new Peshwa, the Nana Sahib. It was not for the revival of either the Moghul power or that of the Peshwa that men were hoping, but for the establishment of their own. If the Rani surrendered Jhansi once again to the British, the old order would never be restored. The rebellion had been successful in Jhansi and the surrounding country. Why, then, should its benefits be voluntarily given up?

The Rani and her supporters were aware of what the British were saying about her, and in March 1858 it was clear that British troops were, at last, coming to Jhansi. With the record of their vengeance preceding them, no one could honestly believe that Jhansi would be spared. All the pressures were for resistance. On 21 March the time of decision arrived. The British under the command of Sir Hugh Rose were outside the gates of Jhansi.

Rose, who had assumed command of the Central India Field Force in December 1857, though a stranger to India was a soldier of intelligence and dash; two characteristics commonly lacking in other British commanders of the time. He had not approached Jhansi directly, but fought a number of sharp engagements to ensure his lines of communications before he did. All this was time-consuming, and it had in fact taken him six weeks to move the 125 miles which separated Saugor, which he occupied on 3 February, from Jhansi.

Within a few miles of his objective, Rose had been faced with a major decision. News reached him that Tantia Topi, little the worse, apparently, for his defeat at Cawnpore, had suddenly appeared at Charkheri, a small state whose raja had remained loyal to the British. Rose was ordered to go to his aid, but decided to disobey. By the time he reached Charkheri it would probably have fallen, and the way to Jhansi would be open to Tantia if he chose to reinforce the Rani. Even though Rose's force was probably too small to take what was believed to be a well-defended fortress city, the effort had to be made. Rose hoped, in any case, to join up with another force commanded by Brigadier Stuart. Jhansi had to be taken, for it had become a symbol of revolt, and in the traditional world symbols were almost always more important than realities.

Though the Rani may well have considered that there was still a chance of negotiation with the British, preparations for the defence of the city were not neglected. The fort of Jhansi was built on a high rock and completely dominated the town. Its granite walls were between sixteen and twenty feet thick. Its south face met the walls of the town itself, and the other sides were completely enclosed by the city walls, themselves of substantial stone construction, loopholed for riflemen. The south face of the fort was almost perpendicular and the only way for an attacking force to take the fort was to break through the town first. On the towers of the fort heavy guns had been placed which could fire without restriction over the surrounding countryside. On one of the towers – known as the White Tower – flew the Rani's flag.

The Rani, in fact, seems to have been extremely active and regularly attended the drill and training of the troops. Her particular interest was in the formation and training of a force of women, who were to fight by the side of the men when the attack came. Others, however, were making different preparations. Some of the wealthy families were known to be shipping gold and jewellery out of the city, most of it to Gwalior, whose ruler was loyal to the British and whose fort was believed to be impregnable. Since the Gwalior Contingent had departed from the state, no one expected further trouble there. Neither the Rani nor her allies made any attempt to stop the exodus of treasure or of people. Nevertheless, though the desertion of a few families hardly mattered, it was possible that their example might upset the rest of the population. Military displays and ceremonies were therefore arranged to impress the people with the strength of the forces in Jhansi as well as with the Rani's determination to use them.

Rose's first act was to issue a proclamation demanding the surrender of the city. If not, it would be destroyed. The decision was put to the Rani's advisors. Her ministers still advocated an attempt at negotiation. The military leaders were, not unnaturally, in favour of a fight, and representatives of the citizens agreed with them. The Rani then issued a proclamation of her own. 'We fight for independence. In the words of Lord Krishna, we will if we are victorious, enjoy the fruits of victory, if defeated and killed on the field of battle, we shall surely earn eternal glory and salvation.' [11]

Rose's bombardment began on 24 March, doing considerable damage to the defences. But the return fire was heavy and repairs to the walls and bastions were carried out during the bombardment, mainly, it appeared to the besiegers, by women. The defenders, hoping for aid from outside had sent messengers with appeals for help to Tantia Topi and to the Nana Sahib's nephew, Rao Sahib. Rose's spies heard of Tantia's movements before the defenders of Jhansi and reported them to Rose, but on the night of 31 March the

119

defenders saw the light of a huge bonfire which Tantia had lit, filling the sky with the promise of relief.

Rose's spies had informed him that Tantia had at least twenty thousand men with him and that he was moving rapidly. Rose could either raise the siege of Jhansi and take his whole force into action against Tantia, or leave part of it to continue the pressure on the city. He decided on the latter course and immediately set off to meet Tantia. The two forces clashed on the banks of the Betwa river, and after a series of engagements Tantia's force was put to flight. Rose then turned back to Jhansi. The terrible news of Tantia's defeat arrived before him. The defenders of Jhansi were alone.

While the battle of the Betwa had been going on, the British force left behind to continue the siege of Jhansi went on pouring shot and shell into the city. For some reason, possibly because of treachery within her own ranks, the Rani made no attempt to leave the city and attack the seriously depleted force still besieging it. British siege guns had managed to widen a breach in the walls and, by 2 April, it was thought to be just large enough for an assault to be made. Rose, who had returned immediately to Jhansi after the defeat of Tantia Topi, planned to launch a false attack against the west wall of the city and, while this was in progress, to send the main storming party into the breach. Attempts would be made at various places to escalade the walls. Rose divided his force into four columns, one of which was to make straight for the breach while another silenced a rocket tower to the right of it.

Three a.m. on 3 April saw all the parties in position, waiting for the sound of the guns in the false attack as the signal to advance. When the sound came, the breach party under Lieutenant-Colonel Lowth moved up and through the breach, while the rocket tower party under Major Stuart, after a sharp engagement, forced its way into the town. The two parties then joined up and made for the Rani's palace. Meanwhile, the other two columns were preparing to attack one of the city gates where the defence, according to a traitor in the Rani's camp, was weakest.

As the British approached, enemy bugles could be heard and very heavy fire was brought to bear on the advance parties carrying the scaling ladders. However, they managed to place their ladders at three positions along the walls. But, wrote Dr Lowe, an eye-witness, 'the fire of the enemy waxed stronger, and amid the chaos of sounds, of volleys of musketry and roaring of cannon, and hissing and bursting of rockets, stink-pots, infernal machines, huge stones, blocks of wood, and trees – all hurled upon their devoted heads – the men wavered for a moment and sheltered themselves behind stones'.[12] Reinforced by a hundred Europeans hurriedly brought up, the stormers rushed to the ladders, but many were too short and others broke as the men began to climb. One group got over, however, and these were soon joined by more. There was bitter hand-to-hand fighting. At this point a party detached by Lowth fell upon the rear of the Jhansi defenders, who broke, and the British continued their movement towards the

120

palace. Each street and house was tenaciously defended, and as the rebels retired on the palace they set fire to the houses surrounding it.

As the stormers moved down the street to the palace which ran by the side of the fort, 'the matchlock and musketry fire on the men . . . was perfectly hellish! The bullets fell so thickly in the dusty road that they resembled the effect of hailstones falling in water when striking it, and the men fell thick and fast here. One point of the street ran quite close to the gateway of the fort and was not passed without severe loss. Here it was that most of our men fell.'[13]

When the British finally forced their way into the courtyard of the palace, each room in the building was bitterly fought over and a quantity of gunpowder exploded. 'When I got into the palace,' wrote an officer who was present, 'I found it crowded with our soldiery, some lying down worn out with the heat and hard work, some sauntering about with two or three puggries [Indian turban scarves] upon their heads and others around their waists, some lying down groaning from their wounds or the explosion, and others busily engaged extinguishing the flames in the rooms where the explosion had taken place. The whole place was a scene of quick ruin and confusion – windows, doors, boxes, and furniture went to wreck like lightning.'[14]

Heavy street fighting continued until the following day and no quarter was given, even to women and children. 'Those [of the rebels] who could not escape threw their women and babes down wells and then jumped down themselves.'[15] The British were not just capturing a city, but were intent on destroying what was to them as much a symbol of cruelty and suffering as the city of Cawnpore. 'No maudlin clemency was to mark the fall of the city,' wrote Dr Lowe.[16] And he was right. Looting and massacre were freely allowed. Although looting was officially forbidden, it was not possible to restrain the troops. What could not be easily carried away was smashed. The British were certainly living up to their reputation.

But the greatest prize eluded the victors. The Rani, after leaving the palace, had retired into the fort. There she discussed with her advisors what should be done next. It was obvious that further resistance in Jhansi itself was useless. For the Rani, there remained suicide. But Lakshmi Bai was persuaded that she must try to leave the city and join Tantia Topi or the Rao Sahib. At midnight on 4 April, accompanied by a small party, she left the fort and made for the north gate of the city. Passing the gate without challenge, the party made its way through Rose's outlying pickets and was miles away before it was discovered that the Rani had gone. The British believed that there had been traitors among their Indian troops who had allowed her to pass, but it is much more likely that the men were too busy looting to notice anything.

When Rose heard of the Rani's flight he sent a cavalry detachment in pursuit. Its commander, Lieutenant Dowker, 'was gaining fast on the Rani who, with four attendants, was escaping on a grey horse, when I was dismounted by a severe wound and would have been almost cut in half but that the blow was turned by the revolver on

121

my hip. I was thus obliged to give up the pursuit and the lady escaped for the time being'.[17] The Rani reached Kalpi before midnight on the 5th, to be joined there by Tantia Topi, who had been making a leisurely journey after his defeat on the Betwa.

The British claimed to have killed five thousand rebels during their attack on Jhansi, but many were innocent women and children. The streets were heavy with the smell of death. 'In the squares of the city the sepoys and soldiers collected hundreds of corpses in large heaps and covered them with wood, floorboards and anything that came handy and set them on fire. Now every square blazed with burning bodies and the city looked like one vast burning ground. By another order the people were given permission to take care of their dead, and those who could afford to give a ritual cremation took away the bodies of their relatives and friends, but the others were just thrown on the fire. It became difficult to breathe as the air stank with the odour of the burning human flesh and the stench of rotting animals in the streets. The carcases of thousands of bullocks, camels, elephants, horses, dogs, cats, donkeys, buffaloes and cows were strewn all over the city. These were collected and removed to the outskirts of the city where a huge pit was dug into which they were all pushed and the pit covered with earth.'[18] British losses were small.[19]

Rose remained at Jhansi to allow his men to recuperate. Meanwhile, at Kalpi – a hundred miles north-east of Jhansi on the river Jumna – the Rani tried to persuade Rao Sahib to reorganise the rebel forces, and some attempt was made to discipline them for the coming battle. The Rani was disliked by the other rebel commanders, possibly for her good sense and certainly for her sex, and Tantia Topi was once again appointed to command the rebels against Rose. The Rani, however, did persuade the other leaders that it would be best to confront Rose outside Kalpi, and the town of Kunch, forty-two miles to the south, was chosen as the place to meet the British. Unfortunately, the Rani's plan of campaign – which showed some awareness of military tactics – was not accepted by Tantia Topi. But the choice of Kunch gave the rebels a strong series of defences, for the town was difficult to approach, being surrounded with temples, woods, and gardens. The town itself was protected by a strong wall and entrenchments were constructed in front of it.

Nevertheless, the rebels could not stand up to Rose who, despite the gruelling heat, took the place on 6 May. His men, however, were too exhausted to pursue the rebels, who fell back again on Kalpi.

The defeat at Kunch aroused considerable recriminations in the rebel headquarters. Everyone blamed someone else, but all were united in their criticism of Tantia Topi, who had fled from Kunch ahead of his men. The divisions were so deep that when rumours reached Kalpi that Rose was on his way many rebels left the town and dispersed into the countryside. According to one report, only eleven soldiers were left in the whole of Kalpi.

The rebels, however, received an unexpected reinforcement. The

Nawab of Banda, a relative of Rao Sahib who had been forced to join the rebels, arrived unexpectedly at Kalpi with two thousand cavalry, some infantry and guns. This revived the rebels' spirits and the sepoys began to return to Kalpi. Rao Sahib held a council of war, under pressure from the Rani, and it was decided to defend Kalpi to the last man. 'We will win or perish but never will we leave the field,' they swore on the sacred waters of the Jumna.

The rebel position at Kalpi was again a good one. Though the town itself was without fortifications, it was approached by many miles of country split by deep ravines. In front, and in the direction of Kunch, elaborate defences had been constructed to bar the road. These outworks were made up of trenches and barricades. The rear of the town lay upon the Jumna itself and the fort was sited on a precipitous rock emerging from the river. The rebels believed that the ravines would severely hamper the movement of Rose's cavalry and guns. If they were driven out of their forward entrenchments, they could fall back on a line of temples each surrounded by walls. Behind the temples were more ravines, then the town itself, with more ravines behind and finally the fort, perched on its rock over the Jumna. The rebels also believed, quite rightly, that they had a powerful ally in the sun. Tantia Topi issued an order to the troops forbidding any action against the British before ten o'clock in the morning. After that, the sun would strike.

But though the heat played its part and Rose's field hospitals were full of men suffering from sunstroke, Kalpi still fell to the British. It was 24 May and Queen Victoria's birthday. It seemed to Rose a very suitable coincidence. The Union Jack was ceremoniously raised on the fort in celebration of the sovereign's birthday and, Rose believed, the end of the campaign.

Everyone agreed. Sir Colin Campbell decided that the Central India Field Force could be disbanded. Sir Hugh Rose, who was ill, could go back to England on sick leave and the rounding up of the defeated rebels could be left to lesser men. Rose issued a farewell proclamation to his troops and made ready to leave.

On 4 June, however, before Rose had actually gone, shattering news arrived at his headquarters. The rebels, whom he had regarded as a demoralised rabble, had taken Gwalior.

After their defeat at Kalpi, the rebel leaders had held a council at which delegates of the sepoys were also present. The situation that faced them was hardly an appealing one. The rebels had lost at Kalpi their last stronghold south of the Jumna river, and a new field had to be found for their operations against the British. The sepoys wanted to join their comrades in Oudh; the Rani of Jhansi wanted a base somewhere in Bundelkhand; Rao Sahib preferred the Deccan, once the heartland of the Maratha empire he was fighting to revive. Then it was suggested, either by the Rani or Tantia Topi, that they should take the fort at Gwalior. Tantia Topi, it is believed, had visited Gwalior after his defeat at Kunch and had come to the conclusion that the Maharaja Sindhia's troops could be persuaded to revolt. The Maharaja had decided that the British would survive the mutiny in their native army and had tried to restrain the Gwalior Contingent which, though paid by him, was officered and trained by the British. When they mutinied, he protected the British in his territory and tried to keep the contingent from leaving the state. In September 1857, however, they had been persuaded by Tantia Topi to join the rebels and had been involved in action near Cawnpore. The departure of the contingent from Gwalior had not, however, diminished sympathy for the rebels. On the contrary, though the Maharaja might have second sight as to the course of future events, others, many of them high officers of state, remembered that Gwalior had once been one of the greatest of the Maratha powers, so great that its ruler had once controlled the Moghul emperor.[20]

The attempt to win over Gwalior, and if possible the Maharaja, was left to Tantia Topi. If he succeeded in the first, it would mean that the rebels would have an important base with an exceptionally strong fort and, what was of more immediate importance, funds and supplies. If Tantia also succeeded in winning over the Maharaja it would be a serious blow to British prestige, and other seemingly 'loyal' princes might throw in their lot with the rebels. Tantia Topi's mission was completely successful with Sindhia's army and his principal nobles, and he received solemn promises that, if the rebels marched on Gwalior, they would meet with no resistance. The Maharaja, on the other hand, would not listen to Tantia Topi's overtures, for he believed that if he could hold out long enough the British would come to his aid. The Maharaja had also heard that the rebel army was without supplies and in a demoralised state.

On 30 May, news came to Sindhia that Tantia Topi, the Rani of Jhansi, and Rao Sahib, with 7,000 infantry, 4,000 cavalry, and twelve guns, had reached Morar, a town not far from Gwalior. Believing reports that the rebels were not in a fit condition to fight, the Maharaja marched out on 1 June to attack them and took up a position two miles to the east of Morar. His army consisted of 1,500 cavalry, his personal bodyguard of 600 men, and eight guns. Dividing these into three bodies, with his guns in the centre, he waited for the rebels to attack. They obliged him at about seven o'clock in the morning.

The rebel advance guard consisted of cavalry and camels. The Maharaja's guns opened fire on them, but as the smoke cleared away, 2,000 rebel horsemen charged and took the guns. At this, most of Sindhia's troops, excepting the bodyguard, went over to the rebels. After a bitter struggle, the Maharaja and his men fled and did not stop until they reached Agra.

The rebels now moved rapidly on Gwalior itself and occupied the town and fort without opposition. No looting was permitted, and most of the officials who had remained behind were confirmed in their appointments. But Rao Sahib did plunder the Maharaja's treasury, the contents of which were used to pay his own and Sindhia's troops. The rebels' next step was to set up a government, proclaiming the Nana Sahib as Peshwa of the revived Maratha dominion, with Rao Sahib as his governor in Gwalior.

There is no doubt that Rao Sahib expected the princes of the Deccan to rise and support him in rebellion against the British. The Rani of Jhansi, however, was rather less sanguine. She knew from her experience at Jhansi that Rose would probably march immediately on Gwalior, and she tried to persuade the rebel leaders to prepare for a British attack. They appeared to be more interested in letting off fireworks to celebrate the capture of the town, and in posturing about the Maratha revival. If the Rao Sahib, instead of staying at Gwalior, had pushed on to the Deccan, he might have raised the princes there. But for some reason he chose to stay where he was. Nor were any real preparations made to defend Gwalior. It was another fatal mistake. Rose, with his characteristic dash, was already on the move.

The Rani of Jhansi is said to have criticised Rao Sahib for making sweetmeats for the celebration of the capture of Gwalior instead of cannonballs to defend it against Rose. But she was ignored. According to later ballads and stories, the Rani withdrew from the rebel councils when her advice was rejected. When, on the arrival of Rose's force, she was once more consulted by Tantia Topi, she replied: 'Rao Sahib has destroyed all hopes of victory by deliberately ignoring the warnings I gave him and by neglecting his war preparations and giving all his attention to trivialities. The enemy is upon us and our army is not ready; everywhere I see nothing but disorder and chaos. How can you expect to win the battle? However, I shall not lose heart. The only thing you can do now is to take out your troops for one glorious attack on the English without caring for the result. You must see to it that the attack is sudden and determined and overwhelming; the enemy must be rolled back.

'I am ready to do my duty. You do yours! Go ahead and God be with you!' [21]

Rose moved with great speed. Morar was taken on 16 June. Three days later the rebels at Gwalior were completely defeated. Another day, and the impregnable fortress had also fallen. So, too, had the Rani of Jhansi. Reports of her death are conflicting, but there is no doubt that she died in action on 17 June. Major Macpherson, the political agent for Gwalior, believed she was shot while trying to escape. Sir Robert Hamilton, after an on-the-spot enquiry, agreed, though with considerable variation over the details. Indian sources are also contradictory, but all insist that she was not retreating when killed. One says she died in hand-to-hand fighting, another that she was wounded by a shell while directing rebel artillery fire against the British. Most agree that she was dressed as a man. The British believed they had found some of her bones at the place where she was said to have been hurriedly cremated by her followers, but this too is open to doubt. Later, a simple shrine was erected at the place where the cremation was believed to have taken place.

Sir Hugh Rose called the Rani 'the bravest and best of the military leaders of the rebels'. Considering the standard of military expertise on both sides, it was no great compliment, even from a victorious general. She had been driven into rebellion, into a totally unnecessary martyrdom, by the weakness and hatred of the British.

In time, the British forgot the Rani – but Indians did not. In ballads and stories, her life was turned into an epic, perhaps rightly so, because her story has the nobility, the harsh sense of unavoidable destiny – and the tragedy – that are the essential elements of legend. Her memory remained alive throughout the years of nationalist struggle against the British. During the second world war, when a women's unit was formed in the Japanese-sponsored Indian National Army, it was inevitable that it should be called the Rani of Jhansi Regiment.

CHAPTER TWO

THE LAST REBEL

While Sir Hugh Rose was occupying Gwalior, Brigadier Napier was moving quickly to intercept the retreating rebels. The Rani of Jhansi was dead, but there remained Rao Sahib and Tantia Topi, both believed by the British to have been involved in the massacre at Cawnpore. Napier caught up with Tantia at Jawra Alipur, a few miles from Gwalior, but though the rebels were defeated again neither Rao Sahib nor Tantia Topi was among the dead or captured. However, this was not considered particularly important. It would only be a matter of time before they gave themselves up or were betrayed.

Once again the British decided that the rebellion was over. The Central India Field Force this time *was* disbanded and its units distributed to new stations. Everyone looked forward to a well-earned rest. Sir Hugh Rose once again prepared to leave for England, and actually left. But the rebellion was not at an end. Again, Tantia Topi had run away only to return. Within a few weeks of his defeat at Jawra Alipur, the villages and jungles of Central India were echoing the name and the exploits of this the most elusive of rebel leaders.

Tantia Topi had been born Ramchandra Panduranga in 1812, in the then independent territories of the Peshwa, Baji Rao. His father was a dependant of the Peshwa and followed his master into exile at Bithur. There Tantia had become a close friend and loyal supporter of the Nana Sahib, giving him, on the death of Baji Rao, his adherence as heir of the Peshwa.

Before the rebellion, John Lang met Tantia at Bithur. He was, wrote Lang, 'a man of about middle height — say five feet — rather slightly made, but very erect. He was far from good-looking. The forehead was low, the nose rather broad at the nostrils, and his teeth were irregular and discoloured. His eyes were expressive and full of cunning, like those,' remarked Lang, 'of most Asiatics; but he did not strike me as a man of eminent ability'.[1]

At the outbreak of the rebellion, Tantia was in Bithur and was given command of some of the Nana's troops. The British were convinced that he had been directly involved in the massacre on the river and in that at the Bibighur, but there is no satisfactory evidence either for or against. Tantia had had no formal military training, but he seems to have inherited the Maratha talent for guerrilla war. He did not know either how to assess the enemy's position and tactics, or how to take advantage of their weaknesses, which were many. At Cawnpore, when he had persuaded the Gwalior Contingent to follow him and had attacked the town while Campbell was away on the final relief of the Residency at Lucknow, Tantia could have taken

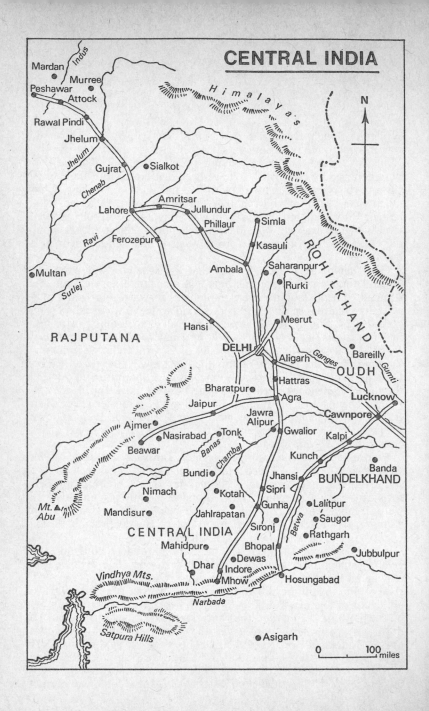

CENTRAL INDIA

N

Mardan
Murree
Peshawar
Attock
Rawal Pindi
Jhelum
Indus
Jhelum
Gujrat
Sialkot
Chenab
Amritsar
Lahore
Jullundur
Phillaur
Simla
Ravi
Ferozepur
Kasauli
Multan
Ambala
Saharanpur
Sutlej
Rurki
H i m a l a y a s
R O H I L K H A N D

RAJPUTANA
Hansi
Meerut
DELHI
Aligarh
Ganges
Bareilly
OUDH
Gumti
Hattras
Bharatpur
Jaipur
Agra
Lucknow
Jawra
Alipur
Cawnpore
Ajmer
Nasirabad
Tonk
Gwalior
Kalpi
Beawar
Banas
Chambal
Kunch
Bundi
Jhansi
Banda
Nimach
Kotah
Sipri
BUNDELKHAND
Mandisur
Jahlrapatan
Gunha
Lalitpur
Saugor
Sironj
Betwa
Rathgarh
CENTRAL INDIA
Mahidpur
Bhopal
Jubbulpur
Dhar
Dewas
Indore
Hosungabad
Vindhya Mts.
Mhow
Mt. Abu
Narbada
Satpura Hills
Asigarh

0   100 miles

10 Cawnpore: the scene in Wheeler's entrenchments before the mutineers' attack

11 The massacre on the river

12 Miss Wheeler defending herself against the sepoys

13 Brigadier-General James Neill   14 The Nana Sahib

15 A village near Cawnpore set alight and its inhabitants driven out by the British

16 Engagement between mutineer cavalry and British infantry at the battle outside Cawnpore

17 'Countrymen Revenge'. Soldiers add an inscription to the walls of the room in which the women and children were massacred

18 Outlying picket of the Highland Brigade at Cawnpore

the town. But he did not move fast enough, or press the advantage once he had won it. His talent, and it was a genuine one – as the British learned in the hardest of ways – was for sudden moves. When a formal battle was obviously lost, Tantia departed the field as quickly as possible. By those with military training, especially the sepoys of the Company's army, this was often viewed as cowardice or treachery.

Tantia seems quickly to have recognised that the time for pitched battles was over. He and Rao Sahib, after Jawra Alipur, crossed into the Rajputana, an area containing a large number of princely states and a people with a long tradition of warfare. Since the general tide was running with the British, Tantia believed that he could no longer count on the active support of the civil population, but thought he might be able to assure their neutrality. Rao Sahib issued a proclamation declaring that the rebel force would pay cash for supplies and that no one need fear either sequestration or reprisal. Parties of men were always sent in advance of the main rebel force to explain that no harm would come to the villagers and that supplies would be paid for in cash. Only if the villagers refused to sell would supplies be taken by force.

Tantia was certain he could persuade the troops of the princely states to side with him. On 27 June, General Roberts, commanding the Rajputana Field Force, heard that Tantia had sent a letter to the nobles of Jaipur inviting them to join him. Roberts immediately marched to Jaipur, but Tantia turned aside and made for the little state of Tonk, where the ruler's army went over to him. By this time, Tantia was being pursued by a flying column under Colonel Holmes.

The rains were now falling heavily and the river Chambal was so swollen that Tantia could not cross it and was forced to make for Bundi, where the ruler closed the gates of the town in his face. Tantia, under the impression that the pursuit was close behind, decided not to waste time in besieging the place. Publicly announcing that he proposed to move south, he in fact turned to the west and made for the country between Nasirabad and Nimach, where the embers of rebellion still glowed. The pursuit, however, was bogged down by the rain and it was not until 5 August that Roberts was able to march on Nimach. Two days later, he received news that Tantia was at Sanganir, some ten miles away. Actually, Tantia's position was midway between Sanganir and Bhilwara, which were separated from each other by a little river. Roberts, knowing that Holmes was moving up behind Tantia's position, decided to attack, though he had only a small force of cavalry.

The rebel position was well sited, but Roberts drove forwards, crossed the river, and brought his artillery to bear on the rebels. During the night, Tantia fled. Holmes was not near enough for immediate pursuit, and Tantia was able to retire to the village of Kotra in Udaipur. Next day, Holmes joined Roberts and the combined forced moved after Tantia. The same day they made contact with the rebel advance guard, and from prisoners taken Roberts learned that the main rebel force occupied a position on the Banas river, seven miles away.

Roberts's intelligence was unusually efficient, for the British had suffered badly from the lack of reliable information throughout the campaign. His method of obtaining information 'was to have about twenty cavalry in advance close to the rebels. They left connecting links of two or three men every few miles, so as to keep up the chain of communication. The advance party was composed half of Baluch Horse, who had no sympathy with the rebels but could not communicate very well with the villagers, and half of horsemen belonging to the Raja of Jaipur, who were supposed, as Rajputs, to be on good terms and able easily to communicate with the villagers, but not to be very warm partisans of the British. By this mixed party, correct and immediate intelligence was constantly supplied'.[2]

On 13 August Tantia left his men and made a pilgrimage to an important Hindu shrine. On his return, about midnight, he heard from his spies that the British were approaching. His first instinct was to move, but his men refused. They were, they said, too tired. Under the circumstances, there was no alternative for Tantia but to stand and fight. Again, his position was naturally strong. The river ran in front of him and also protected his right. To his left lay steep hills. On the opposite bank of the river a flat plain 800 yards wide offered no cover to his attackers.

When Roberts arrived, the rebels' four guns opened up, but despite casualties the British infantry forded the river and scaled the hill while the cavalry attacked the centre. The charge broke the rebel line and the cavalry pursued for nearly fifteen miles, cutting down stragglers and capturing three elephants and a quantity of baggage. The pursuit was abandoned when the rebels reached the jungle, where cavalry could not operate.

Tantia now made for the river Chambal, followed by Roberts who, when he reached Punah, near Chitor, met up with a brigade under Brigadier Parke who had come up from Nimach in order to cut off the rebels from the south. Roberts handed over the pursuit to Parke.

Unfortunately, Parke's cavalry horses were not in good shape and he was compelled to return to Nimach for remounts. There he was told by some self-styled experts that Tantia would not be able to cross the Chambal as it was swollen by the rains. Parke chose to believe them rather than the political agent in Udaipur, who assured him that Tantia would undoubtedly cross the river. When Parke received information that Tantia was indeed making the crossing, he arrived too late and found only 'a few disabled ponies standing on the left bank and the rebels disappearing among some mango trees in the west horizon'.[3] Parke returned to Nimach.

Tantia, still moving rapidly, now arrived at the town of Jhalrapatan in Jhalwar state. Here the state troops welcomed him and the raja was forced to pay a large ransom before he was able to contrive his escape. Tantia also obtained thirty guns with ammunition horses, which he badly needed, having had to abandon his artillery at the

Banas river engagement. The rebels remained five days in Jhalwar, as the Chambal had risen and blocked pursuit. Jhalwar was only fifty miles from Indore, and Tantia conceived the plan of making for that town and raising the rebellion there once again.

The British, however, had not been idle, and General Michel, commanding in Malwa, sent a force to cover Indore from a position at the town of Ujjain. At the same time, a small force moved out from Mhow. Michel himself, who had now also assumed General Roberts's command, joined the two forces at Nalkera, where he received reports that Tantia was moving in a north-easterly direction. Though it was now September, heavy rain was still falling and movement was difficult. Michel, however, pushed on until he met up with the rebels near Rajgarh.

Michel's men were extremely fatigued, night was coming on, and it was decided that the attack could wait until the morning. But when the next day dawned, Tantia and his men were nowhere to be seen. All that remained were the tracks of his elephants and the wheelmarks of his artillery. Michel at once sent his cavalry in pursuit and discovered the main rebel force deployed for battle. By the time the infantry and guns had caught up with the cavalry, however, the rebels were already in flight. In their haste to depart, they abandoned twenty-seven guns.

Tantia now disappeared into jungle country on the way to Sironj. The British began to close in again. Brigadier Parke controlled the approaches to Indore and Bhopal. Smith's brigade was moving down from the north. The column from Jhansi under Colonel Liddell was closing in from the north-east. Michel himself continued to move in from the west.

While General Michel was making his preparations and Tantia Topi was moving silently through the jungles near the river Betwa, Napier, operating out of Gwalior, had also been busy. Gwalior state, though reoccupied, was not pacified and the countryside was still disturbed. In August, a tributary of the Maharaja, named Man Singh, quarrelled with his overlord and, raising an army of twelve thousand followers, attacked the fort of Paori, eighty-three miles from Gwalior along the road to Sipri.

Napier ordered Smith, then still at Sipri, to march on Paori. When Smith neared the town, Man Singh sent a messenger with a letter asking for an interview and claiming that he was not in rebellion against the British but only against the Maharaja, who had, he said, robbed him of his ancestral right to the little state of Narwar. Man Singh, in fact, told the truth when he claimed: 'I have no connection with the rebels and no quarrel with the English.' Unfortunately, in the prevailing circumstances rebellion was rebellion, however justified the cause, and the British commander informed Man Singh that he must surrender and be punished for breaking the peace.

Paori was well fortified and amply supplied with ammunition. Smith's force was too small to attempt a successful siege. He therefore sat down outside and waited for reinforcements. Napier, deciding that Man Singh showed no signs of surrendering, gave the order that he must be attacked in case others followed his example. Smith received the reinforcements he required and after a twenty-four-hour artillery bombardment Man Singh and his men quitted the fort on the night of 23 August, leaving the British to occupy – and destroy – the fort next day. Man Singh was pursued and some of his men, under his uncle, Ajit Singh, were caught up with and dispersed near Gunah. Man Singh himself disappeared.

Meanwhile Tantia Topi had reached Sironj, in about the middle of September. After a few days' rest he took and plundered a town south of Sipri and there contemplated his future plans. He decided to divide the rebel force. Tantia, with the bulk of the men and five guns, was to make for Chanderi in Bundelkhand while Rao Sahib, who was still with him, was to take six guns and fewer men in the direction of Jhansi.

At Chanderi, Tantia found himself unable to capture the fort, which was held by one of Sindhia's men, and after three days of wasted effort he moved off towards the west bank of the Betwa. But Michel was now close behind and caught up with him at Mangrauli on 10 October. There Tantia stood his ground for a short while, then, as before, abandoned his guns and fled. Michel did not pursue him because he was without cavalry.

Tantia, always a little ahead of his pursuers, stopping now and again to fight them, seeming to be defeated but always reappearing somewhere else, at the end of October joined up once again with the Rao Sahib. They crossed the Narbada river and entered Nagpur, a former Maratha state where they expected to be joyously and actively received. A year earlier, they probably would have been, and the rebellion might well have spread south into the territory of the Nizam of Hyderabad. But now it was too late. The British were clearly winning and no one was prepared to join in a dying rebellion. British forces were also in a position to bar a further move southwards.

The rebels did receive some reinforcement at Kurgaon and, despite every effort by the British, recrossed the Narbada and made for Baroda, another Maratha state where there was considerable sympathy for the rebels. They were not destined to reach there, however, for they were overtaken by Parke at Chota Udaipur, fifty miles from Baroda, and once again defeated.

From Chota Udaipur, Tantia and Rao Sahib entered the little Rajput state of Banswara and then made for Pratabgarh where, on 25 December, they had a brush with a small British force. From there Tantia moved to Mandisur and then to Zirapur, almost due south of Gwalior. Despite his rapid progress, the British were still closing in, and the rebels marched to Nahergarh where they joined up with Man Singh.

Another rebel leader now appeared on the scene. Firuz Shah, a victim of Campbell's campaign in Rohilkhand, had crossed the Ganges and made for Kunch and Kalpi. Napier had marched to intercept him and did so at Ranod, a large town fifty miles north-east of Gunah. There Napier inflicted a severe defeat, and Firuz, with the remained of his force, moved away and met up with Tantia Topi at Indargarh.

The rebels, however, whose combined force numbered scarcely two thousand men, now seemed to be caught in a trap from which it would be impossible to escape. But escape they did. A British force caught up with them at Daosa, between Jaipur and Bharatpur, on 14 January 1859. The rebels lost a tenth of their men, but the remainder, with their leaders, contrived to get away. They rested for a day or so at Sikar in Jaipur state. Again they were surprised and routed on 21 January, and again the leaders escaped.

After their defeat at Sikar, the three rebel leaders decided to separate and so make it easier to evade their pursuers. Tantia, now with only three horses and a pony, left the others for the jungles of Paron. There he met Man Singh who, according to Tantia's own deposition, asked: ' "Why did you leave your force? You have not acted right in so doing." I replied that I was tired of running away and that I would remain with him whether I had done right or wrong.'[4]

As far as the British could learn from their spies, there was no indication of the whereabouts of any of the rebel leaders. Soon, however, Rao Sahib and Firuz Shah put out feelers for terms of surrender. Neither would accept the terms offered, and both escaped the net the British spread to catch them. Rao Sahib remained a fugitive until 1862, when he was betrayed and afterwards hanged. Firuz Shah died in poverty in Mecca in 1877.[5]

But it was Tantia Topi the British wanted most of all. He had kept them rushing around difficult country for months. To them, he was the last rebel. Until he was caught or killed, the rebellion would not really be over.

The British decided that Tantia's weak link was Man Singh. Though Man Singh had been treated as a rebel by the British, his real quarrel was with his overlord, the Maharaja of Gwalior. If a reconciliation could be achieved, he might surrender, especially as it was known that Man Singh was not enjoying his life as a fugitive.

The opportunity to open up negotiations came when Captain Meade, who commanded a detachment of Irregular Cavalry, learned that the landlord of a village near where he was stationed was connected with Man Singh. Meade went to the village and persuaded the old man to return with him to his base. After some talk, the landlord agreed to bring Man Singh's confidential agent to see Meade and said that he would use such influence as he had to persuade Man Singh to surrender. A few days later, Meade met the agent, and promised Man Singh his life and possibly the return of some of his confiscated property. He also suggested that if Man Singh sent in his wives and children they would be given shelter and protected from any reprisals by the Gwalior maharaja.

After more than a week in which nothing happened, Meade was ordered to put pressure on Man Singh. He moved out with his force into the jungle area, and was surprised when, on 25 March, about seventy members of Man Singh's household arrived in his camp with the agent, who informed Meade that the raja himself would surrender in a few days' time. Further negotiations took place, mainly concerned with those ceremonies so essential to status in India. One of the points of protocol on which Man Singh insisted was that he should be met at some distance from the British camp by a native of rank. This was easily arranged, and the raja surrendered on 2 April.

Tantia Topi was now alone, and only Man Singh knew where he was. The British had found the local inhabitants not only hostile but silent, and could obtain no information from them on Tantia's movements. It was time to play upon the hopes of Man Singh. He had his life, but he might have more. If he could perform some particularly outstanding service for the British, they would ensure that the Maharaja of Gwalior forgave him and returned at least some of his possessions. Meade worked on the raja for two days. He got a betrayal – but of Man Singh's uncle, not of Tantia Topi. And even when Man Singh led the British to the place where his uncle was supposed to be, there was no sign of him. Meade now became more pressing. 'I have,' he reported to his superiors, 'done all I could by kind and encouraging counsel to urge him to establish, by so signal an act of service [the betrayal of Tantia] his claim to the consideration of the Government, promised him . . . [on] the 27th ultimo.'[6]

Man Singh's problem was that he had to make up his mind before Tantia moved away from the area. While in Meade's camp, the raja appears to have been approached by an emissary of Tantia's who informed him that Tantia was considering rejoining Firuz Shah. For Man Singh, there was no point in betrayal if the rewards were not specific. General promises were not enough. He asked Meade for an assurance that certain territories which had formerly been part of his little state would be returned to him. This assurance Meade was not empowered to give. As time was running out, Man Singh reluctantly accepted Meade's promise that 'he might rely on any claim he might establish being faithfully considered by Government'.[7]

The raja's cooperation won, Meade now faced the problem of preparing to capture Tantia without everyone knowing his plans. He knew there were spies in his camp. If he sent off a detachment consisting only of Europeans it would be obvious that something important was afoot. Meade therefore decided to send a party of Native Infantry under an Indian officer. The officer was told to obey Man Singh's orders and to arrest any suspicious persons the raja might point out to him. Tantia's name was not mentioned.

Man Singh had already prepared the way by telling an emissary of Tantia's that he, Man Singh, would meet Tantia to discuss whether or not Tantia should join Firuz Shah. It is surprising that Tantia should have trusted Man Singh, but he did. On 7 April Man Singh and the troops were near the spot where Tantia was waiting with two attendants. The party was on foot, as Man Singh had insisted that no horses be taken in case Tantia should hear them and disappear into the jungle. About midday, Man Singh placed the infantry in ambush and then went on foot to meet Tantia. They talked for many hours, and then lay down to rest. At about midnight, Tantia was asleep and Man Singh brought in the troops. 'Tantia Topi was secured and pinioned, his arms being secured by Man Singh himself.'[8] In the slight struggle that took place, Tantia's two attendants escaped, or were allowed to escape. The rebel leader had with him only a sword and a large knife, three gold armlets, and 118 gold coins.

Next morning Tantia was taken to Meade at Sipri, but even in captivity the British still considered him a danger. A man who could lead some of their best generals such a dance, who could be caught only by treachery, might still slip out of their hands. Man Singh, in fact, reported that attempts were made to bribe the guard, though this may only have been his way of trying to hurry the British into action. If so, he was successful, and on 15 April Tantia was brought before a court martial at Sipri on the charge of having been in rebellion and having waged war against the British government between June 1857 and December 1858.

Tantia's defence was simple. 'I have only obeyed in all things I did, my master's [the Nana Sahib's] orders, up to the capture of Kalpi;[9] and afterwards those of Rao Sahib. I have nothing to state except that I had nothing to do with the murder of any European men, women or children; neither had I at any time given orders for anyone to be hanged.'[10] Tantia's own position was clear to him, and to many others who had joined in the rebellion. His master the Peshwa had been sent into exile, but the loyalties had remained the same. During British rule, his service to his master was only suspended. When the last Peshwa's heir had called for his service, it was given as a duty.

Tantia, in fact, did not put forward this argument at his trial. No doubt he felt that it was self-evident. But he was very much concerned with absolving both himself and the Nana Sahib of guilt for the two massacres at Cawnpore. His story of events at the river side was that he had been responsible for the arrangements for the British to sail down river to Allahabad. 'I went and got ready forty boats, and having caused all the gentlemen, ladies, and children to get into the boats, I started them off to Allahabad. In the meanwhile the whole army, artillery included . . . arrived at the river Ganges. The sepoys jumped into the water and commenced a massacre of all the men, women, and children, and set the boats on fire.'[11] As far as the murders at the Bibighur were concerned, neither Tantia nor the Nana was in Cawnpore at the time. Oddly enough, Tantia was *not* charged with the murder of British men, women and children, perhaps because it would have been too difficult to prove even to a prejudiced court martial. Later evidence, taken from informers, though it satisfied many cannot be trusted.

The court martial's verdict was a foregone conclusion. The sentence was death by hanging. Tantia had expected it, and asked only that his family should not be punished for anything he had done.

The execution was fixed for 4 p.m. on 18 April 1859. It was to be something of a ceremony. A scaffold had been erected in a square in the town and troops were assembled on all four sides. There was a large audience of Indians scattered at vantage points behind the soldiers. Tantia was brought to the square in irons, but after the charge had been read and the sentence repeated those round his legs were struck off. 'He mounted the ricketty ladder,' reported an eye-witness, 'with as much firmness as handcuffs would allow him; was then pinioned and his legs tied, he remarking that there was no necessity for these operations; and he then deliberately put his head into the noose, which being drawn tight by the executioner, the fatal bolt was drawn.' [12] Tantia did not die immediately; some servants had to be called to hang on to his legs.

'Thus finished the career of the rebel chief . . . with all the due solemnities of British military routine. When the suspended body became motionless, the troops were all marched off, and the body remained hanging for the remainder of the evening. After the troops left, a great scramble was made by officers and others to get a lock of hair . . .' [13]

PART SIX

The Queen's Peace over all

For we must bear our leader's blame,
    On us the shame will fall,
If we lift our hand from a fettered land,
    And the Queen's Peace over all,
        Dear Boys,
    The Queen's Peace over all.

Rudyard Kipling: *The Running of Shindand*

CHAPTER ONE

A KING ON TRIAL

The British were not quite sure what they should do with Bahadur Shah, king of Delhi by their courtesy, emperor of Hindustan by that of the rebels. There was delay in putting him on trial, and it aroused considerable controversy in the press. 'Prudent delay was imputed to weakness and indecision; and every act of mitigated punishment, where a native was concerned was, irrespective of the merits of the case, cried down as an exhibition of mistaken and mischievous leniency.'[1] The governor-general was the obvious target for criticism. Trying to decide between, on the one hand, 'the impulsive and all but national cry for unmitigated vengeance; and on the other, the calm and prudent dictates of high policy and humanity'.[2]

Lord Canning was quickly given the nickname 'Clemency'. The newspapers were full of inaccurate and inflammatory stories. 'We would call the attention of the government of India,' thundered one, 'to the state of things existing in the city of Delhi, which demand instant and stern reform. The youngest son of the king, eighteen years of age, has been declared innocent on account of his youth, and rides through Delhi on an elephant, with two British officers behind him to do him honour. The statement appears so incredible, that it may be set aside as a mere newspaper report; but we entreat the government to believe that it is one which we would not publish without such information as produces absolute certainty. The king also, it is said (but for this we have only the authority of the *Lahore Chronicle*), has a retinue who attend him, and coolly insults the British officers who visit him. It is things such as these – the honours paid to our murderers – which exasperate Europeans to frenzy.'[3]

The reports were entirely untrue. The king was certainly not treated with any indulgence. Nor were members of his family. Mrs Hodson, the wife of the man who had captured the king, visited him in December 1857. 'We mounted,' she wrote, 'a flight of stone steps, at the bottom and top of which was a European sentry. A small low door opened into a room, half of which was partitioned off with a grass matting . . . behind which was a woman cooking some atrocious compound, if I might judge from the smell. In the other half was a native bedstead – that is, a frame of bamboo, on four legs, with grass ropes strung across it; on this was lying, and smoking a hookah, an old man with a long white beard; no other article of furniture whatever was in the room; and I am almost ashamed to say that a feeling of pity mingled with my disgust, at seeing a man recently lord of an imperial city almost unparalleled for riches and magnificence, confined in a low, close, dirty room, which the lowest slave in his household would scarcely have occupied in the very palace where he had reigned supreme.'⁴ Another lady, Mrs Coopland, who saw the king at about the same time, confirmed Mrs Hodson's story, with a little additional colour. 'Pushing aside the [screen] we entered a small, dirty low room . . . At our entrance [the king] laid aside the hookah he had been smoking, and he, who had formerly thought it an insult for any one to sit in his presence, began salaaming to us in the most abject manner, and saying that he was "very glad" to see us.'⁵

The king's condition had not been improved when William Howard Russell saw him in June 1858. Russell found the whole atmosphere depressing. What had once been a magnificent palace was now a wreck. After passing among a collection of 'mean houses in various stages of ruin', Russell was led into a court, 'only partially paved, and the stones in places had been removed to repair the decaying houses'. From there he was 'taken by a breach made in the walls of the houses' into 'a large garden in a state of utter neglect and overrun with weeds', and finally arrived 'at a rude stone staircase' which led to a 'very small open court'. At last he was actually reaching the apartments assigned to the king. 'In a dingy, dark passage, leading from the open court or terrace in which we stood to a darker room beyond, there sat, crouched on his haunches, a diminutive, attenuated old man, dressed in an ordinary and rather dirty muslin tunic, his small lean feet bare, his head covered by a small thin cambric skullcap. The moment of our visit was not propitious . . . In fact, the ex-King was sick; with bent body he seemed nearly prostrate over a brass basin, into which he was retching violently.' Russell courteously turned away. 'That dim-wandering-eyed, dreamy old man, with feeble hanging nether lip and toothless gums,' he wondered, 'was he, indeed, one who had conceived that vast plan of restoring a great empire, who had fomented the most gigantic mutiny in the history of the world, and who, from the walls of his ancient palace, had hurled defiance and shot ridicule upon the race that held every throne in India in the hollow of their palms?'⁶

Russell 'could not help thinking, as I looked at the old man, that our rulers were somewhat to blame for the crimes he had committed'.⁷ But there were few, if any, who shared his view. Even Zinat Mahal had had enough. 'Why,' said she, 'the old . . . fool goes on as if he were a king; he's no king now. I want to go away from him. He's a troublesome, nasty, cross old fellow, and I'm quite tired of him.'⁸ Overhearing this, the ex-king 'merely asked one of his attendants for a piece of coffee-cake or chocolate, put a small piece in his mouth, mumbled it, smiled, and pointing with his thumbs over his shoulder in the direction from which the shrill and angry accents of queenly wrath were coming, said, with all the shrug and *bonhomie* of a withered little French marquis of the old school, "*Mon Dieu!* – I mean, Allah! listen to her!"'⁹

It would perhaps have been better, certainly more humane, if the old king had been sent into exile as quickly as possible. His treatment at Delhi had all the cruelty of indifference. But it was decided that there must be a trial. What the British hoped to gain from it is not clear – perhaps the salving of their conscience, perhaps a demonstration that a new era had begun. The trial was not organised as a show, a kind of nineteenth-century Nuremberg, for the British realised that to Indians it did not really matter. To them, power was the law and there was little purpose in invoking justice as well. It was a pity that the king had not decided to die with the rebels – which would have saved the British trouble. But he had not, and something had to be done, even if only to satisfy the newspapers.

In January 1859 a commission was appointed to try the ex-king. The gravamen of the charge was that Bahadur Shah, 'being a pensioner of the British government in India', had abetted the mutinous sepoys 'in the crimes of mutiny and rebellion', had supported his son, Mirza Moghul, conveniently dead, in his plan to 'rebel and wage war against the state', and, 'being a British subject . . . and not regarding his allegiance', had allowed himself 'to proclaim and declare himself the reigning king and sovereign of India'. It was also charged that he did 'feloniously cause and become an accessory to the murder of forty-nine persons, chiefly women and children of European and mixed European descent', and did 'encourage and abet divers soldiers and others in murdering European officers and other English subjects . . . both by promising such murderers service, advancement and distinction'.[10]

Bahadur Shah was to be tried by a military court, and because of his indifferent health and a change in the personnel of the court, it was not until 27 January 1859 that the first sitting could take place. The court met, with some sense of theatre, in the Hall of Private Audience in the Red Fort at Delhi. For various reasons, the accused was kept waiting for some hours before he was led into court, supported on one side by his youngest son. The charges were read out by the prosecutor, who reminded the court that the ex-king's life had been guaranteed to him, even if the verdict were guilty. When the charge was put to Bahadur Shah and he was asked to plead, he would not reply. After some argument, a plea of 'not guilty' was entered in the record.

The first day of the trial was taken up with the presentation of documents by the prosecution. These were designed to prove that Bahadur Shah had, in actuality, assumed power. Each document bore his signature and incorporated orders written by him. During this procedure Bahadur Shah dozed, and when asked to identify his signature claimed that he knew nothing of it. So the trial continued. Documents were produced and attested by people whom the British considered to be reliable witnesses. Evidence of the most damning sort was given, originating with informers. For the murder of Europeans, there were the most harrowing details, though none from really reliable eye-witnesses. One, Mrs Aldwell, the Eurasian wife of a Company official, had survived – so she said – by becoming a Muslim. Her evidence was damning, to the late Mirza Moghul if not to the ex-king. It was still written into the record.

On the charge of conspiracy, the testimony of one of the ex-king's

141

secretaries, Mukund Lal, was decisive in the eyes of the judges. According to him, Bahadur Shah had sent envoys to the Shah of Persia. A proclamation said to have come from the Shah had certainly been posted up on a wall in Delhi before the actual outbreak, but no lawyer would have been satisfied with the proof offered. The soldiers who comprised the court were easier to convince. Their purpose was to convict the ex-king and to pronounce sentence; such evidence as they were collecting was designed to prove to posterity that the verdict was justified.

During the giving of evidence and the examination of witnesses, Bahadur Shah – obviously senile – seemed sometimes concerned and sometimes angry at the statements made. But it did not matter. The verdict was, as everyone expected, that the ex-king was guilty on all charges. As he could not be executed, the sentence was that he should be transported for life either to the Andaman Islands or to some other place selected by the governor-general.

The problem of disposing of Bahadur Shah took some time. The Andaman Islands, in the Bay of Bengal, had been chosen as a prison for many of the rebels. But it was decided that it would be a mistake to send the ex-king there in case, once again, he became a focus for rebellion. South Africa was suggested. So, too, was Hong Kong. The final choice was Rangoon, in Burma.

While the decision was being made, the ex-king was still held with his immediate family in close confinement in the palace. Some of his time was spent in writing sad verses on his predicament. His situation aroused some sympathy in Britain, and the then member of parliament for Aylesbury, a Mr Layard, who had visited the prisoner, took up the ex-king's case at a public meeting held in London in May 1858. 'Many persons,' he said in his speech, 'regret that the king of Delhi had not fallen in just punishment for his offence. I saw the king of Delhi; and I will leave the meeting to judge, when it has heard me, whether *he is punished*! I will not give any opinion as to whether the manner in which we are treating him is worthy of a great nation. I saw that broken-down old man – not in a room, but in a miserable hole of his palace – lying on a bedstead, with nothing to cover him but a miserable tattered coverlet. As I beheld him, some remembrance of his former greatness seemed to arise in his mind. He rose with difficulty from his couch; showed me his arms, which were eaten into by disease and by flies – partly from want of water; and he said, in a lamentable voice, that he had not enough to eat! Is that a way in which, as Christians, we ought to treat a king? I saw his women, too, all huddled up in a corner with their children; and I was told that all that was allowed for their support was 16s. a-day! Is not that punishment enough for one that has occupied a throne?' [11]

Mr Layard's attack produced a strong denial from the doctor in attendance on Bahadur Shah. He maintained that his patient was in excellent health – 'for a man of his years . . . particularly active and intelligent'. His room was not 'a miserable hole', but a large apartment opening on to a pleasant square and overlooking a garden. The 'tattered coverlet' was merely the single sheet customarily used in northern India in the hot weather. The doctor did admit that Bahadur Shah had suffered at one time from 'a disease not uncommon in India but rarely mentioned in polite English ears', which accounted, he said, for the disfigurement of the skin. The ex-king was not short of food. The normal wage of a Delhi labourer was seven shillings a *month*, and 'very few adults consume more than three pence worth of common food in twenty-four hours'. The doctor considered himself an expert on such matters, as 'the accounts of the lunatic asylum pass through my hands and in that institution the dietary for the patients, of different social conditions, is without stint'.[12]

This reply seems to have silenced any doubts in Britain about the ex-king's treatment.

In October 1858, the decision had been made on his place of exile, and preparations to remove him from Delhi were begun. The departure was handled with some secrecy. Bahadur Shah was not informed as to his real destination, and was told only that he was being sent to Calcutta. In charge of the party of Lancers which was to escort the prisoner was a lieutenant, his low rank a last gesture of humiliation for the king. Bahadur Shah and two of his sons, Jawan Bakht and a young son by a concubine, were to travel in a single, closed carriage. In another travelled Zinat Mahal and a few attendants. A third carriage held another wife and her attendants. Five store carts were assigned for the baggage, and twenty male and female servants were permitted to accompany the exile.

The cortège left Delhi at an early hour on 7 October and moved slowly across northern India. Lieutenant Ommanney found the speed much to his liking, even though he had to rise at 1.30 a.m. in order to get the party organised for the road. This he found 'rather hard', especially as he did not manage to return to his tent for breakfast until 9 a.m. 'But,' he assured the commissioner at Delhi, 'I don't care a straw for the amount of work and am very jolly. I am Honorary Member of the Lancers Mess, breakfast, dinner, and tiffin, good stags at dinner twice a week, a pack of Hounds accompany the column on the march, and we have a run when we succeed in getting a jackal, there is a Hook[ah] Club and in short it is as comfortably and perfectly managed as any.'[13]

By coincidence, the ex-king's party with its accompanying Lancers and pack of hounds arrived at Allahabad on the day the governor-general announced there the assumption of power in India by the British Crown.

The party embarked at Allahabad on a flat attached to a steamer for Calcutta. There it transferred to an ocean-going vessel and arrived at Rangoon on 9 November. Bahadur Shah died and was buried in a suburb of that city in 1862.

Forty days of a tedious trial had proved Bahadur Shah's guilt to the satisfaction of the British. But what had he really been guilty of? He was a victim of his times. To the rebels, his person was unimportant; he was the symbol of a romantic past, no more. Later, it was to

143

be argued that it was the East India Company, not he, who was the rebel, for at no time had the Company formally renounced the position of feudatory it had accepted after the battle of Plassey in 1757.[14] But the supreme legality is power; that was what resurrected the Moghul empire for a few short weeks in 1857, and what condemned its symbolic head to exile in Rangoon in 1858.

For nearly ninety years the memory of the last king of Delhi was submerged in the shadows. Then in 1943 the heroes of the rebellion were paraded once again as examples in a new attempt to drive the British from India. A year later, at a ceremony before the tomb of Bahadur Shah, men of the Indian National Army took an oath to free their country. 'Blood is calling to blood,' their leader, Subhas Chandra Bose, reminded them. 'Arise! . . . Take up your arms. There in front of you is the road our pioneers have built. We shall march along that road . . . The road to Delhi is the road to freedom. On to Delhi!' But this rebellion was also to fail. The men who finally disposed of the British had other heroes.

CHAPTER TWO

THE WHITE MUTINY

On 1 November 1858, a proclamation was read at various places throughout India announcing that the long rule of the East India Company was over. The pretence of double government was finally at an end. The British Crown now ruled India directly and a new era had come, even if the rebellion was not yet officially over.

The governor-general was at Allahabad. Outside the fort a platform had been raised, covered with crimson cloth embroidered with the royal arms. On the platform, under a canopy of crimson and gold, stood a richly gilded chair. Lord Canning, attired in court dress and riding a large black horse, was accompanied by military and civil officers in a variety of elegant uniforms, and all were surrounded by Indians wearing scarlet, each carrying a silver wand of office. After a salute of guns, the governor-general – now, in fact, 'viceroy' – ascended the platform and read the long proclamation in English. It was then read in Urdu. More salutes followed, and the viceroy and his staff left the ground. In the evening there was a dinner in the fort, and a display of fireworks.*

William Howard Russell, who was present, found the ceremony 'cold and spiritless'. He was told that ordinary Indians had been 'actually prevented or dissuaded from coming to listen to the royal promises of pardon, forgiveness, justice, respect for religious belief, and non-annexation'. It was certainly obvious that 'the natives who were present consisted, for the most part, of officials in the various public offices'.[1] But there was also present a large body of troops, some of whom did not much like what they had heard. To the text of Queen Victoria's proclamation, Canning had added one of his own. One paragraph, in particular, caused some unease among the European soldiers of the Company's army 'From this day,' it ran, 'all men of every place and class who under the administration of the Honourable East India Company have joined to uphold the honour of England will be the servants of the Queen alone.'[2] This appeared to mean that the Company's European troops had been transferred into the queen's service without any consultation whatever.

The Company's European troops had never been considered in any way part of the British Army. The soldiers did take an oath to serve the Crown as well as the Company, but it was on the understanding that they should serve only in India. A soldier's life in India had not been particularly enviable, however. His stay was usually indefinite, but the period of service was taken to be twenty-one years if death or disease did not intervene. They frequently did. The mortality rate among common soldiers was extremely high. Indeed, the

* For the text of the proclamation, see Appendix 3, p. 168.

145

life expectation of a European soldier in India was less than half what it was in England. The only compensation was that the rate of pay was higher than in Her Majesty's forces and, if the soldier survived, he received a reasonable pension.

The odds against survival were high. Discipline was extremely harsh and though flogging had been abolished in the native army white soldiers could still face sentences of from five hundred to a thousand lashes. Such sentences were by no means rare. Three out of every four men in the Company's forces – and the queen's soldiers were no different – could show the stigmata of a back scarred by the lash into lumps of thick, calloused flesh and hideous weals. Men often died in their early twenties from the effects of the lash.

Outside the bounds of this harsh and unmerciful discipline, the common soldier had ample leisure in which to do nothing. There was, in fact, nothing for him to do. Drunkenness and fornication were his principal activities. No attempt was made to control the soldiers' relations with Indian women, and some settled down into permanent relationships which contributed not only to the men's happiness but to the number of the Eurasian population. There were even some English wives, whose morals were notoriously lax.

No one cared very much about the soldiers or their children until in 1846 Henry Lawrence, appalled by the conditions in which they were forced to live in barracks, drew up a plan 'to provide for the orphan and other children of soldiers, serving, or having served in India, an asylum from the debilitating effects of a tropical climate, and the demoralising influence of barrack life; wherein they may obtain the benefits of a bracing climate, a healthy moral atmosphere, and a plain, useful, and above all religious education, adapted to fit them for employment suited to their position in life, and, with the divine blessing, to make them consistent Christians, and intelligent and useful members of society'.[3] During the rebellion, the schools had at least given asylum to some of the soldiers' children, but many more had died with their mothers at the hands of the rebels.

Despite the trials of service in India, the Company's soldiers – at least on the surface – appeared to have a real attachment to their employers. And they soon showed that they were not prepared to be transferred, like so many slaves, to another master. The first sign of unrest showed itself among the European cavalry at Meerut, who respectfully conveyed their protest through their officers. It was passed on to the commander-in-chief and then to the viceroy. But the rebelion was still in progress, and no decision could be made without the authority of the cabinet in London. This, of course, would take time.

Campbell was at first sympathetic, but ill-informed. He could not, he wrote, even obtain a copy of the oath taken by the Company's soldiers. He thought that the government should be prepared for a large number of requests for discharge. When he was able to give more consideration to the matter, he came to the conclusion that the soldiers should be given a choice between re-enlistment under new terms, and the right to take their discharge. With this opinion the cabinet in London could not agree. The constitutional lawyers gave their ruling that there was no injustice, and no case to argue. 'No wrong has been done,' wrote the new secretary of state for India to the viceroy on 28 January 1859. 'No real grievance exists. The utmost that can be pleaded on the part of the men is that there may be, on a hasty survey of the case, an appearance of injustice: a semblance of having transferred their service from one authority to another, without their consent previously obtained. I say a semblance only, for in truth the authority is the same. It has changed its name, and that is all.'

This ruling was not made known to the soldiers until a general order was issued on 8 April. Its terms were unequivocal. 'Her Majesty's Government have decided that the claim made to discharge, or re-enlistment with bounty, is inadmissible.'

It took some time for the order to reach all the stations, but on 2 May the viceroy learned that the European troops at Meerut were on the edge of mutiny. There were reports that slogans had appeared on walls. 'Stick up for discharge or bounty: if refused, immediately for Delhi', read one, in frightening echo of what had happened at Meerut almost two years before. There was also unrest at other stations, and at Allahabad the officer commanding wanted to disarm the white troops. He was ordered not to. As the summer went on, there were minor outbreaks at other places.

Again the cumbrous machinery of courts of enquiry was set up. A petition was sent to England from the discontented soldiers, and a change of government there brought hopes of a more sympathetic hearing. Yet there was still the danger of real mutiny, a danger all the more alarming in a country where military rebellion had only recently been suppressed and where the peace was still brittle with resentments and fears. In June, the viceroy prepared a proclamation to the effect that every soldier who so wished could take his discharge and would be given free passage to Britain; but the viceroy could hold out no hope of a change of mind on the matter of re-enlistment. Discharge would be final.

Just as this order was about to be circulated, General Hearsey, still commanding at Barrackpur, reported that men of the 5th European Regiment stationed at Berhampur had 'refused to do any duty and are in a positive state of mutiny'. The government could afford to stand no nonsense. A force of five hundred men of the royal army was hurriedly sent to restore order. It did so promptly and without bloodshed. The report that followed criticised the officers of the regiment, who seemed to have been incapable of maintaining discipline.

With this sudden outburst, as suddenly crushed, the 'white mutiny' ended. From then onwards, the requests for discharge poured in. Of the fifteen thousand men of the former Company's army, over ten thousand left for England. It cost the government more than £250,000 in passage money.

Even after their departure, it could not be said that all was well. When a new commander-in-chief took office in June 1860, he advised the viceroy to take harsh measures against continuing indiscipline. Once again, it was the 5th Regiment that broke into near-mutiny. This time a soldier was sentenced to death. The commander in-chief refused to accept a strong recommendation for mercy. 'The state of the 5th is quite hopeless,' he wrote. 'All the elements of order and discipline are the wrong way in them . . . Fancy, the 5th, last year, in May 1859 after the order was read stating that they were not going to get their Discharges, giving "Three cheers for the Company and three groans for the Queen"! Nothing will stop the mutinous and insubordinate conduct of the 5th but capital punishment. They do not seem to care for Penal Servitude, even for life. I fear that the Army at large has a very erroneous impression of it.'[4]

With the execution and the later disbanding of the regiment, the Company's army had finally ceased to exist. No longer would a permanent force of white soldiers be stationed in India. A force which had been created to protect the warehouses of English merchants ended with a military execution and a coffin paraded before the condemned man to the sound of the Dead March. Was it really nostalgia for India and the Company that had inspired unrest and mutiny? It seems unlikely. It was more as if the men wanted to get away from a country they hated with something of the same intensity as many of their 'betters' – and with more justification. Or perhaps the Company's European soldiers had recognised instinctively that after the rebellion India would never be the same again.

CHAPTER THREE

A FETTERED LAND

It was not until July 1859 that the governor-general was able formally to announce the end of the rebellion. He called for a day of solemn thanksgiving. 'War is at an end; Rebellion has been put down; the Noise of Arms is no longer heard where the enemies of State have persisted in their last struggle; the Presence of large Forces in the Field has ceased to be necessary. Order is re-established; and peaceful Pursuits have everywhere been resumed.' [1]

The words were optimistic but the realities were daunting. The queen's government had taken over direct responsibility for the government of India, new ideas were in the air, and the problems of reconstruction were immense. Indian finances had been crippled by the rebellion, and the government faced a debt amounting to the then enormous sum of £38 million. The government was also faced with large claims for property destroyed by the rebels or during the operations to suppress them. The revenue-collecting administration had to be reorganised. Above all, the anarchy of the rebellion had ravaged the economic fabric of large parts of northern India.

If only in the interests of future security, the British were anxious to establish not only the causes of the rebellion but the reasons why it had come as such a surprise to the authorities. The solution to the latter question was simple enough, and once arrived at easily remedied – or so the British thought. There would have to be more Englishmen in positions close to the people; only then could the government learn of the people's feelings, their fears and their ambitions.

The causes were more difficult to define, and the number of explanations which had gained currency only made understanding more difficult. Some Englishmen were convinced that English education was at the root of the rebellion. That argument was easily disposed of. The educated classes had not only demonstrated their loyalty to the British, but had openly and strongly condemned the rebels. Herbert Edwardes claimed that the rebellion had been sent to chastise the British; Indians had been given all the material benefits of British civilisation, but not the moral ones. 'To the Bible and Christianity,' Edwardes wrote in a long memorandum in March 1858, 'England owes the soundness of her social heart, the God-fearing manliness of her sons, the excelling purity of her daughters, the happiness of her homes, the loyal yet unenslavable character of her people, and that progressive prosperity which marks the nation that, as a rule, honours and is honoured by God. Yet this same England has forbidden her own religion to be taught in the Government schools of India, and withheld the Bible.' [2] His solution to the problems of India included the abolition of caste, the replacement of Hindu and Muslim law by British law, and a number of other measures which would most certainly have stirred up, all over again, the main cause of the rebellion – a conflict of religious beliefs.

Others saw, quite clearly, that at least one of the causes had been British interference with long-standing customs and a social organisation which had the sanction not only of tradition but of religion. The answer, they believed, was to abandon such interference and to conciliate those who had resented it to the point of revolt. The problem was how to identify the resentful elements. Did they represent specific social classes? The answer was obviously no, for the rebellion had demonstrated that all classes of Indians, except for the tiny educated minority, had been divided in their attitude. Very few of the princes had rebelled, and by no means all of the landholders. A small number of Europeans had supported the rebels. The sepoys – and practically everybody agreed that they had formed the spearhead of the revolt – had also been divided. In fact, the British could not have suppressed the rebellion without the assistance of Indian soldiers and camp followers. On the Ridge before Delhi, over half the fighting men had been Indian, and, as William Howard Russell noted in his journal, all the other essential supporting tasks had been done by Indians. 'Look at us here in camp,' he wrote. 'Our outposts are native troops – natives are cutting grass for and grooming our horses, feeding the elephants, managing the transport, supplying the Commissariat which feeds us, cooking our soldiers' food, cleaning their camp, pitching and carrying their tents, waiting on our officers, and even lending us money. The soldier who acts as my amanuensis declares his regiment could not live a week but for the regimental servants, dooly-bearers, hospital-men, and other dependents.'[3]

At least it was a fairly straightforward matter to reorganise the native army in such a way that it could never risk mutinying again. The number of Indian regiments in the Bengal Army was halved, and the balance of native to white troops reduced to two to one. This still unavoidable imbalance was corrected by putting the artillery into exclusively white hands. The artillery, wrote Lord Canning, was 'to India what a Channel Fleet is to England. As long as it is strong we are all but secure against any attempt at disturbance. It will keep all in check.'[4] The real danger would only come if a war in Europe prevented the sending of white troops to India or even required that they be withdrawn from there. Canning was convinced that 'there is but one way of meeting this danger, and that is to bring the influential classes – the native states first and afterwards our own chief subjects – into that condition and temper in which, when the moment comes, we may as completely as possible throw the reins on their necks and entrust to them the keeping of internal peace and order.'[5]

The first step in reconciliation was a general one. It was necessary that those who had rebelled should be pardoned as quickly as possible. Even those found guilty of the murder of Europeans should be imprisoned rather than executed. Where property and land had been confiscated, as much as possible should be restored to the owners.

Narrower areas for reconciliation concerned the princes, and the talukdars of Oudh. Canning held two durbars, one at Agra and the other at Lahore, to which loyal princes were summoned and confirmed in their rank and titles. In some cases, they were given a gaudy jewel of an imperial Order. Most of the princes were rewarded in some way, whether with land, or with titles such as 'Most Cherished Son of the True Faith.' [6] All were assured that the 'doctrine of lapse' had been abandoned and they could adopt what heirs they wished if they had no natural son. The Maharaja of Rewa, who was a childless leper, received the news with joy, and said that 'the viceroy's words had dispelled an evil wind which had long been blowing over him'.[7]

The princes were more than satisfied, but the talukdars of Oudh were frankly incredulous at the generosity with which they were treated. They had expected to be annihilated, and instead they found themselves better off than they had ever been. Not only were their lands restored to them. They were also granted judicial and financial powers. 'These measures are an experiment,' wrote Canning, 'which will require careful watching. They may fail ... At least we will have shown unmistakably that we desire to hold out a friendly hand to those amongst the great chiefs of the province who appear deserving of favour and trust.' [8]

It was hardly surprising that, in April 1861, a deputation of nineteen of the principal talukdars should have waited on the viceroy in Calcutta to thank him for his leniency and for the restoration of the privileges they had lost at the time of annexation. Lord Canning replied that there was 'no part of Hindustan more flourishing or more full of promise for the future. The ancient system of land tenure has been restored, but has been placed on a new and clear foundation. The preservation of the great families of the soil has been encouraged and facilitated. The rights of the humbler occupants have been protected. Garrisons have been reduced, police diminished. The country is so tranquil that an English child might travel from one end of it to the other in safety; so thriving that its people have been the most prompt and liberal of all the natives of India in responding to the cry of their famishing brethren in the north-west'.[9]

The conservative bias of the government in attaching to itself the landed classes was not allowed to interfere with the modernisation of both the administration and the economy. The British had not realised that the modernisation process itself was a cause of tension and unease. The Victorian certainty that progress was not only inevitable, but good and desirable, could not be put aside. There was no chance of the government of India becoming either traditional, in an Indian sense, or static. The purpose which justified Britain's imperial rule could not be sustained by inactivity.

There was to be no cessation of the modernising process itself. But a significant change of attitude did come about. The essential belief which had buttressed earlier policies, that cooperation between the British and the Indian middle classes would produce sweeping reform, was abandoned. A new spirit animated the government, and

151

resulted in 'the breakdown of the old system; the renunciation of the attempt to effect an impossible compromise between the Asiatic and the European view of things, legal, military, and administrative'.[10]

On the surface, the new spirit seemed very little different from the old, stern paternalism of the Punjab school. But the men who were to operate the system were cold, bureaucratic, and racially arrogant. Paradoxically, the system was also cautious. There was to be no open interference in matters of religion and social custom. But interference there was. Traditional institutions were not destroyed; instead, they were superseded by new systems and allowed to decay. A wide range of archaic institutions therefore survived in parallel with the most advanced. There was no planned substitution of modern economics for traditional ones, but new markets, new techniques, expanding communications, a money-based economy and rapidly fluctuating prices turned traditional India upside down. Yet the British felt that as long as they did not interfere with religion they were safe.

There was no attempt to deny Indians the boons of Western education. On the contrary. At the height of the rebellion, the first universities were established at Calcutta, Bombay and Madras. But the British no longer believed that a Western-educated minority could act as mediator between the majority of Indians and their rulers, that it could be an instrument of modernisation. By the end of the nineteenth century, in fact, they were convinced that instead they had created a monster which threatened their rule, and did so in the vocabulary of modern Europe. When the British denied democracy to those whom they had educated to believe in it as the highest form of political sophistication, there were Indians who remembered the rebellion of 1857.

The memory of those times had never died in either the British or the Indian mind. The British were haunted by the rebellion. If they later saw their rule as a partnership, it was as a partnership between the soldier and the engineer, not one between British and Indians. They might have found a metaphor for the nature of that partnership in an episode which had occurred in March 1858. Then, Lord Canning had opened a section of railway line linking Allahabad and Fatehpur. Before the governor-general passed along this great symbol of Victorian progress, it was considered prudent to burn the villages on either side of the track and to line it with armed troops.

The failure of constitutional agitation for participation in the governing of their own country was to turn some Indian nationalists to violence. They looked back to 1857, saw the rebellion as a war of national liberation and cultivated legends around it. These legends inspired the Indian National Army of Subhas Chandra Bose, though not the non-violent followers of Mahatma Gandhi. But it was a mutiny in the Indian forces of the empire in 1946 – a small mutiny, easily quelled – which reminded the British of the fragility of their rule and led, a year later, to the raising of the flag of independent India over the palace of the last of the Moghuls at Delhi.

APPENDIX 1

Principal events in the rebellion, January 1857–April 1859

1857

January   Rumour of 'greased cartridges' started in Dum Dum
February 2   Mutiny of the 19th Native Infantry at Berhampur
March 30   Disbandment of the 19th Native Infantry at Barrackpur
April   Unrest and incendiarism in Ambala
May 3   Mutiny in Lucknow prevented by Sir Henry Lawrence
   Disbandment of 7th Irregular Cavalry
May 6   Disbandment of 34th Native Infantry in Barrackpur
May 10   Mutiny and massacre at Meerut
May   Meerut mutiny followed by outbreaks in Delhi, Ferozepur, Bombay, Aligarh, Mainpuri, Etawah, Bulandshar, Nasirabad, Barcilly, Moradabad, Shahjahanpur, and many smaller stations. Disarming of sepoys in Lahore, Agra, Lucknow, Peshawar, and Mardan
   Delhi Field Force advances to Karnaul
   Death of General Anson, British commander-in-chief
June   Mutinies at Sitapur, Hansi, Hissar, Azamgarh, Gorakhpur, and Nimach. Surviving Europeans besieged in Nimach fort
   Mutinies at Gwalior, Bharatpur, and Jhansi
   Mutiny at Cawnpore, then siege of European survivors (4–25 June) and massacre
   Mutiny in Banaras forestalled. Sepoys and doubtful Sikh battalion dispersed by gunfire
   Mutinies at Jewanpur, Allahabad, Jullundur, Phillaur, Nowgong, Rhoni, Fatehgarh, Aurungabad (Deccan), Fatehpur, and Jubbulpur. Aurangabad mutiny suppressed after a few days; rebels flee
   Forcible disarming of Indian units at Nagpur and Barrackpur
   Mutinies at Faizabad, Sultanpur, and Lucknow. Order is restored in the latter town, but the city and surrounding area remain disturbed. Europeans take shelter in the Residency
   British defeated at Chinhat (30 June) near Lucknow
   Siege of Lucknow begins
   Also in June:
   Battle of Badli-ke-serai (8 June)
   Delhi Field Force takes up position on the Ridge and begins operations against Delhi
   Throughout June, the revolt spreads through the Ganges plain, the Rajputana, Central India, and affects parts of Bengal
July   Mutinies at Indore and Mhow, Auggur, Jhelum, Saugor,

153

Sialkot, Dinapur, and Agra. Europeans concentrate in the fort at Agra

Siege of Lucknow Residency continues throughout July, as do Delhi Field Force operations against the city of Delhi. General Barnard, commanding at Delhi, dies 5 July

General Havelock's force, advancing from Allahabad to the relief of Cawnpore, arrives on 17 July, one day too late to save the women and children from massacre

Indian units in Rawalpindi disarmed

Sialkot mutineers defeated by General John Nicolson at Trimmu Ghat (16 July)

August   Mutinies at Kolhapur (Bombay Presidency), Poonamali (near Madras), Jubbulpur, Bhopawar (near Indore), Mian Mir (near Lahore)

Rebellion spreads through Saugor and Narbada districts

Also in August:

Surprise disarmament of Indian units in Berhampur (1 August)

Siege of Lucknow Residency continues; Havelock's first attempt to relieve it fails

September   Outbreak fails in Karachi (14 September)

Further outbreaks in Saugor and Narbada districts

Beginning of siege of Saugor

City of Delhi assaulted and recaptured by the British (14–20 September)

Lucknow Residency relieved by Havelock and Outram (25 September); new siege of the reinforced garrison begins

October   Mutiny at Bhogalpur (near Dinapur)

Unrest in Bihar, North Bengal, and Assam.

Mutiny in Bombay city forestalled (15 October)

Revolt in Kotah state (15 October); Major Burton, the political agent, murdered

November   Lucknow relieved by Sir Colin Campbell (17 November); garrison evacuated and Residency and city temporarily abandoned

General Windham defeated outside Cawnpore (28 November); line of retreat from Lucknow threatened by mutineers

December   Decisive battle of Cawnpore (6 December). Armies of the Rao Sahib – nephew of the Nana Sahib – and of Tantia Topi routed by Sir Colin Campbell

Campaign in the Doab. Capture of Fatehgarh

1858

January   Beginning of Sir Hugh Rose's Central Indian campaign

Sir Colin Campbell begins campaign to recapture Lucknow

Gurkha army of Nepal comes to assistance of British in Lucknow campaign

February   Saugor relieved by Sir Hugh Rose (3 February)

Assembly of Sir Colin Campbell's 'Army of Oudh' along

Cawnpore–Lucknow road to await arrival of Gurkha army under Jang Bahadur

March   Lucknow recaptured (21 March) and rebel armies dispersed into Oudh

Continuation of Sir Hugh Rose's campaign

April 1   Battle of the Betwa; Tantia Topi defeated

April 3   Jhansi stormed

April 4   Rani of Jhansi flees

April 6   Final capture of Jhansi

Azamgarh recaptured and garrison relieved

April 25   Sir Hugh Rose resumes advance on Kalpi

Also in April:

Sir Colin Campbell begins reconquest of Rohilkhand

Fresh rising in Bihar, led by Koer Singh; after campaign against him, he retreats wounded to his stronghold of Jagdispur where he dies of his wounds

May 5   Battle of Bareilly

May 7   Bareilly recaptured

Battle of Kunch; defeat of Tantia Topi

May 10   Jagdispur recaptured

May 23   Kalpi reoccupied by the British

May 24   Battle of Mohamdi. End of resistance in Rohilkhand

May 27   Rebels begin guerrilla warfare in the jungle

Tantia Topi and Rani of Jhansi at gates of Gwalior

June 1   Gwalior army deserts to rebels

Tantia Topi and Rani of Jhansi seize Gwalior

June 6   Sir Hugh Rose marches from Kalpi

June 16   Arrival of Sir Hugh Rose at Gwalior

June 17   Battle of Kotah-ke-serai; this date is supposed to be that of the death of the Rani of Jhansi

June 19   Battle of Gwalior

June 20   Capture of the fortress; flight of Tantia Topi

Also in June:

Suppression continues of scattered guerrilla forces in Oudh, Bihar, and along Nepalese frontier

July–December   Guerrilla bands gradually suppressed everywhere except in the Rajputana and Central India, where Tantia Topi remains free and continues active resistance

1859

April 7   Tantia Topi is betrayed by Man Singh and captured

April 15   Trial of Tantia Topi

April 18   Execution of Tantia Topi

APPENDIX 2

Contemporary Reaction

The following extracts from official and private correspondence, government orders, speeches in the House of Commons and elsewhere, correspondence and leaders in newspapers in Britain and India, have been selected to give a general overall view of contemporary British reaction, both public and private, to the rebellion, its suppression, and to the 'problem' of administering India. The extracts appear in chronological order, but it should be remembered that there was not infrequently a very considerable time lag between events in India and the arrival of the true facts in other parts of the country and in Britain.

Bring the matter, without further delay, *to the bayonet*. This disaffection will never be talked down. It must be *put* down.

Herbert Edwardes to John Lawrence, 12 May 1857

Let us propose a Bill for the flaying alive, impalement, or burning of the murderers of the women and children at Delhi. The idea of simply hanging the perpetrators of such atrocities is maddening. I wish that I were in that part of the world, that if necessary I might take the law into my own hands.

You do not answer me about the Bill for a new kind of death for the murderers and dishonourers of our women. I will propose it alone, if you will not help me. I will not, if I can help it, see fiends of that stamp let off with a simple hanging.

As regards torturing the murderers of the women and children: If it be right otherwise, I do not not think we should refrain from it, because it is a Native custom. We are told in the Bible that stripes shall be meted out according to faults, and if hanging is sufficient punishment for such wretches, it is too severe for ordinary mutineers. If I had them in my power today, and I knew that I were to die tomorrow, I would inflict the most excruciating tortures I could think of on them with a perfectly easy conscience. Our English nature appears to me to be always in extremes. A few years ago men (frequently innocent) used to be tortured merely on suspicion. Now there is no punishment worse than hanging, which is a very easy death, for atrocities which could not be exceeded by fiends. We have different scales of punishment for different kinds of theft, assault, forgery, and other crimes – why not for murder?

John Nicholson, letters to Herbert Edwardes, May and June 1857

156

Even in the Punjab . . . where the people are as yet on the whole loyal, the execution, by order of Mr Montgomery, of a subahdar of a Sikh battalion, of the resaldar of the mounted police, and of the gaol darogah, for *having failed in their duty to the State*, was necessary to show publicly in the eyes of all men, that, at all events, the Punjab authorities adhered to the policy of overawing, by a prompt and stern initiative (the only way to strike terror into its semi-barbarous people) and to the last would brook nothing short of absolute, active, and positive loyalty. Government could not condescend to exist upon the moral sufferance of its subjects.

George Cooper, deputy commissioner of Amritsar, writing of events there in May 1857

I must say a few words for some of the Fifty-fifth prisoners. The officers of that regiment all concur in stating that the Sikhs were on their side to the last. I would, therefore, temper stern justice with mercy, and spare the Sikhs and young recruits. Blow away all the rest, by all means, but spare boys scarcely out of their childhood, and men who were really loyal and respectful up to the moment when they allowed themselves to be carried away in a panic by the mass.

John Nicholson to Herbert Edwardes, June 1857

In respect to the mutineers of the Fifty-fifth, they were taken fighting against us, and so far deserve little mercy. But, on full reflection, I would not put them all to death. I do not think that we should be justified in the eyes of the Almighty in doing so. A hundred and twenty men are a large number to put to death. Our object is to make an example to terrify others. I think this object would be effectually gained by destroying from a quarter to a third of them. I would select all those against whom anything bad can be shown – such as general bad character, turbulence, prominence in disaffection or in the fight, disrespectful demeanour to their officers during the few days before the 26th, and the like. If these do not make up the required number, I would then add to them the oldest soldiers. All these should be shot or blown away from guns, as may be most expedient. The rest I would divide into batches: some to be imprisoned ten years, some seven, some five, some three. I think that a sufficient example will then be made, and that these distinctions will do good, and not harm. The Sepoys will see that we punish to deter, and not for vengeance. Public sympathy will not be on the side of the sufferers. Otherwise, they will fight desperately to the last, as feeling certain that they must die.

John Lawrence to Herbert Edwardes, June 1857

By Act No. XIV of 1857, passed on the 6th of June, provision was made for the punishment of persons convicted of exciting mutiny or sedition in the army . . . and the Supreme and Local executive governments were authorised to issue commissions in any district, for the trial by single commissioners, without the assistance of law officers or assessors, and with absolute and final power of judgement and execution, of any crime against the State, or any 'heinous offence' whatever; the term 'heinous offence' being declared to include every crime attended with great personal violence, or committed with the intention of forwarding the designs of those who are waging war against the State.

Despatch of Government of India to the Court of Directors of the East India Company (11 December 1857)

It may also be alleged against us that we have deposed the kings and ruined the nobles of India; but why should the world sigh over that result? Monarchs who always took the wages, but seldom performed the work of government, and aristocrats who looked upon authority as a personal right, and have never been able to comprehend what is meant by the sovereignty of the people, are surely better out of the way. No Englishman in these days deplores the wars of the Roses, and would like to see the Cliffords and Warwicks restored again to life. France bears with calmness the loss of her old nobility; Europe at large makes steady contributions to the list of kings out of employment. Had princes and rajahs in Hindostan been worth conserving, they would have retained their titles and power. The class speedily dies out in the natural course of mortality, and it is not for the benefit of society that it should be renewed.

Array the evil against the acknowledged good; weigh the broken pledges, the ruined families, the impoverished ryots, the imperfect justice, against the missionary and the schoolmaster, the railway and the steam engine, the abolition of suttee and the destruction of the Thugs, and declare in which scale the balance lies! For every anna that we have taken from the noble we have returned a rupee to the trader. We have saved more lives in peace than we have sacrificed in war. We have committed many blunders and crimes; wrought evil by premeditation, and good by instinct; but when all is summed up, the award must be in our favour. And with the passing away of the present cloud, there will dawn a brighter day both for England and India. We shall strengthen at the same time our hold upon the soil and upon the hearts of the people; tighten the bonds of conquest and of mutual interest. The land must be thrown open to the capital and enterprise of Europe; the ryot lifted by degrees out of his misery, and made to feel that he is a man if not a brother, and everywhere heaven's gifts of climate and circumstance made the most of. The first centenary of Plassey was ushered in by the revolt of the native army; the second may be celebrated in Bengal by a respected government and a Christian population.

From a leading article, 'The Centenary of Plassey', in *The Friend of India*. June 1857

I fear in your case your natural tenderness. But consider that we have to crucify these affections as well as our lusts. The magistrate bears not the sword in vain. The Word of God gives no authority to the modern tenderness for human life which would save even the murderer. I believe that your duty now is to be firm and resolute, to execute the law rigorously in its extreme penalties, and to set your face as a flint against all concessions. It is necessary in all Eastern lands to establish a fear and awe of the Government. Then, and not till then, are its benefits appreciated. Previously, they are ascribed to weakness. We must be sternly, rigorously just against all treason, violence, and treachery, and hand down a tradition of our severity. Otherwise these troubles will recur.

Letter to Henry Tucker, commissioner of Banaras,
from a gentleman described by J. W. Kaye as
'one of the purest hearts and one of the soundest
heads in all our Christian community' – in fact,
Colonel James Neill. July 1857

9. It is unquestionably necessary, in the first attempt to restore order in a district in which the civil authority has been entirely overthrown, to administer the law with such promptitude and severity as will strike terror into the minds of the evil-disposed among the people, and will induce them by the fear of death to abstain from plunder, to restore stolen property, and return to peaceful occupations. But this object once in a great degree attained, the punishment of crime should be regulated with discrimination.

10. The continued administration of the law in its utmost severity, after the requisite impression has been made upon the rebellious and disorderly, and after order has been partially restored, would have the effect of exasperating the people, and would probably induce them to band together in large numbers for the protection of their lives, and with a view to retaliation – a result much to be deprecated. It would greatly add to the difficulties of settling the country hereafter.

From instructions issued by Lord Canning in
clarification of the terms of Act XIV, July 1857

Lenity towards any portion of the conspirators is misplaced, impolitic, and iniquitous, and is calculated to excite contempt and invite attack on every side, by showing to the world the Government of India so powerless to punish mutiny, or so indifferent to the sufferings which have been endured by the victims of the rebellion, that it allows the blood of English and Christian subjects of Her Majesty to flow in torrents, and their wives, sisters and daughters to be outraged and dishonoured without adequate retribution.

From a leading article attacking Lord Canning's
instructions, in *The Bengal Hurkuru.* August 1857

It is the deliberate conviction of your Majesty's petitioners that all these calamities, the result of the spread of the mutiny, are directly attributable to the blunders, weakness, and incapacity of the local Government of India of which the present Governor-General is the responsible head; and in support of this charge your Majesty's petitioners submit the following facts . . . The Governor-General by pertinaceously refusing at first to acknowledge the existence of the mutiny, by the subsequent feebleness and vacillation of his measures, when it could no longer be denied, by pursuing an ill-timed and hopeless policy of conciliation towards the rebels and mutineers, and by his wanton attacks on the valued rights of your Majesty's British and Christian subjects in this country has, as your Majesty's petitioners believe, been a principal cause of the great calamities which have desolated this land, has strengthened the hands of the enemy, weakened or destroyed the respect before entertained for the name of Englishman in the East, imperilled British rule, exposed the Capital of British India to massacre and pillage, excited the contempt of all parties, estranged from the Government of India a large and loyal body of Christians, and in every way proved himself unfit to be further continued in his high trust.

Petition by D. Mackinlay, Merchant, and 682 European
Citizens of Calcutta to Queen Victoria. August 1857

There is something quite new to English minds in hearing of the dreadful outrages committed upon the persons of English men and women. We thought we were lifted above such a dreadful risk, that our higher-than-Roman citizenship would shield us, that some Palladium would protect one of English blood from the last indignities, even in such terrible extremities as these. It seems we are mistaken. Here are men who know us well, know our power, our superiority, our discipline, who have been actually raised far above their native resources by us, and can yet treat the persons of English people in this way . . .

The more cringing and servile they were before – the more they crouched under the commanding eye which controlled them then – the more boundless is their insolence now. They revel and wallow in the absence of respect as the greatest luxury they can enjoy, and having once torn away the veil, rush with a voracious relish to the pollution of the sanctuary. This is the extravagance of vulgar irreverence, to soil the marble surface of the temple with vilest filth, to spit in the face of Majesty, and kick the Royalty which has won such deference, in very revenge for the deference it has won.

From a leading article in *The Times.* August 1857

VICTORIA R. – We, taking into our most serious consideration the grievous mutiny and disturbances which have broken out in India, and putting our trust in Almighty God that He will graciously bless our efforts for the restoration of lawful authority in the country, have resolved, and do, by and with the advice of our privy council, hereby command that a public day of solemn fast, humiliation and prayer, be observed throughout those parts of our united kingdom called England, and Ireland, on Wednesday the 7th day of October next, that so both we and our people may humble ourselves before Almighty God in order to obtain pardon of our sins, and in the most devout and solemn manner send up our prayers and supplications to the Divine Majesty for imploring His blessing and assistance on our arms for the restoration of tranquillity; and we do strictly charge and command that the said day be reverently and devoutly observed by all our loving subjects in England and Ireland, as they tender the favour of Almighty God: and, for the better and more orderly solemnising the same, we have given directions to the most reverend the archbishops and the right reverend the bishops of England and Ireland, to compose a form of prayer suitable to this occasion, to be used in all churches, chapels and places of public worship, and to take care the same be timely dispersed throughout their respective dioceses.

Given at our court at Balmoral, this 24th day of September in the year of our Lord 1857, and in the 21st year of our reign.

Proclamation of Queen Victoria, printed in the
London Gazette. September 1857

These hordes of savage mutineers seem to have cast aside the commonest feelings of humanity, and to have not merely resumed the barbarity of their ancient condition, but borrowed the ferocity of the tiger in his jungle, to torture, to mutilate, to agonise, and to destroy. Nay, if we had imagined to ourselves the unchecked excesses of fiendish fury by which legions of demons let loose against a tribe accursed of God would have marked their progress of devastation, the picture would have fallen short of what has been perpetrated, in a land that we called our own, and thought we had blessed with earthly happiness, on those whom many around us know, whom some near us may have tenderly loved.

*Cardinal Wiseman. Pastoral letter following the
issue of the Queen's proclamation*. September 1857

I have no doubt, and I expect, that all that retribution – if I may use the expression – which the solemn necessity of the case requires will be exacted. But I may be permitted to add, that I trust nothing more will be exacted than the necessity of the case does require. The horrors of war need no stimulant. The horrors of war, carried on as the war in India is at present, especially need no stimulant. I am persuaded that our soldiers and our sailors will exact a retribution which it may, perhaps, be too terrible to pause upon. But I do, without the slightest hesitation, declare my humble disapprobation at persons in high authority announcing that, upon the standard of England, 'vengeance' and not 'justice' should be inscribed . . . I protest against meeting atrocities by atrocities. I have heard things said, and seen them written of late, which would make me almost suppose that the religious opinions of the people of England had undergone some sudden change; and that instead of bowing before the name of Jesus, we were preparing to revive the worship of Moloch.

Benjamin Disraeli. Speech at Newport Pagnell.
September 1857

When the rebellion has been crushed out from the Himalayas to Comorin; when every gibbet is red with blood; when every bayonet creaks beneath its ghastly burden; when the ground in front of every cannon is strewn with rags, and flesh, and shattered bone – then talk of mercy. Then you may find some to listen. This is not the time.

Speaker in the first debate of the Oxford Union.
Michaelmas Term, 1857

Monument of the Mutinies: Sir, – I have just finished reading an article on the Cawnpore horrors, copied into your columns of the 10th October from the *Examiner* of the 5th September. *The Times* recommends that Delhi should be razed to the ground, as a memorial of just retribution.

I would do this and *more*. I would pile the *débris* of its ruins over the palace of its King, until a pyramid was raised rivalling that of Egypt's *Gizeh*. In the centre of this pyramid should be built a circular well 20 feet diameter, its base resting on the choicest spot of the King's palace . . .

The reader may with reason ask by whose hands is this '*Retributive Monument*' to be raised? I say, by every mutineer against whom even collective cruelty can be charged. Who is to superintend the erection of this great *Gomorrah* monument? I again say, 'Nana Heliogabalus', *Saheb* no longer. The name of Heliogabalus is so appropriate, and events in both their lives are so singularly alike, that one is half led to believe that Nana's soul must have resided in the body of Heliogabalus, in accordance with the belief in the transmigration theory . . .

Economists may enquire who are to feed the mutineers while engaged on this great work? I say again, every village whose inhabitants abetted the villains should have a grain tax imposed to feed the Memorial builders. As the pyramid and its charnel tube were raised inch by inch, so would its builders die of toil one by one: Brahmin, Mussulman . . . would find a common grave in its circular depths, till the pile was finished and the Golgotha circle arched over, *except a hole two feet square*. Over this sepulchre of fiends I would then raise a Titan figure of *Justice*, built of stone, rough, but massive, to accord with the pyramid. The figure should be armed with the sword of *Retribution*. When all was finished, and Nana Heliogabalus had viewed the *Avengers' Pyramid* from various points of a hundred mile circle, then I would take him to the fatal opening in the well, and thrusting him through head-foremost, say 'Down, down to hell, monster! and say I sent thee there!'

'Tom Cringle'. Letter to the editor of the
Bombay Gazette. October 1857

What atrocities have the rebels committed against us Europeans? I approach this subject with some hesitation and difficulty. It requires some courage now to venture to hint to Englishmen that perhaps their wives and daughters, and fathers and mothers and sons, have not been ravished and tortured and dishonoured to such an extent as has been lately asserted . . . I thoroughly believe that by far the greater part of the stories of dishonour and torture are pure inventions, and that the mutineers have generally, in their blind rage, made no distinction between men and women in any way whatever. I do not pretend to have ascertained accurately what *did* occur in each case – that never will be known; but . . . this I will say positively of my own knowledge, that nine-tenths of the stories told are not to be heard at all on the spots to which they have reference; it is only as we get farther and farther off that they grow and acquire force and circumstantiality. At Delhi for months the belief was that men, women, and children had been indiscriminately massacred, but no more. I never heard there a story of dishonour pretending to anything like authenticity . . . I never heard a word of anything of the kind at other stations in those parts; indeed it was repeatedly a subject of surprise and remark that such things were so little alleged, and that no distinction of sexes seemed to have been made in any way. But I *did* hear when I was on the Delhi side that the most horrible and unmentionable atrocities had been committed at Cawnpore. Well, I went to Cawnpore; what did I hear there from impartial and well-informed persons? Why, simply this, that the matter had been particularly inquired into, and that the result was the assurance that there had not been dishonour or prolonged torture, but that the women and children had been massacred all together and thrown into a well. But, it was added, though it has not been here there is no doubt that it was so at Delhi . . . Such is the difference of version according to distance . . .

'Judex' (George Campbell). Letter to the editor of
The Times. October 1857

A large meeting, principally of Irishmen, was held at New York on the evening of the 17th September to express opposition to British enlistments in the United States for the war in India, and sympathy with the sepoy mutiny.

Report in *The Times*. October 1857

I am most anxious that everything possible should be done to relieve the sufferers in India; let us, however, have some security that the funds collected will not be supplied to the foundation of protestant asylums for the perversion of poor catholic orphans.

Archbishop Cullen of Dublin, commenting on the
India Relief Fund, as reported in the *Daily News.*
October 1857

I cannot agree with those who view this revolt as a national one. I see no indication of its being a general movement on the part of the people, rising against misgovernment, oppression, and wrong. The masses of the population are with us; the industrial, the agricultural, the commercial class are all on our side; and, even in the neighbourhood of warlike operations, the resources of the country are at our command. Look, too, at the native chiefs and princes, who, with an insignificant exception, are all on our side, and have given us the readiest help. Both princes and people have shown, by their conduct, that they respect our character and value our rule. The revolt, then, is a purely military one, confined to a portion of our army only, though certainly a large portion.

*J. P. Willoughby, a Director of the East India Company
and member of parliament for Leominster. Speech to his
constituents.* October 1857

The wives and daughters of our countrymen have been publicly violated; their children have been put to death with circumstances of cruelty surpassing all we read of in history and the punishments inflicted by God upon the offending Jews. It has not been deemed sufficient to destroy us. We were first to be dishonoured, and this in a country through which we have proudly – perhaps too proudly – stalked as conquerors for a hundred years. Do you suppose that, if we could submit to this in India, we should not be threatened with it in England? Do you imagine that the great military powers of Europe, always prepared for war, offended by our pride, resentful of our former victories, and coveting our present wealth, would long permit us to enjoy in peace the luxuries we cling to, and the dreams of irresistible strength in which we fatuously indulge? Be assured that if, under the strongest necessity ever imposed upon a people, we do not rise as one man to vindicate our national honour, and to re-establish our Indian empire, the horrors we read of with shuddering as perpetrated at Meerut and at Delhi, will not for ever be averted from our island home.

*Lord Ellenborough, a former governor-general of India.
Speech to his tenants.* October 1857

I wonder not that the sepoy has no reverence for our faith . . . I believe there is no part of her majesty's dominions which has, from time to time, given to God truer, better servants than in India; but who does not know that there is yet a very dark side to the picture – that those to whom the natives should have looked, as from their position planted to be lights on a hill, to shine to God's glory, have yet, in their unconcealed profligacy, been a disgrace to that very faith the Hindoo was to be led to think so much purer than his own.

'S.G.O.' Letter to the editor of *The Times*.
October 1857

1. To double (at least) the number of the society's European missionaries in India, and to promote, by every available means, the education, training, and ordination of the more advanced native converts for the work of the Christian ministry among their own countrymen.
2. To found new, and strengthen existing missions, in the presidential and other principal cities of India, wherever there may appear to be the best opening, with a view to bring the truths of Christianity before the minds of the upper as well as of the lower classes in those great centres of population.

*Resolution passed at a meeting of the Society
for the Propagation of the Gospel. London, November 1857*

The cobweb notions which have infested some brains of educating Mohammedans and Brahmins until the polished heathen shall be capable of participating in a silken administration, seeking the happiness and good of all, have been swept away by the besom of the Cawnpore destruction ... A polished Brahmin or a polished Mohammedan is a savage still; and I trust that henceforth, instead of confining ourselves to the cultivation of the native intellect, we shall administer India not merely for our own temporal advantage, but for the benefit of the people and the support of Christian truth.

*The Bishop of Oxford at the meeting of the
SPG. London, November 1857*

He referred to the slaughter of the native princes at Delhi [by William Hodson]. He could not, without infringing on the rights of conscience, designate that act by any other name than one of the foulest murders and atrocities recorded in human history. ('Oh! Oh!') He could assure the honourable gentleman who said 'Oh!' that in parts of this country a very different sound was raised on finding that this great dishonour had been done to the English name – a dishonour which would never be got over while history lasted . . . A British officer in these days was tantamount to an executioner.

*General Thompson, M.P. for Bradford. Report of
a speech in the House of Commons. February 1858*

All these kinds of vindictive, unChristian, Indian torture, such as sewing Mohammedans in pig-skins, smearing them with pork-fat before execution, and burning their bodies, and forcing Hindus to defile themselves, are disgraceful, and ultimately recoil on ourselves. They are spiritual and mental tortures to which we have no right to resort, and which we dare not perpetrate in the face of Europe.

William Howard Russell, special correspondent of
The Times in India. May 1858

As cruel as covenanters without their faith, as relentless as inquisitors without their fanaticism, these sanguinary creatures, from the safe seclusion of their desks, utter stridulous cries as they plunge their pens into the seething ink, and shout out 'Blood! more blood!' with the unfailing energy and thirst of a Marat or St Just. 'We want vengeance!' they cry – 'We must have it full; we care not if it be indiscriminate. We are not Christians now, because we are dealing with those who are not of our faith; rather are we of the faith and followers of him who preached "The study of revenge, *immortal hate!*"' May their school perish for ever, and that right soon, or India is lost – lost with the approbation of the world – to the Crown of Great Britain.

William Howard Russell. October 1858

O Almighty God, who by Thy Providence orderest all things, both in Heaven and earth; we desire to approach Thee this day with the voice of praise and thanksgiving. Thou hast graciously hearkened to the supplications of Thy people, who humbled themselves before Thee, and turned to Thee for succour in the hour of danger. Thou hast heard our prayer: Thou hast maintained our cause: Thou hast frustrated the treacherous designs which were formed against our sovereign and her rule, and threatened British India with wasting and destruction. It hath pleased Thee to scatter our enemies and to give victory to our arms . . .

And now, O Lord, when through Thy goodness tranquillity has been restored to our rich and fruitful territory in the East, direct, we pray Thee, the minds of its inhabitants to the Author of our strength, and the source of our power, even to Thee the only true God, and Jesus Christ, whom Thou hast sent. Let the light of the everlasting Gospel disperse the darkness of idolatry and superstition which has encouraged their murderous rebellion. Teach them to prize the benefits which they have long enjoyed through the supremacy of this Christian nation, and so dispose the hearts of those who sojourn there, that they may set forth, both by word and good example, the blessings of Thy holy religion. So shall the calamities from which we have been mercifully relieved be overruled to the promotion of Thy glory, and the advancement of the kingdom of Thy blessed Son, our only Lord and Saviour: To whom, with Thee and the Holy Ghost, be all honour and glory, for ever and ever. Amen.

Form of prayer to be used on a day of thanksgiving (1 May 1859), prescribed by Royal Proclamation in the *London Gazette*. April 1859

APPENDIX 3

Two Proclamations

On 24 June 1858 a Bill was introduced into the House of Commons and received the royal assent on 2 August. The new Act abolished the Court of Directors of the East India Company and the Board of Control. The British Crown took over direct rule of India.

Such a major change had to be made known to the people of India, and this was done through a proclamation of Queen Victoria on 1 November 1858. The text was translated into seventeen languages, including Burmese, Karen, and Malay, and arrangements were made for it to be read in the presence of the governor-general at his camp at Allahabad, and simultaneously at all other places of importance. Lord Canning, who was to be the first viceroy under the new dispensation, told the last president of the Board of Control that it would be read in English 'and in the vernacular language of the Presidency or Province, not only here at Allahabad and at the three Presidency capitals, but at Lucknow and Lahore, at Peshawar under the Afghan Hills, at Karachi at the mouth of the Indus, and at Rangoon on the Irrawaddy. The proper Salutes and Parades have been ordered; as also two days of Holiday to the Public Offices. At Calcutta and Allahabad there will be Illuminations and Fireworks (the show most congenial to natives) and the same probably at Madras and Bombay'.*

The terms of the proclamation were not received with unqualified enthusiasm. Their sincerity was questioned by one of the surviving rebel leaders, the Begum Hazrat Mahal of Oudh, in a counter-proclamation issued in the name of her son, Birjis Qadr. Her proclamation dissected Queen Victoria's text paragraph by paragraph, and though the sentences read somewhat clumsily in translation, they enshrine the fears and misunderstandings that had led to the outbreak of the rebellion.

QUEEN VICTORIA'S PROCLAMATION

Victoria, by the Grace of God of the United Kingdom of Great Britain and Ireland, and of the Colonies and Dependencies thereof in Europe, Asia, Africa, America, and Australasia, Queen, Defender of the Faith:

Whereas, for divers mighty reasons, we have resolved, by and with the advice and consent of the Lords Spiritual and Temporal, and Commons, in Parliament assembled, to take upon ourselves the

* Canning to Lord Stanley, 19 October 1858.

168

government of the territories in India, heretofore administered in trust for us by the Honourable East India Company.

Now, therefore, we do by these presents notify and declare that, by the advice and consent aforesaid, we have taken upon ourselves the said government; and we hereby call upon all our subjects within the said territories to be faithful, and to bear true allegiance to us, our heirs and successors, and to submit themselves to the authority of those whom we may hereafter, from time to time, see fit to appoint to administer the government of our said territories, in our name and on our behalf.

And we, reposing our especial trust and confidence in the loyalty, ability and judgement of our right trusty and well-beloved cousin, Charles John, Viscount Canning, do hereby constitute and appoint him, the said Viscount Canning, to be our first Viceroy and Governor-General in and over the said territories, and to administer the government thereof in our name, and generally to act in our name and on our behalf subject to such orders and regulations as he shall, from time to time, receive through one of our Principal Secretaries of State.

And we do hereby confirm in their several offices, civil and military, all persons now employed in the service of the Honourable East India Company, subject to our future pleasure, and to such laws and regulations as may hereafter be enacted.

We hereby announce to the native Princes of India, that all treaties and engagements made with them by or under the authority of the Honourable East India Company are by us accepted, and will be scrupulously maintained, and we look for the like observance on their part.

We desire no extension of our present territorial possessions; and, while we will permit no aggression upon our dominions or our rights to be attempted with impunity, we shall sanction no encroachment on those of others.

We shall respect the rights, dignity, and honour of native princes as our own; and we desire that they, as well as our own subjects, should enjoy that prosperity and that social advancement which can only be secured by internal peace and good government.

We hold ourselves bound to the natives of our Indian territories by the same obligations of duty which bind us to all our other subjects, and those obligations, by the blessing of Almighty God, we shall faithfully and conscientiously fill.

Firmly relying ourselves on the truth of Christianity, and acknowledging with gratitude the solace of religion, we disclaim alike the right and the desire to impose our convictions on any of our subjects. We declare it to be our royal will and pleasure that none be in any wise favoured, none molested or disquieted, by reason of their religious faith or observances, but that all shall alike enjoy the equal and impartial protection of the law; and we so strictly charge and enjoin all those who may be in authority under us that they abstain from all interference with the religious belief or worship of any of our subjects on pain of our highest displeasure.

And it is our further will that, so far as may be, our subjects, of whatever race or creed, be freely and impartially admitted to office in our service, the duties of which they may be qualified by their education, ability, and integrity duly to discharge.

We know, and respect, the feelings of attachment with which the natives of India regard the lands inherited by them from their ancestors, and we desire to protect them in all rights connected therewith, subject to the equitable demands of the State; and we will that generally, in framing and administering the law, due regard be paid to the ancient rights, usages, and customs of India.

We deeply lament the evils and misery which have been brought upon India by the acts of ambitious men, who have deceived their countrymen by false reports, and led them into open rebellion. Our power has been shown by the suppression of that rebellion in the field; we desire to show our mercy by pardoning the offences of those who have been misled, but who desire to return to the path of duty.

Already, in one province, with a view to stop the further effusion of blood, and to hasten the pacification of our Indian dominions, our Viceroy and Governor-General has held out the expectation of pardon, on certain terms, to the great majority of those who, in the late unhappy disturbances, have been guilty of offences against our Government, and has declared the punishment which will be inflicted on those whose crimes place them beyond the reach of forgiveness. We approve and confirm the said act of our Viceroy and Governor-General, and do further announce and proclaim as follows:

Our clemency will be extended to all offenders, save and except those who have been, or shall be, convicted of having directly taken part in the murder of British subjects. With regard to such the demands of justice forbid the exercise of mercy.

To those who have willingly given asylum to murderers, knowing them to be such, or who may have acted as leaders or instigators of revolt, their lives alone can be guaranteed; but in apportioning the penalty due to such persons, full consideration will be given to the circumstances under which they have been induced to throw off their allegiance and large indulgence will be shown to those whose crimes may appear to have originated in too credulous acceptance of the false reports circulated by designing men.

To all others in arms against the Government we hereby promise unconditional pardon, amnesty, and oblivion of all offences against ourselves, our crown and dignity, on their return to their homes and peaceful pursuits.

It is our royal pleasure that these terms of grace and amnesty should be extended to all those who comply with these conditions before the 1st day of January next.

When, by the blessing of Providence, internal tranquillity shall be restored, it is our earnest desire to stimulate the peaceful industry of India, to promote works of public utility and government, and to administer the government for the benefit of all our subjects resident therein. In their prosperity will be our strength, in their contentment our security, and in their gratitude our best reward. And may the God of all power grant to us, and to those in authority under us, strength to carry out these our wishes for the good of our people.*

COUNTER-PROCLAMATION BY THE BEGUM OF OUDH

At this time certain weak-minded foolish people have spread a report that the English have forgiven the faults and crimes of the people of Hindustan; this appears very astonishing, for it is the unvarying custom of the English never to forgive a fault, be it great or small; so much so, that if a small offence be committed through ignorance or negligence, they never forgive it.

The Proclamation of the 10th November 1858, which has come before us, is perfectly clear, and as some foolish people, not understanding the real object of the Proclamation, have been carried away, therefore, we, the ever abiding Government, Parents of the people of Oudh, with great consideration put forth the present Proclamation, in order that the real object of the chief points may be exposed, and our subjects be placed on their guard.

First. It is written in the Proclamation, that the country of Hindustan which was held in trust by the Company, has been resumed by the Queen, and that for the future, the Queen's Laws shall be obeyed. This is not to be trusted by our religious subjects; for the Laws of the Company, the Settlement of the Company, the English Servants of the Company, the Governor General, and the Judicial administration of the Company, are all unchanged; what then is there new which can benefit the people or on which they can rely?

Second. In the Proclamation, it is written that all contracts and agreements entered into by the Company will be accepted by the Queen. Let the people carefully observe this artifice. The Company has seized on the whole of Hindustan, and if this arrangement be accepted, what is then new in it? The Company professed to treat the Chief of Bharatpur as a son, and then took his Territory; the Chief of Lahore was carried off to London, and it has not fallen to his lot to return; the Nawab Shamsuddin Khan on one side they hanged, and on the other side they took off their hats and salaamed to him; the Peshwa they expelled from Poona, and imprisoned for life in Bithur; their breach of faith with Sultan Tippu, is well known, the Raja of Banaras they imprisoned in Agra. Under pretence of administering the Country of the Chief of Gwalior, they introduced English customs; they have left no name or traces of the Chiefs of Bihar, Orissa and Bengal; they gave the [nawab] of Farukhabad a small monthly allowance, and took his territory . . . Our ancient possessions, they took from us on pretence of distributing pay; and in the 7th Article of the Treaty, they wrote on Oath, that they would take no more from us, if then the arrangements made by the Company are to be accepted, what is the difference between the former

* Parliamentary Papers 1859. Session I, xviii, pp. 296–97.

171

and the present state of things? These are old affairs; but recently in defiance of treaties and oaths and notwithstanding that they owed us millions of rupees, without reason, and on the pretence of the mis-Government and discontent of our people, they took our country and property worth millions of rupees. If our people were discontented with our Royal predecessor Wajid Ali Shah, how comes it they are content with us? and no ruler ever experienced such loyalty and devotion of life and goods as we have done! what then is wanting that they do not restore our country?

Further, it is written in the Proclamation, that they want no increase of Territory, but yet they cannot refrain from annexation. If the Queen has assumed the Government why does Her Majesty not restore our Country to us, when our people wish it? It is well known that no King or Queen ever punished a whole Army and people for rebellion; all were forgiven; and the wise cannot approve of punishing the whole Army and people of Hindustan; for so long as the word 'punishment' remains, the disturbances will not be suppressed. There is a well known proverb 'a dying man is desperate'. . . it is impossible that a thousand should attack a million, and the thousand escape.

Third. In the Proclamation it is written that the Christian religion is true, but no other religion will suffer oppression, and that the Laws will be observed towards all. What has the administration of Justice to do with the truth, or falsehood of a religion? That religion is true which acknowledges one God, and knows no other; when there are three Gods in a religion, neither Muslims nor Hindus, nay – not even Jews, Sun worshippers, or fire worshippers, can believe it true. To eat pigs, and drink wine, to bite greased cartridges, and to mix pigs' fat with flour and sweetmeats, to destroy Hindu and Muslim temples on pretence of making roads, to build Churches, to send clergymen into the streets and alleys to preach the Christian religion, to institute English schools, and pay people a monthly stipend for learning the English Services, while the places of worship for Hindus and Muslims are to this day entirely neglected; with all this, how can the people believe that religion will not be interfered with? The rebellion began with religion, and for it millions of men have been killed. Let not our subjects be deceived; thousands were deprived of their religion in the North West, and thousands were hanged rather than abandon their religion.

Fourth. It is written in the Proclamation that they who harboured rebels, or who were leaders of rebels, or who caused men to rebel, shall have their lives, but that punishment shall be awarded after deliberation and that murderers and abettors of murderers, shall have no mercy shown them; while all others shall be forgiven, any foolish person can see, that under this proclamation, no one, be he guilty or innocent, can escape; everything is written and yet nothing is written but they have clearly written that they will not let off anyone implicated; and in whatever Village or Estate the army may have halted, the inhabitants of that place cannot escape. We are deeply concerned for the condition of our people on reading this Proclamation, which

172

palpably teems with enmity. We now issue a distinct order, and one that may be trusted that all subjects who may have foolishly presented themselves as heads of Villages to the English, shall before the 1st of January present themselves in our camp, without doubt their faults shall be forgiven them, and they shall be treated according to their merits. To believe in this Proclamation it is only necessary to re-member, that Hindustani rulers are altogether kind and merciful. Thousands have seen this, millions have heard it. No one has ever seen in a dream that the English forgave an offence.

Fifthly. In this Proclamation it is written that when peace is restored public Works, such as roads and canals will be made in order to improve the condition of the people. It is worthy of a little reflection that they have promised no better employment for Hindustanis than making roads and digging canals. If people cannot see clearly what this means, there is no help for them. Let no subject be deceived by the Proclamation.*

* Foreign Political Consultations, No. 3022, 31 December 1858.

APPENDIX 4

The Muse and the 'Mutiny'

Poets in the nineteenth century may not have been the 'unacknowledged legislators of the world', as Shelley claimed, but they were certainly the purveyors of popular history – and the perpetuators of myths. The following is only a small selection from the large quantity of verse produced in Britain and India during, and immediately after, the rebellion of 1857. Only extracts from the longer poems are reproduced.

> Ere now
> The secret has been told – the country through,
> Has heard the sacred message, it is known
> From India unto Brahmapootra's wave
> Since last we met, the mystic cake has sped.
> And cursed be he of Hindoo race who sees,
> But answers not the summons. May the Gods
> Reject him as unworthy of his name,
> His country and his race! may he become
> A wanderer upon the earth! From Delhi's home
> North, east, south, west, with rapid foot 'twas borne
> By many a way, and many an ancient stream
> To towns and villages; and the sacred fanes,
> Of temples and the citadels of kings,
> Revealing the command – the daring deed,
> And then the place of meeting. Soon our swords,
> Shall drink the life-blood of our enemies.

A Graduate of Oxford : *The Moslem and the Hindoo, a Poem on the sepoy Revolt.* London 1858

> They gathered round the evening meal,
> Not now with joke or song.
> Scarce trusting, and yet loath to doubt
> Men they had led so long.
> Yet each day gloomy rumour brought
> Fresh tiding dark and dread;
> Midst tales of horror and of blood
> That last 'good night' was said ...

> 'Tis the same moon that shines above
> My own dear English home;
> One Lord, one Faith, one Baptism,
> However far we roam.

And Heaven we know, is just as near,
   Whether by land or sea;
If only soldiers of the Cross
   To their Colours faithful be ...

No; England's sons have fallen now,
   And England's daughters, too,
By foul and treacherous murder,
   Hundreds against the few.
And shall her sons and daughters
   And babes thus slaughtered lie?
Sure every English soldier
   Will know the reason why!

'The Boy Soldier', from D.M.:
Scenes from the late Indian Mutinies. London 1858

CAWNPORE

They ranged themselves to die, hand clasping hand –
That mournful brotherhood in death and woe, –
While one with saddened voice, yet calm and slow,
Read holy words about yon better land,
Upon whose ever-blushing summer strand
Comes never shadow of a fiendish foe
Nor hellish treachery like to that below
Is with malignant hatred coldly planned, –
Then prayed. O Crucified, didst Thou not stoop
Down from above with Thy deep sympathy,
Soothing the suffering, bleeding, huddled group,
While the fierce volleys poured in hurriedly,
And with uplifted swords the yelling troop
Rushed to complete their deed of perfidy?

But all is over; – the fierce agony
Of men who could not their beloveds save
From unheard tortures, and a common grave
Heaped high with quivering, crushed humanity, –
The frantic woe of women forced to see
Their tiny infants, unto whom they clave
With love which could all fear and torment brave,
Dashed down upon the ground unpityingly:
And nought remains but the wet, bloody floor,
And little rings of soft, white baby-hair
Mingled with long, dark tresses, dimmed with gore,
In hopeless tangles scattered here and there,
And God's own blessed Book of holy lore,
Sole comforter amid that deep despair.

Mary E. Leslie:
Sorrows, Aspirations and Legends from India. London 1858

Who pules about mercy. The agonised wail
    Of babies hewn piecemeal yet sickens the air
And echoes still shudder that caught on the gale
    The mother's – the maiden's – wild scream of despair.

Our swords come for slaughter: they come in the name
    Of Justice: and sternly their work shall be done:
And a world, now indignant, behold with acclaim
    That hecatomb, slain in the face of the sun.

And terrified India shall tell to all time
    How Englishmen paid her for murder and lust;
And stained not their fame with one spot of the crime
    That brought the rich splendour of Delhi to dust.

But woe to the hell-hounds! Their enemies know
    Who hath said to the soldier that fights in His name –
'THY FOOT SHALL BE DIPPED IN THE BLOOD OF THY FOE,
    AND THE TONGUE OF THY DOGS SHALL BE RED THROUGH
    THE SAME'.

'Liberavimus Animam', from
Punch. September 1857

LORD CANNING
And what did he, within whose hand was placed
    The guidance of the empire? A great name,
    The high inheritance of a father's fame,
Were his, and at the first were not disgraced.
The laws, too nerveless for the times, were braced;
    New powers were granted, as such crises claim;
    And from all sides to quench the rising flame,
The British troops were summoned up in haste.
All efforts were exhausted to dispel
    The Sepoy's mad delusion ere it grew:
Measures of stern repression passed, to quell
    Those bent on mutiny; and he withdrew
A doubtful proclamation: so far well,
    And praise shall not be stinted where 'tis due.

Ex Oriente. Sonnets on the Indian Rebellion
London 1858

And, England, now avenge their wrongs by vengeance deep and dire,
Cut out this canker with the sword and burn it out with fire;
Destroy these traitor legions, hang every Pariah-hound,
    And hunt them down to death, in all the hills and cities round.

Martin Tupper. 'Avenge O Lord thy slaughtered
saints', in *Naval and Military Gazette*. 5 September 1857

THE RELIEF OF ARRAH, AUGUST 2, 1857

Pent in our fortressed bungalow as yet our ground we stood
Six thousand rebel foes around, all thirsting for our blood,
Full feeble seemed our little force amid the mutineers;
Ourselves, with fifty faithful Sikhs and a few volunteers.

But gallant hearts had thought for us, though they were distant far,
And gallant men soon hasted on, to aid us from Buxar:
'Oh! shall we come too late to save?' this was the only fear
Of every British soldier there – of every volunteer.

Alas! another gallant force had tried to aid in vain,
Surprised at night, by thousands crushed, and beaten back again,
We seemed by God forsaken, yet help was drawing near
Th' Artillery – the 5th – and the Buxar Volunteers.

We heard the murderous musketry at midnight from afar,
And our hearts grew cold within us, for we knew th' unequal war,
We knew brave men had died for us, and we knew not then how near
Th' Artillery – the 5th – and each gallant volunteer.

Still hope failed not within us, relaxed we not the fight,
Though for our deaths some new device each morning brought to
    light;
We scarce dared on the future think, yet our faces showed no fears,
Whilst, all unknown to us, marched on the troops and volunteers.

All day we were surrounded – bitter foes were lurking nigh,
Oft startling up the hush of night we heard their fiendish cry
Each chance of life seemed lessened, days lengthened into years,
While still pressed onwards to our aid the troops and volunteers.

One night our foes forsook us, at first we knew not why,
But hope soon changed to certainty, that friends and help were nigh;
We knew them soon victorious, and we gave three hearty cheers,
When spurring came to bring the news, the helmed volunteers.

Like water to the thirsty wretch in deserts bleak and bare,
Like hope within the sailor's breast when he sees his guiding star,
Was the ray of joy that o'er us beamed, when we saw our friends
    appear,
Th' Artillery – the 5th – and each hardy volunteer.

And memory fond shall bring again those grateful feelings back,
While they our brave deliverers still follow Glory's track;
Yes! restored to those who love us, we will think in after years
On th' Artillery – the 5th – and the Buxar Volunteers.

John James Halls; *Arrah in 1857*
Dover 1893 (privately printed).

THE DEATH OF CAPTAIN SKENE AND HIS WIFE

A hundred, a thousand to one; even so;
Not a hope in the world remained;
The swarming, howling wretches below,
Gained, and gained, and gained.

S—— look'd at his pale young wife: –
'Is the time come?' 'The time is come!'
Young, strong, and so full of life;
The agony struck them dumb.

'Will it hurt much?' 'No, mine own:
I wish I could bear the pang for both.'
'I wish I could bear the pang alone:
Courage, dear! I am not loth.'

Kiss and kiss: 'It is not pain
Thus to kiss and die.
One kiss more.' 'And yet one again.'
'Good bye!' 'Good bye!'

Christina Georgina Rossetti

THE DEFENCE OF LUCKNOW

Banner of England, not for a season, O banner of England, hast thou
Floated in conquering battle or flapt to the battle-cry!
Never with mightier glory than when we had reared thee on high
Flying at the top of the roofs in the ghastly siege of Lucknow—
Shot through the staff or the halyard, but ever we raised thee anew,
And ever upon the topmost roof our banner of England blew . . .

Frail were the works that defended the hold that we held with our
     lives –
Women and children among us, God help them our children and
     wives!
Hold it we might – and for fifteen days or twenty at most.
'Never surrender, I charge you, but every man die at his post!' . . .

Ever the day with its traitorous death from the loopholes around,
Ever the night with its coffinless corpse to be laid in the ground,
Heat like the mouth of a Hell, or a deluge of cataract skies,
Stench of old offal decaying and infinite torture of flies,
Thoughts of the breezes of May blowing over an English field,
Cholera, scurvy and fever, the wound that *would* not be healed . . .

Alfred Tennyson

178

All honour to those,
Who, encompassed by foes,
Grew stronger in courage and might:
All honour to them,
Who, like brave Englishmen,
Are ready, aye ready, to fight!

All hail to the dead,
Who by treachery fled
From husbands, from parents, from friends.
There are brave hearts still here
Who your memory revere,
And will trample the heads of the fiends.

You wretches without,
Who go sneaking about,
A terror to none but the weak,
Beware of the wrath
Which your acts have brought forth –
'Tis the vengeance of Britons you seek!

Think not that your babes
Shall redden our blades,
Or their mothers have reason to care;
For an Englishman's pride –
It is known far and wide –
Is the innocent always to spare.

The aged he'll respect,
And the feeble protect,
And the simple he'll pass them with scorn;
But the vicious – ah! they
Shall remember the day
That an Englishman's vengeance was born.

Anonymous poem, written on a
wall at Lucknow during the siege

AFTER THE DEATH OF JOHN NICHOLSON
When Nicholson to Delhi came, right solemnly he swore,
If God will only spare my life, her name shall be no more;
Proud Jumna's flood shall wash her streets, her battlements I'll raze,
And nought but blacken'd mounds shall meet the wond'ring traveller's
    gaze . . .

But British hearts are merciful, and vengeance is forgot,
E'en injured serfs obtain their rights, and bless their happy lot;
Where erst a vicious emperor sat, an honest ruler sways,
Aiding the ruined citizens, who murmur grateful praise.

Oh, Nicholson was bravest brave that English Chief could be;
My brother, such a gallant man seems very God to me.
And thus the dying hero wrote, to Lawrence at Lahore,
'Thou art lord of the Khalsa's land, my brother chief of yore;
List to my pray'r for Hyat Khan, my brave Towana guard:
Make him a noble of the land, with him my all is shared.
Write, and let India's Viceroy hear, a childless Captain's prayer,
Regard my troops as dearest sons, make them my country's care,
To recompense my children's deed the choicest gifts I crave.'
Oh, brother! we can ne'er forget John Nicholson the brave.
Oh, dearest spark of chivalry, let a Punjabi cry
All shame that British soldiery left Nicholson to die!
Upon our father's honoured grave, thy Khalsa [Sikh] soldiers weep,
Towanas brave and stout Pathans lament thy lifeless sleep;
Mourning we say, hadst thou but lived, what riches were in store
For us, who war for stranger chiefs, since thou canst fight no more!

John Lawrence sent a missive sad to Britain's gracious Queen,
Recounting first proud Delhi's fall, and the great hero's mien,
How gallantly he stormed the breach, above the Kashmir gate,
And ever foremost in the van, had met a soldier's fate.
The Queen, with gentle sympathy, in tears this letter read,
And then her chieftain's mother called, whose only son was dead.
She soothed the mother's bitter grief, and from her royal neck,
Weeping, a priceless necklet took, her sobbing guest to deck;
'Oh! mother's heart, be comforted, nor mourn thy soldier son;
God owns thy child, in England's Queen thou hast a mother won.'

From a Punjabi ballad 'recently sung' in the streets
of Delhi. L. J. Trotter: *John Nicholson*. London 1898

The following poems were collected by William Crooke, a retired
member of the Indian Civil Service, and published by him in the
original, and in translation, in *The Indian Antiquary*, vol. XL, 1911.
The versions of the extracts given here are, however, by Michael
Edwardes.

THE SETTLEMENT OF OUDH
The English were in the Baillie Guard
And there were no supplies, only the mercy of Providence,
Yet they were full of fight.
Though dying of hunger, they did not run away.

When the English came out and attacked,
The rebels sprang mines on their guns,
But though they tried to hide and ran from place to place
The white men cut off their heads wherever they found them.

Sword and shell and bayonet they used,
When the mines exploded, hundreds were maimed,
The very earth shook at the sound of it,
And babies fell from the wombs of women with child.

What kind of bravery did Birjis Qadr and the Begum show?
Her name has not been forgotten.
But who now will show the same courage?
When she fled, what resistance was possible?

Verses sung by Ghirdhari Das Chaube,
and recorded by Ram Gharib Chaube

MEERUT 1857
Others got shawls, big and small: my love got a handkerchief.
   At Meerut there is a rich bazaar. My love did not know how to
   plunder.

Others got fine china, cups and dishes: my love got a cheap glass.
   At Meerut the bazaar is rich, my love did not know how to plunder.

Others got coconuts and dates: my love got an almond.
   At Meerut there is a great bazaar, my love did not know how to
   plunder.

Others got coins made of fine gold: my love got one of copper.
   At Meerut the bazaar is rich, my love did not know how to plunder.

Song of the Gujar [professional thief]
women of Saharanpur

FAIZABAD 1857
The soldiers of the talukdar caused great trouble in Oudh, my Ram.
The governor-general wrote a letter: Come and join us, talukdar.
From London I will get you a grant of military honours and will make
   you governor of all Oudh.
The talukdar replied: 'Do not trifle with me.
As long as my body has life, I will throw you down and hurl you
   aside'.
All the others who held land came together and joined the English,
Then were my master's followers destroyed, then was his fort razed
   to the ground.

Sung and recorded by Banda Ali Sayyid
of Unahi, near Faizabad

OUTBREAK OF THE MUTINY
It began in Meerut in the year 1857.
When the time of destruction came, the British panicked. The goddess
   Kali wished to destroy England.
The cartridges were of cow and pig's fat and when the soldiers heard
   that this was so they threw off their uniforms.

181

Dhawal Ram says: 'In the year 1857 have the English fled and deserted Calcutta.'

Song sung during the rebellion, and
remembered by Rameshwar Dyali Misra

THE RANI OF JHANSI

She fought well, that brave one, the Rani of Jhansi.
There were guns in the towers, and the magic shells were fired.
O the Rani of Jhansi, how well she fought that brave one.
Her soldiers were fed on sweetmeats but she took only coarse sugar and rice.
O Rani of Jhansi, how well she fought, that brave one ...

Part of a song sung by Rameshwar
Dyali Misra

KHUDAGANJ (FATEHGARH) 1857

They marched from Cawnpore and faced their enemy at Fatehgarh,
They had dug trenches all around them, they fought well those English ...

The Hindus shouted 'Ram Ram' and the Muslims 'Allah Allah!'
Without fear they fought with all the strength they could.

The sepoys fought in small groups, and would not give way,
Yet the English dug themselves in and they fought well, those English.

When they first met, both sides used cold steel, terrible was the fight.
The brave sepoys fought at Fatehgarh, above the river ...

The brave English came to the field like elephants on heat
With no fear of death in their faces ...

How wise were the Europeans, they conquered the army,
Making a double march they entered the city ...

The bankers met the general with costly presents.
He stopped the looting of the city and the merchants were able to start trading again.

Said Kamalapati: 'In Manik Ram did the English invest authority.
O the rule of these great English; theirs is the sword that conquers.'

Sung by Shital Prasad Shukla, and
recorded by Ram Gharib Chaube

APPENDIX 5

The narrative of Syed Mubarak Shah

The author of this previously unpublished narrative, which is now in the India Office Library, London (MS Eur. B 138), was the chief police official in the city of Delhi during its 'siege' by the British. When the city was recaptured, Mubarak Shah fled and remained in hiding until – as part of Queen Victoria's proclamation of November 1858 – an amnesty was declared for certain categories of rebel.

Mubarak Shah's narrative was translated, and rather cursorily edited, in the following year by R. M. Edwards, Magistrate and Collector of the district of Muzaffarnagar (which lies between Saharanpur and Meerut) from July 1857.

Compared with the enormous number of personal narratives of the rebellion written by British participants, very few survive from the rebel side and even fewer have been published. One, which supplies another dimension and some confirmation of Syed Mubarak Shah's, is by Hakim Ahsanullah Khan, the personal physician and trusted advisor of Bahadur Shah, king of Delhi.*

The narrative of Syed Mubarak Shah printed here includes R. M. Edwards' footnotes. The spelling of names and places has, however, been modernised. Editorial interpolations by the present author are contained within [square brackets].

From the preface by R. M. Edwards

Previous to the outbreak Syed Mubarak Shah, for that was his name, had served under me as a Police Officer in the district of Saharanpur. He was of good family and far better educated than the usual run of Police Officers and his statements may I think be for the most part relied on. He surrendered to me under the amnesty in 1858 and declared himself penniless and almost starving which was probably correct as I had confiscated all his property and the people generally were at that time afraid of assisting noted rebels. I could not employ him under Government – but as there was no evidence of his having been involved in the murder of Europeans or loyal Natives, during the outbreak, it struck me that he might be useful in supplying information as to what had taken place in the city of Delhi during the siege. We were well acquainted with what had occurred outside but knew absolutely nothing of events inside the walls. I therefore sug-

---

* Metcalfe, T. C. *Two Native Narratives of the Mutiny at Delhi*, London 1898. Others can be found in Muir, W. *Records of the Intelligence Department of the Government of the North-West Provinces of India during the Mutiny of 1857*, 2 vols, Edinburgh 1902. The manuscript of Ahsanullah Khan's narrative is, with other accounts, in the India Office Library, London (Home Miscellaneous vol. 725).

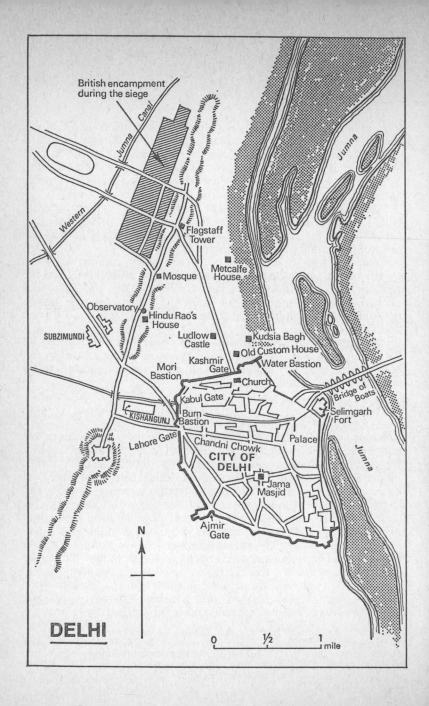

British encampment
during the siege

Jumna Canal

Western

Flagstaff
Tower

Mosque

Metcalfe
House

Observatory

SUBZIMUNDI

Hindu Rao's
House

Ludlow
Castle

Kudsia Bagh

Old Custom House

Mori
Bastion

Kashmir
Gate

Water Bastion

Kabul Gate

Church

Bridge of
Boats

KISHANGUNJ

Burn
Bastion

Selimgarh
Fort

Lahore Gate

Chandni Chowk

Palace

CITY OF
DELHI

Jumna

Jama
Masjid

Ajmir
Gate

Jumna

N

DELHI

0   ½   1
                     mile

gested his compiling a narration of events *in Delhi* and said that while thus employed he might accompany my camp and I would support him. The only proviso I made was that he should record nothing that he did not know to be absolute facts. He agreed and this work is the result.   R.M.E.

NARRATIVE OF SYED MUBARAK SHAH

About 9 a.m. on the 11th May 1857, a rumour spread through the city of Delhi that four Troops of Regular Cavalry and two Poorbeah [Bengali] Regiments which had mutinied on the previous day in Meerut and successfully resisted the European troops had arrived at the Bridge of Boats over the Jumna after burning the Toll-house. This report reached Simon Fraser, Commissioner and Governor General's Agent when taking his morning bath and greatly alarmed him. A Telegram had been received by him the night before describing the events at Meerut – but as the city gates had been already closed as usual, he appears to have thought that nothing could happen before morning and no precautionary measures would be necessary until then. Mr Fraser's house and office were in the building known as Ludlow Castle, a short distance from the Kashmir gate of the city. He had not believed it possible that the mutineers could reach Delhi so quickly, or otherwise than a broken and disorganised body after their encounter with the European troops quartered at Meerut – or he would have made arrangements to prevent their gaining admittance within the city, for he was a sagacious and brave man – but 'it was written and so it came to pass'. The 3rd Cavalry troopers were the first to arrive, seven of their number proceeding in advance accompanied by numerous convicts from the Meerut Jail and Gujars [robbers] and others from the villages round about Delhi. It was these seven troopers who had looted and burnt the Toll-house. As they rode on towards the city gate they killed some servants of European gentlemen whom they happened to meet on the way

In the meantime the Commissioner determined to go at once into the city, ordered his buggy and called for his gun but the latter could not be brought as the key of the case was not forthcoming. Mr Le Bar the Judge and Mr Hutchinson the Officiating Magistrate now arrived and the three gentlemen left in buggies. The Commissioner had the Calcutta gate of the city closed immediately and the Judge and Magistrate drove on to arrange matters at the Delhi gate. At this time the seven troopers, who had come from the Bridge of Boats by the [Rajghat] road, were approaching the Palace at the Delhi gate and Daryaganj, and the two gentlemen saw them riding at speed with their swords drawn. Being unarmed both judge and magistrate turned their horses and tried to escape – the judge's buggy got clear but the [troopers] surrounded that of the magistrate and cut at him with their swords – wounded and bleeding he jumped from the buggy and ran into the house of Ramji Das [a banker], from which the [troopers] dragged him and put him to death. Shortly before, these men had

185

met Chamanlal, Native Doctor, and being told by some of the city people that he had been educated as an English Doctor one of their number drawing a pistol from his holster shot him dead.

Sir Theophilus Metcalfe, the Joint Magistrate, who had also gone into the city on hearing of the disturbance was wounded in the hand but it is not known by whom. He went to the [Police Headquarters] and desired [the Chief of Police] to be on the alert – then mounting a horse belonging to Muhammad Khan of Jhujhur rode through the Girdon bazaar and escaped to Jhujhur via Pahargunj and Zardubpir in the thana [police jurisdiction] of Najafgarh.

One of the above mentioned [troopers] went towards the palace and seeing the Commissioner [Simon Fraser] who had not yet entered it, rode at him with the intention of cutting him down. Mr Fraser seized a musket from a [guard] who was standing by and shot him. The [trooper] wounded in the chest retired, and the Commissioner went into the palace and had the gate closed. The wounded man when passing through the bazaar fell from his horse – one of the shop-keepers brought him water but he soon after died.

The rest of the troopers went to the Calcutta gate but finding it shut passed along the bank of the river and thus got beneath the back windows of the palace where they shouted to the guard on duty to open it. This they at first refused to do, but on the mutineers threatening to kill them and calling on them as true Muhammadans they complied and the whole of the 3rd Cavalry men then passed into the city.

Captain Douglas, Commandant of the Palace Guards and assistant to the Agent to the Governor General, lived with his family in apartments over the Lahore gate of the palace. He was at the time suffering from serious illness, but he went at once to . . . the King, and asked him to remonstrate with the Troopers. The King proceeded in person and in a loud voice ordered all his retainers then present to take no part whatever with the mutineers and ordered the 3rd Cavalry men to leave the city, adding that he would do his utmost to get their crime pardoned and use all his influence to obtain for them whatever they demanded. The mutineers replied: 'We have come with the express intention of putting all the Europeans to death because they have condemned us to bite the cartridges after having smeared them with the fat of swine. We have already commenced a [Holy War] and have come to Delhi considering you the Muhammadan King, but it appears that you are in league with the Christians. You will see what will happen.' They were turning their horses' heads when a trooper rode up and cried out: 'The city gate is open, come along.' They at once left for the Calcutta gate, and the King entered the Hall of Devotion, saying to Captain Douglas; 'Come with me and I'll place you for safety in the zenana [women's quarters].' Captain D. replied: 'I could never do such a thing. Do you mean that I should go and hide myself?' On this he came out of the Diwan-i-Khas [Hall of Private Audience] intending to go up to his quarters where Mr Fraser the Commissioner had already arrived [but] he was attacked by the King's [attendants] who assaulted him with their sticks of office. He staggered on until he reached his rooms. The Rev. Mr Jennings and his daughter, Miss Clifford and the Commissioner, were all assembled there with the Douglas family. Mr Fraser seeing the true state of affairs and the lamentable condition of Captain Douglas left the room and went down the stairs, unarmed, and saw one of the 3rd Cavalry troopers standing outside and insisting on the palace gate being opened. He spoke to him in severe terms and began going up the stair to get a musket when an Afghan [attendant] of the King's, Khalihdad Khan, struck him with his sword wounding him severely on the face and as Mr Fraser fell struck him repeatedly, killing him on the spot. While the Commissioner was being murdered the gate of the palace was opened. Khalihdad Khan accompanied by other [attendants] then went to Captain Douglas's quarters and forcing their way into the room killed every soul they found.

Captain Douglas was cut to pieces when lying in a state of insensibility, then Padre Jennings and the rest were butchered by Khalihdad Khan aided by the other miscreants who were only armed with bludgeons – but Miss Jennings got hold of a large bamboo and defended herself most gallantly, repeatedly striking the [Afghan] and the others but was eventually overpowered and killed by the sword of Khalihdad Khan.

Some hours had now elapsed from the time the 3rd Cavalry men had reached the Bridge of Boats. During this time the waves of revolt and of hell were rolling into the city of Delhi – an enormous amount of property was plundered by the bad characters of the town and by the convicts who had escaped from the Meerut Jail. Every man of the Magistrate's office who had made any show of resistance had been killed along with the guard. Those alone escaped who joined the rioters or who throwing away their weapons succeeded in concealing themselves. Every soul from the oldest man to the youngest infant, who could in any way be regarded as Christian, was put to death by the city [hooligans] and the large mob which by this time had joined the mutineer cavalry. Numbers of people began to point out where Christians lived, or were concealed, and the troopers rushed about slaying every man, woman, or child they could discover.

About this time the three Native Infantry regiments which had been stationed at Delhi, viz, the 74th, the 54th and the 38th were marched down to the Kashmir gate with the object of expelling the Meerut mutineers from the city. When the 54th had gone a short distance within the walls some of the 3rd Cavalry approached and on seeing the regiment their leader rode out in advance and raising his sword above his head reversed it, with the point downwards, calling out: 'Brother are you with those of the true faith?' on which the 54th halted to a man. From this it would appear that matters had been previously arranged and that both parties were acting on a preconcerted plan. The officers called on their men to fire, but they, one and all, grounded their arms and ran on one side, leaving their officers alone, three or four of whom were at once shot by the Cavalry while the rest, seeing they could do nothing with their men, fled from

187

the city in various directions. The sepoys then fired their muskets in the air and many embraced the troopers. The three Native Infantry regiments now made common cause with the Cavalry mutineers and accompanied them into the heart of the city.

In a house near the palace of Nawab Hamid Ali Khan and close to the Kashmir gate lived Mr Collins with his family – he was Deputy Collector in charge of the Government Treasury. The 3rd Cavalry men and above mentioned sepoys murdered the entire Collins family, including father, mother, six young children and some grown-up young ladies. One of the Miss Collins was a great beauty – when she saw her relations killed she called out to the trooper who was about to cut her down: 'You will gain nothing by thus killing me. Your religious faith will not spread over the land, nor will your rule succeed; show some pity.' Gummur Khan, son of Gulab Shah, a resident of the Meerut district, a trooper in the 3rd Cavalry, struck her with such violence that she was cleft through the head down to the bosom.

The mutineers then went to the late Colonel Skinner's house and found no one, but in the neighbourhood a European lady and gentleman lived and the troopers and sepoys entered the enclosure and put them also to death. The gentleman was overpowered and killed immediately, but the lady who was in an upper and rather lofty verandah, seeing her husband murdered, leant over and cut down one of the sepoys with a sword wounding him severely on the head and hand. The mutineers however got up to where she was and cut her to pieces.

Another English gentleman escaped from the city by the Ajmir gate and hid himself in one of the [potters'] pits. These men on seeing him told the troopers who came and shot him.

When the Native Infantry regiments had as already described marched into the city, parties of the sepoys and troopers left the main body and went to the Jail where they demanded that the gates should be opened. The guard made a show of resistance at first and fired a few harmless shots but very soon opened the Jail, released all the prisoners and removed their fetters.

In the meantime the 11th and 20th Native Infantry which had mutinied at Meerut arrived in Delhi and the whole five regiments, joined by the convicts released from the Meerut and Delhi jails together with a large number of the city [hooligans] and masses of men from the neighbouring villages roamed about plundering the respectable inhabitants and committing every species of enormity. Several European officers and gentlemen who resided with their families outside the city or in cantonments, after remaining for some hours at the Flagstaff Tower on the Ridge and being abandoned by their men fled to Meerut, Ambala and other stations. During that night the sepoys and rioters enriched themselves with the plunder of gold and silver coin, valuable jewellery, and costly embroidered cloth.

Mr Galloway the Assistant Magistrate who held office in the early morning was sitting alone in his [court] room, all his [clerks] having disappeared, when a 38th Native Infantry sepoy, one of the Treasury

188

Guard, shot him in his chair – the rest of the guard then looted the treasure.*

The troopers of the 3rd Cavalry did not join in the general pillage but the Sepoys especially the 74th Native Infantry and 20th Native Infantry from Meerut distinguished themselves in the indiscriminate slaughter of defenceless women and children in a manner that in no other country or under any form of religion or government has ever been equalled – no not from the creation of the world up to the present day. This was especially shameful because from the very commencement of British rule in India the English have respected the faith and religious observances of both Muhammadan and Hindu, have meted out equal justice to all, have treated with honour and distinction the native nobility, have aided in the ceremonies of both religions, have added to the dignity and wealth of the people and have invariably treated them with that consideration and kindness which is said to have been the practice of those ancient Kings who are now always spoken of as the protectors and benefactors of their people. They have also always respected the sanctity of the zenana and the honour of native women of all classes and ranks, in the same manner as they respect their own. What then must we the people of India think when after such basic ingratitude, foul treachery and massacre, the Queen – whom may Heaven reward, with a magnanimity which no language can describe, has returned good for evil and forgotten and forgiven such black offences. All the local officers in accordance with the spirit of Her Majesty's instructions have dealt leniently with the people so that those who had abandoned their homes are returning and settling to their former peaceful pursuits. Why should not the Almighty strengthen the roots of such a Government and preserve it forever?

It must always be a matter of surprise and astonishment why or from what special causes these heinous crimes were committed. All that can be said is, that it was decreed by the Supreme Being, the Creator of the world, and that man is powerless to resist God's will.

* The above account is incorrect and in justice to Arthur Galloway I give the true one –

On hearing of the disturbances in the city on the early morning of Monday 11th May 1857, Galloway went to his post at the Treasury and only quitted it for a time to procure aid from the main guard at the Kashmir gate as the Sepoys of the Treasury guard were in almost open mutiny though up to that time they had not attacked him or broken into the strong room. The officers deserted by their men and many of them wounded could give no assistance and Galloway was repeatedly urged to remain and take his chance with them as by returning to the Treasury he could do no good and would certainly lose his life. He said he was well aware what the result must be but it was his duty to stick to his post – he did so, and stood on guard at the door of the Treasury with a drawn sword – our solitary Englishman, among a seething mass of armed and excited Sepoys who soon attacked and overpowered him resisting to the death.

I received this information from officers who had seen and spoken with Galloway at the Kashmir gate on that occasion – and the scene at the Treasury was told me by respectable natives of Delhi who had heard it from the Sepoys and others.

In the very midst of the outbreak in the city a European lady disguised in native clothes, entered the Palace unobserved. The King's favourite wife, Zinat Mahal Begum, placed her for safety in the zenana, but some of the [attendants] discovering the fact told the sepoys, about a hundred of whom forced their way into the Diwan-i-khas and shouted to the King: 'Deliver up immediately the memsahib whom you have concealed in the Palace or we will break into your zenana, drag her out and dishonour you forever.' On this the King handed her over to the sepoys but made them promise not to kill her. They took her outside the Palace and when they had reached the main bazaar they began beating her with the butt-end of their muskets. She lost her temper and reproached them saying: 'You are treating me as you would a poor coolie – if you want to kill me why don't you shoot me at once instead of subjecting me to these indignities?' On this one of their number shot her dead.

Numerous bodies of sepoys, Cavalry troopers and others went through the streets, alleys and lanes of the city plundering and maltreating respectable citizens, while many others proceeded to the Government Magazine. The several gates of the walled enclosure had been made fast by the four or five European sergeants who were inside. These men seeing that they could not resist for any length of time the vast hordes of assailants by which they were surrounded, collected a quantity of small arms ammunition and fired it. One of their number was blown to pieces and one of the Magazine buildings blown into the air at the same time – upwards of two hundred men including sepoys, troopers and lookers on . . . were killed by the explosion and a vast number wounded. The bullets from the exploded cartridges reached the Palace, some falling in the King's private apartments. The rest of the Europeans were, it is believed, all killed,* by the mutineers and town rabble who soon effected an entrance. In the height of their insane exultation they took no measures to prevent a general plunder of the magazine stores, the result being that enormous quantities of gunpowder and ordnance supplies of every description were carried off not only by the mutineers but by the townspeople and the men of the surrounding villages. This looting of the Magazine continued for several days, but was at length stopped and a sepoy guard stationed at the main gate. Orders were also issued requiring the people to give up what they had taken but these had little effect. The residences of the European officers situated in Cantonments were burnt or otherwise destroyed.

Mr and Mrs Beresford with three grown-up daughters and some European clerks lived in the Delhi Bank House situated in the Begum Sumru's garden in the heart of the city close to the Chandni Chowk. The gentlemen had armed themselves with guns, the ladies with pistols, and they kept up a heavy fire from the roof killing and wounding several of the sepoys and city blackguards who had come to loot the Bank. Some of their assailants, however, managed to effect an entrance where they collected the books and papers in a large pile

* This is incorrect.

and set fire to the mass. The house speedily caught and the Europeans were forced to descend when one and all were butchered.

In the general confusion caused by the riotous proceedings in the city, a party of eight [Muslim Rajputs] assembled a body of dacoits and sometimes along with and sometimes apart from them gutted one portion of the town, loaded their camels with gold coins, jewellery and other valuables and started for their native village . . . The plundering of the city continued for the whole of that day and night. On the following day a European sergeant who had up to that time remained concealed . . . was betrayed to the sepoys, dragged to the Fatehpur Masjid [one of the city's mosques] and there put to death.

The landowners and Native gentlemen of respectability and position remained during these days within their houses, in the hope, vain in most instances, of being able to protect their property, but in constant dread of an attack by the mob. Some 80 or 100 sepoys went to the house of Ram Surrum Das, Deputy Collector, who had died a few weeks before and who had been a very able and trusted servant of the British government, but between whom and the townspeople feelings of animosity had long existed, and then and there disgraced and maltreated the women of the family some of whom did not recover from the violent treatment to which they were subjected.

The troopers of the 3rd Cavalry were picketed in the Mehtab Bagh adjacent to the Hyat Bagh while the infantry regiments were distributed in the shops in the several bazaars.

The city was being rapidly ruined by the indiscriminate pillage which was carried on. The bodies of the English officers and other European residents along with many native corpses were lying about in the streets and the large and up to then flourishing city became the abode of fear, dismay and pestilence.

On the third day several European ladies married and unmarried with children of various ages from one to seven, one lady far advanced in pregnancy, and one European gentleman, in all about forty souls, were betrayed to the sepoys by the townspeople, taken out of a house in Daryaganj belonging to the Nawab Wazir of Lucknow where they had hitherto remained concealed, and removed to the Palace where they were all imprisoned together near the Lahore gate. For four days the King fed them . . . from his own table. Hakim Ahsanullah Khan [the king's physician] and Mirza Alahi Baksh [a relative of the king's] together with Husain Mirza, the King's minister, constantly besought the King to issue injunctions to the sepoys forbidding them on any account to kill these Europeans, but to detain them in confinement, urging 'these are all women and children – What harm have they done and what advantage can their death be to you?' The King acted on the representations and issued orders to the mutineers but when these last learnt that he had fed them during their detention they suspected he was in league with the English and determined to involve him in their death. Consequently on the fourth or fifth day of their imprisonment the whole party was taken out . . . in front of a shallow tank by a *pipal* tree and surrounded by sepoys and troopers. The

King wept and besought the mutineers not to take the lives of helpless women and children, saying to them: 'Take care – for if you commit such a deed the vengeance and anger of God will fall on me – Why slay the innocent?' The mutineers refused to listen and replied: 'We'll kill them and in your Palace so whatever be the result you too shall be considered *one* in this business and you will be thought equally guilty by the English.' At length the King's [attendants], the chief of whom was Jemadar Hamid Khan of Rampur, and the 3rd Cavalry men slaughtered the women and children with their swords but the [attendants] were the most active in the massacre and killed by far the greater number. *The instigators of this massacre were Talyar Khan, subadar [native officer] of the 3rd Cavalry from Meerut, and Mirza Moghul*, the King's son.*

News of the occurrences at Delhi had by this time spread east, west, north, and south. The country roads were no longer safe and those who attempted to travel along them were waylaid. Lines of communications were closed. Village attacked village. The strong preyed upon the weak – crime reigned supreme and weapons of every description were prepared in large quantities – 14,000 battleaxes and 8,000 matchlocks [in three regions] in eleven days. Agriculture was to a great extent abandoned and the country people soon became even worse [off] during the time of the Marathas or the Sikhs. Peace, confidence and safety deserted the land and a very different regime took their place. Thousands of lives were sacrificed. Those who had been ruined by the resumption of *jagirs* [grants of land], or beggared by Civil Court decrees, or ousted by moneylenders, joined heart and soul in the disturbances so that large numbers were killed. The assailants were in their turn the victims of the rapacity of others and property which had escaped the fangs of the law was frequently destroyed in these raids. It must however be stated that the warlike preparations made by the people were not against the British government but with a view to protect themselves against their neighbours, with whom in most instances feuds of long standing were renewed – feuds which were not forgotten though they had for years been suppressed by the strong hand of government. Moreover a general plunder of the amassed gains of the moneylenders was set on foot and spread like fire in a forest. Great numbers of the Muhammadan population repaired to Delhi to take part in the war of extermination against the English. As far as in them lay, the mutineers did not leave a Christian alive in the capital. The sepoys now began to add murder to indiscriminate robbery and killed many highly respectable people on pretence that they were in collusion with the British, but really because they would not accede to their demands.

At length the mutinied regiments in Delhi assembled in council and determined to get reinforcements from other stations. The King, too, with a view to restore order in the city and curb the excesses of the escaped convicts and [hooligans] after consulting the officers of the Cavalry and Infantry, appointed Mir Nawab . . . [Chief of Police] in

* Afterwards shot by William Hodson.

19 Lucknow: defenders on the lookout
20 The first relief of Lucknow: General Havelock meets the defenders

THE RANI OF JHANSI

21 The Begum Hazrat   22 The Rani of Jhansi
Mahal of Oudh

23 The death of Captain Skene and his wife at Jhansi (see the poem by
Christina Rossetti, p. 178)

24　The British and Tantia Topi meet at the battle of the Banas river

25　Colin Campbell　　　　　26　Tantia Topi awaiting execution

27 The end of the mutiny: rebel sepoys were tied to the cannon-mouth and blown to pieces

28 and the last emperor of Hindustan dwindled into an 'attenuated old man, dressed in an ordinary and rather dirty muslin tunic . . . his head covered by a small thin cambric skull-cap'

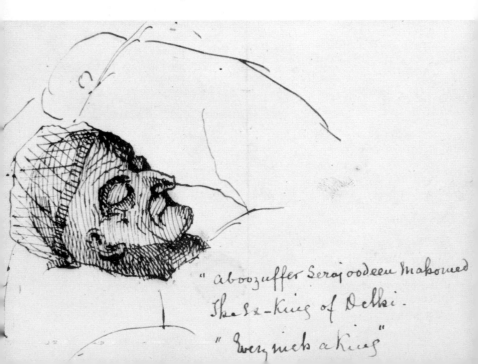

"aboozuffer Seraj oodeen Mahomed
The Ex-King of Delhi.
"Every inch a King"

the room of [the previous holder] who had fled on the commencement of the outbreak.

Some four or five European gentlemen including one known as the 'Captain Sahib' had succeeded in concealing themselves for four days in the [cellars] of the house of the Wazir of Lucknow – but unable to stand the intense thirst any longer one of their number crept out to procure water. Unfortunately he was seen by one of the neighbours who went and told the sepoys that Europeans were in hiding . . . Upwards of a hundred mutineers went to the house at once – one party surrounding it while another went down to the basement. The Captain Sahib, who alone had a gun, shot one of the sepoys, when the rest retired for a time but soon returned in force, effected an entrance, and killing all the others took the Captain Sahib away with them. He was a man of Herculean strength, tried courage, and noble appearance. They dragged him to the [Police Headquarters] and murdered him in front of that building.

Two days after this, young Skinner, son of Joseph Skinner and grandson of the celebrated Colonel Skinner, was passing along by the Sahiba Bagh disguised in native costume when some of the townspeople recognised him and informed the sepoys who came and seized him and intended shooting him then and there but a Cavalry man remonstrated and proposed they should take him to the Palace and there put him to death – they started with this intention but had only reached the [Police Headquarters] when one of the party shot him. He received the ball in the body but had not fallen when a trooper dealt him a blow separating his head from his body.

Another European known as the *bajawala* [bandmaster] – who played the Church organ and whose young son was very intimate with Jawan Bakht [one of the King's sons] had at the commencement of the outbreak sought shelter of Zinat Mahal, hoping thereby to save his own and his boy's life. She concealed them in her apartment for five days but told them on the sixth that if they remained they would certainly be killed, so after disguising themselves father and son left the palace, barefoot. On their arriving at the Fatehpur Masjid they were recognised by the people who after beating them severely took them to the sepoys and had them shot.

The people of Delhi complained so bitterly at this time of the plundering and violence to which they were daily and almost hourly subjected that their accusations reached the King who dismissed the [Chief of Police] as incompetent and placed Muizuddin Husain, Thanadar [senior police officer] of Paharganj, in the vacancy, but he was unable to stop the general robbery and pillage and after a few days was also discharged . . .

All who were seized as Christians were kept in close custody either in the Palace or city [Police Headquarters] until the facts were enquired into when their release or execution solely depended on the will of the sepoys whose power was supreme. Few indeed ever reached either of these [places] as in most instances the sepoys who had seized them, either believing them to be really Christians, or for ends of their own, or at the instigation of others murdered them at once.

The following arrangements for the defence of the city were now made.

Four hundred sepoys and two guns were stationed at each gate. Large parties of Cavalry were kept inside the Palace – a troop being placed at the main gate and another by the Diwan-i-khas. Six Horse Artillery guns fully equipped were in front of the Diwan-i-am [Hall of Public Audience]. Mir Nawab who was [now] head and chief of the city rebels after consulting with the mutineer officers determined to seize the district of Gurgaon and capture the Civil Officers at that station. He left with a strong force for that purpose but Mr Ford the Magistrate managed to escape . . . The Mir's party then made common cause with the villagers and after burning the houses and public offices returned to Delhi. The Deputy Collector and most of the native officials of Gurgaon succeeded in concealing themselves and escaped the grasp of the oppressors.

The mutineer army despatched a single sepoy with a letter to Abdul Rahman Khan, Nawab [ruler] of Jhujhur requiring him to join and aid their cause and in the event of his refusal threatening to march against him. He sent fifty horsemen, nominally to assist but really to mislead the mutineers and prevent their attacking him, saying that he sent this party at once as an advance guard but was preparing a much larger force for them. He at the same time presented the sepoy messenger with two hundred rupees. The movement against Jhujhur was consequently postponed and a force assembled for Rohtak instead, the command of which was given to Mirza Abu Bakr, grandson of the King, Mir Nawab being associated with him.

About this period news reached Delhi that Rao Tula Ram of Rewari had seized that part of the country, proclaimed himself raja, and was looting in every direction. The King was much enraged as this same Tula Ram had a short time before sent [petitions] to him tendering his allegiance. The raja of Ballabhgarh had sent a similar [petition] on which the mutineers ordered him to join them at once or take the consequences. On receiving their communication the raja left for Delhi with an escort of one hundred horse and arriving near the city before dawn sent notice of his arrival to Hakim Ahsanullah Khan, who, being a man of experience and rare sagacity and moreover a well-wisher of the British, replied, telling him on no account to come into the city, but to return at once and if the mutineer army threatened to attack him to collect his vassals and defy them. On this the raja retraced his steps.

Rawalji, an influential and very wealthy landholder in Jaipur, had been living in Delhi for some time having left his own country in a huff at being dismissed from the maharaja's service. He had a body of Horse and Foot with him and was in like manner required by the mutineers to join them. Being an astute individual he replied that he was ready and willing to do so, that he had indeed been rather impatiently waiting for such an invitation but that as the force with him was small he would march back at once to Jaipur, collect a formidable body of troops and speedily return and ally himself with them and their cause. The leading mutineer officers highly approved and Rawalji departed in great pomp for Jaipur and never returned . . .

The Ramadan [a Muslim festival and feast] was now over and the first of the Id [a festival which followed Ramadan] had arrived – a rumour prevailed throughout the city that the English troops would assault and enter Delhi on the Meerut side when the King and his followers had gone in procession to the Idgarh [a place for celebrating festivals] for prayer. The old King, on account of his great age or from fear of an attack did not accompany the party, but his sons Mirza Moghul, Mirza Khizr Sultan, and his grandson Abu Bakr went in great pomp with drums beating and banners flying, escorted by 250 Cavalry – a regiment of Infantry and three guns. Now it so happened that Bishen Singh and Bhagwat Singh of Ghaziabad, influential zamindars [landowners] were coming at the same time to Delhi to pay homage and present a nazar [ceremonial gift] to the King and a large mass of Muhammadans were also on their way to the city for the Id. The King was sitting in [a tower room] which overlooks the river and seeing this vast assemblage of people at once concluded that the report above alluded to was correct and that the English army had really arrived, so he despatched a [camel-rider] in hot haste to the Idgarh ordering his son to leave the troops to their fate and instantly return to the palace, as from the great clouds of dust an army was evidently approaching and was already near the Jumna bridge. On receipt of this order the princes sprang on their horses and fled in a state of terror such as no language can adequately describe. The troops followed helter skelter, a confused, panic-stricken mob, leaving their guns, most of the Cavalry chargers, and even many of their weapons behind at the Idgarh. On reaching the city they learned that the Ghaziabad zamindars had been the sole cause of the panic.

Hakim Ahsanullah Khan contrived to send a secret messenger to the representative of the British government at Meerut with a letter as if from the King detailing these facts and saying: 'I am powerless to strike – you have left me so. The mutinied portion of your army of their own will and pleasure, entered this city and murdered your people and your women and children. Up to the present moment the pillage of the place continues. I am really under surveillance. In the manner which may seem best to you take or send for your army, and turn them out of Delhi.'

Up to this point the King appears to have remained true and upright as far as the British government was concerned, but that very evening by the advice and guile of Mir Nawab and Mirza Abu Bakr, the King's grandson, two infantry regiments with three guns and some regular cavalry were despatched to Rohtak.

On the Rohtak road about [twelve miles] from Delhi in the Police Thana [station] of Mundh, the Thanadar was Syed Mubarak Shah.*

* The compiler of this narration.

195

This officer had remained at his post from the commencement of the outbreak, although constantly threatened with death or expulsion. Daily expecting the arrival of a British force he had maintained order to the best of his ability and restrained the villagers from crime, assuring them that the suspension of governmental authority was but for a day and that all would shortly be restored as before. As long as Mubarak Shah remained the men of Mundh committed no excesses but those of the surrounding villages were mixed up in numerous dacoities and murders.

When the Thanadar found that he was the only government official left in the Delhi division he sent a petition to the Magistrate of Rohtak describing the state of the country round and begging for a reinforcement of two hundred horsemen to enable him to resist the rebels. A reply arrived to the effect that no troops could be sent as those who should have composed the party had mutinied – but that if unable to hold on where he was the [police station] of Samplah was at his disposal. On the arrival of the Delhi rebels at Mundh they called up the Thanadar and asked whose Thana it was. He replied: 'The King's' – on this they said: 'On whose side are you?' He answered: 'On that of the true faith.' Then the detachment passed on towards Rohtak – and the Thanadar by these answers saved his own life. It halted at Samplah and from there communicated by letter with the Rohtak Treasury Guard who told them to approach without fear as they were 'with them'. Mr Locke the Magistrate, finding that the sepoys would not obey orders and that they had practically taken possession of the Treasury, left the station with four or five faithful natives and escaped in safety to Panipat. The following day the rebel force entered Rohtak, plundered and burnt every house in the civil lines; looted the city, maltreated the males and outraged the women – Mir Nawab himself carried off three fair Hindu girls loaded with costly ornaments. Mirza Abu Bakr and his army of oppressors then returned to Delhi bringing the whole of the government treasure and accompanied by the traitorous sepoy guard. When passing Mundh they seized the Thanadar Mubarak Shah and took him along with them as they suspected him to be a friend of the English.*

The Thanadar was threatened with instant death if he ventured outside Delhi city, so he remained with an old friend Abdul Wahud.† a resident of Saharanpur who had been employed in Mr Fraser the Commissioner's office. Both eagerly looked for an opportunity to escape but were unable to venture in consequence of the strict watch kept night and day at all the gates.

As already stated the Magistrate of Rohtak reached Panipat safely and halted there in hopes of obtaining troops to take back to his station. The 60th Native Infantry was eventually ordered to go, but

* The compiler of this narration makes out a good story for himself – but there is no doubt that he threw in his lot with the rebels and mutineers and took an active part against the British.

† This man had been head of my vernacular office at Saharanpur and was an exceptionally clever but unscrupulous fellow. He joined the rebels in Delhi – of his ultimate fate I know nothing.

on arrival at Rohtak heard all particulars of the Delhi force which had preceded them and themselves broke into open mutiny but did not raise their hands against their officers. They simply told them to 'be off' so they and the Magistrate left while the 60th started for Delhi.

The treasury guard at Hissar consisted of a company of the Hariana Light Infantry stationed at Hansi. When news of the mutineer troops being in Delhi reached the former place the cavalry of Bahadur Jang Khan [ruler of Hissar] who were on duty with the Magistrate began a system of highway robbery. Mr Wedderburn sent for Shah Nur Khan the [cavalry officer] and enjoined him to maintain order as disturbances were rife throughout the country. On this the [officer] wrote to his master the raja for a hundred additional men who arrived in due course . . . and encamped in a garden outside the Fort, altogether separate from Shah Nur Khan and his men.

The Hariana Infantry Regiment and the detachment of the 4th Irregular Cavalry which had been left at Hansi by Major Martin when he marched with the main body to Karnal determined to mutiny and sent five troopers to Hissar with instructions to their comrades to rise, murder the Europeans and seize the treasure as they intended doing at Hansi. The officers at the latter place on learning of these plots resolved to blow up the magazine but were prevented by the sepoys who were on the alert and had taken possession of the place. Captain Stafford commanding the regiment, Tapsill the Collector of Customs, Dr Rich and all the ladies and children escaped in the Jind direction, but the doctor and three or four Europeans fell into the hands of the sepoys and were put to death.

A European [landowner] named Paul, on seeing the critical state of things at Hansi left for Hissar with his wife and nine children and on the way met the five troopers (who had been sent to that place as already stated) and the company of the Harianas which after mutinying at Hissar was proceeding to join the headquarters of the regiment. They seized the helpless Paul and his family and though he repeatedly assured them that he was unconnected with the government and their grievances, his remonstrances were of no avail and he with his entire family were butchered. The company of sepoys had possessed themselves of the Rs. 19,000 of government treasure besides seizing all the money in the several stations along the Customs line.

The five troopers of the 4th Irregulars who had been deputed to Hissar, rode up to the Fort on arrival and ordered the gates to be opened as the Russian army had arrived. All the European residents as well as sepoys forming the Treasury Guard were inside the Fort. When the latter heard details of the events at Hansi they sounded the alarm and [Lieutenant] Barwell the Adjutant going to the spot was shot down. Mrs Barwell, Mrs Wedderburn and her infant were taken prisoner by the sepoys and eventually handed over by the [commander] of the regiment to a party of Muhammadans who had joined the outbreak, the chief of whom was a relation of the Muhammadan

Deputy Magistrate. This fiend took the ladies into one of the [bath-houses] and there murdered them, the infant sharing the fate of its mother. It is said that Mrs Wedderburn's long hair had fallen down and she asked permission to put it up so that it should not interfere with the effect of the sword blow and so delay death. Mr Smith escaped from the [courthouse] into the high grass jungle. Mrs Smith and her children hid for some time in their garden but as they were suffering agony from thirst she ventured to the canal to procure a little water and was seen and murdered – the poor children were pointed out by their Muhammadan servant and all butchered. Mr Wedderburn was the first person killed having been shot in the [courthouse] by the sepoys on duty at the Treasury. Mr Jeffrey, the Collectorate Clerk, was sheltered and concealed by a son of Dhian Singh.

When the company of Hariana sepoys had thus disposed of all the Europeans they could find they took possession of the treasure amounting to one lakh and fifty-six thousand rupees [156,000] and placing it in commissariat carts which they seized for the purpose, brought it with them to Hansi. The public offices at Hissar and Hansi were burnt and totally destroyed. The whole of the Hariana Light Infantry with 100 men of the 4th Irregulars then set off for Delhi taking the treasure and magazine stores along with them and marching via Najafgarh but avoiding the main road. While en route they divided the greater part of the spoil but laid aside a portion for the King.

Three companies of the Hariana corps and 200 of the 4th Irregular Cavalry were stationed at Lirza under Imam Khan. When information of the mutiny of the headquarters of their regiment at Hansi reached this detachment they determined to follow the example and persuaded the troopers to join them. On learning their intentions Captain Robertson, the Superintendent, wanted the people of the town and villages to disarm the troops but they refused professing their inability to cope with the sepoys. Both Cavalry and Infantry soon broke into open mutiny, the [commanding officer of the Infantry] telling his men to slaughter all the Europeans, while the [Cavalry commander] refused to join or permit any bloodshed saying that the gentlemen had never done them any harm but on the contrary had invariably treated them with consideration. Both Horse and Foot took possession of the money in the Treasury, thirty-six thousand rupees, and marched direct for Delhi. They did not keep any portion of the treasure but took it entire to the King.

So large a force of mutineer troops had now arrived in Delhi that Mirza Moghul the King's son and the chief officers of the rebel army, after holding a council determined to occupy the Ridge at the Flagstaff Tower and for this purpose detached two infantry regiments, two hundred Regular Cavalry – one hundred of the 4th Irregular – two guns of a Bullock Battery and one Field Battery – but of this number fully one half, sometimes two thirds were in the habit of

198

leaving their posts and coming into the city during the night. On more than one occasion the guns were left quite deserted.

Although enormous supplies of military stores had been plundered from the government Magazine a vast amount still remained, as can be well imagined when we recollect that five crores of rupees [50 million] had been expended on them. All this had now fallen into the hands of the mutineers so they began to erect bastions and mount guns at the points they considered the strongest and most tenable.

A British force of about two thousand men of all arms, European and Native, which had come by forced marches from Meerut arrived at the Hindan river about [ten miles] east of Delhi and encamped on its bank. The system of plunder and robbery which [landowners] had since the commencement of the disturbances carried on along their line of road was at once stopped by the approach of this column. Reprisals were taken as the troops advanced and hundreds of innocent travellers as well as dacoits [bandits] and highway robbers were seized and hanged.

When the mutineer forces learned of the approach of the British they arranged to march on [Ghazi-ud-din Nagar] and give them battle; and the leading officers deemed it advisable so to act that the people of the country generally should believe that the King was . . . with them in all they had done or were about to do. They thought this the more necessary as from the delay in the arrival of the British , , , and the great number of regiments which had mutinied throughout the length and breadth of the land, a belief existed in the rebel army and indeed among the [Delhi princes] themselves that with the exception of the force at the Hindan river the whole of Hindustan was now clear of the English – as without any real cause of grievance, or any inducement offered by King or prince, the Company's army, its own sworn servants, had turned upon their masters and driven them from the country. The regimental officers went in consequence to the King in a body and besought His Majesty to mount and accompany them to the first battle . . . 'You will thus see how we will fight for you.' The King replied that he was old and infirm, could with difficulty move about and had been unable to go even as far as the Idgarh on the great day of prayer though it was close outside the city walls. Nor had he or his ancestors from the time of [the emperor Farrukhsiyar] a period of [138] years, ever seen a battle – adding: 'I know nothing whatever of military tactics but you do.' The officers replied that if unable to go himself he must send one or more of his sons. The King thus importuned told them to consult with Mirza Moghul, Mirza Khizr Sultan and Abu Bakr. The two last prepared to accompany the rebel army which was to march before daybreak the next morning. The force consisted of three regiments, four Horse Artillery guns, one gun of a Bullock Battery and four hundred Cavalry. Mir Nawab, the same man who had gone to Rohtak, accompanied the princes.

The British column was smaller than that of the mutineers and their information was bad so they were not aware of the near approach of their enemies, but they had a strong picket of the 9th Lancers thrown out on both flanks and their troops were hidden from view by rising ground. The mutineers advanced and fired their heavy guns which were immediately replied to by the British. Both parties of Lancers advanced slowly to the rebel troops shaking their lances and making them glisten in the sun. The mutineers did not like the look of the Lancers and their artillerymen losing nerve withdrew one of the guns. The rebels advanced firing slowly and irregularly while the British guns were discharged with great rapidity. Mirza Khizr Sultan not liking the turn matters were taking got out of his buggy and mounted his horse, and the British fire becoming each moment heavier while that of the rebels got weaker, he turned to Mir Nawab and said: 'What is to be done now?' to which the latter replied: 'Come along, your Highness – look the English are advancing along the line and the Lancers are coming on with those fearful lances.' On hearing these words the Mirza turned his horse's head and the mutineers seeing him retiring, first by twos and three, but soon in one mass fled panic-stricken from the field. The European cavalry followed for a short distance and captured one heavy gun and three Horse Artillery guns. The rebel troops threw away their arms in their flight and in sore straits and inconceivable confusion reached the Jumna late in the afternoon.

The narrow bridge could not hold the crowds pressing over it so that hundreds from sheer terror and believing that the dreaded lances of the 9th were close to their backs rushed into the river and perished. The English did not pursue for any distance. If even a small portion of their troops had followed closely their first battery might have been at the gates of Delhi and they would assuredly have got into the city, as the beaten army had communicated their fears to the entire rebel force which had remained in the city and one and all had become incapacitated from fear and were helpless as far as fighting was concerned. The English commander however did not deem it expedient to carry on the pursuit.

Next day the rebel army, trying to look very valorous, made arrangements for the defence of the city and recommended oppressing the townspeople on the pretence that they were conveying information to the advancing column. Shamelessly forgetful of their own utter discomfiture they continued to bully the respectable citizens and to disgrace them in every possible way.

The officers of the regiments which had been engaged the previous day laid the blame for the defeat on Mirza Khizr Sultan and Mirza Abu Bakr and finding it necessary to do something to retrieve their name and prestige, left again for [Ghiza-ud-din Nagar] with two additional guns under Mir Nawab. Artillery fire was carried on for some time with the English forces, in which [Colonel Chester] on the British side, an officer of great prowess, was killed, and a grapeshot struck Mir Nawab on the hand. [This action took place at Badli-ke-serai.] At 4 p.m. the rebel force retired and re-entered Delhi. On that day they were not attacked by the English so they escaped in safety with their guns.

At this time the British commanders deemed it advisable to move from [Badli-ke-serai], join the column which had marched from Ambala under General Anson [actually, Sir Henry Barnard] and if possible take up a position on the Ridge between Delhi city and the cantonments. Their route was by the Bajpat ferry.

As the column left [Badli-ke-serai] Mr Greathed, Commissioner of Meerut and Civil Commissioner with the force, remarked: 'If we can seize the Ridge we may consider we have possession of Delhi, because in the first place we shall have the benefit of the old cantonment and secondly, the city will be within range of our guns, while the Ridge will protect us from those of the enemy.'

[From the Jumna ferry] the column moved to Alipur. On the rebel leaders learning this they sent three infantry regiments – five hundred Horse, composed of Regulars and Irregulars – four heavy guns, Bullock Battery and two troops of Horse Artillery under command of Mirza Khizr Sultan and Mir Nawab. On that night a spy of the British disguised as a maulvi [Muslim divine] came into Delhi and informed the ... Native Officers that four hundred of the 4th Irregular Cavalry then with the British would during the fight come over and join them – they must not interfere with them in any way as they were friends and easily recognisable being dressed in green tunics and green turbans and that he had been sent secretly with the information. As proposals for mutiny and desertion had been going on for some time between this regiment and the troops in Delhi the latter believed the story and were greatly elated at this accession to their strength which coming at so favourable a moment would ensure them victory. The rebel army marched that night taking the maulvi with them and arrived at [Badli-ke-serai]. Before sunrise the artillery opened from both sides. Mirza Khizr Sultan was distinguished by a very brilliant [helmet] which glistened and sparkled in the sun. The English guns commenced a heavy fire of round shot some falling on the prince's right, others on his left and so close that he was greatly alarmed and said to [one] who was close by: 'What shall I do now?', who replied: 'Fly, your Highness, for you have come out today without asking leave of your dear Mother.' On this Mirza Khizr Sultan on the pretence of bringing up magazine stores, separated from the main body and was the first to fly. He and the chief officers of the rebels saw the four hundred Horse as described by the maulvi and fully satisfied, allowed them to advance unmolested but when close to the guns they began with sword and lance to cut down and kill the artillerymen. The 3rd Cavalry advanced to oppose them and they met in the melee. The fight was well contested, both sides losing some 200 or 250 men, when it became apparent to the rebels that their opponents were Europeans not [Indian] horsemen, and as they had captured the guns in the first onslaught, the infantry commenced retreating followed by the remaining artillery and 3rd Cavalry on which a general flight ensued. Numbers of the European troopers fell from sunstroke and were put to death. Four heavy guns fell into the hands of the British. When news of the defeat reached the King he summoned the 4 Troops of [the] Irregulars and after consulting the native officers who happened to be with him . . . ordered them to go and reinforce the beaten army. They obeyed and outside the city walls met the flying troops and did their utmost to encourage and reassure them. [The] Cavalry went [six miles] beyond the Ridge and saw that the entire British column was advancing. On the English observing this body of Horse they sent some round shot among them. The Irregulars had no guns and when the wind of a shot slightly injured their commander . . . they commenced retiring feeling quite unequal to the task of opposing the Europeans – some separating fled to Delhi by the Chaudur bridge, a few only making a show of resistance at Rohilla Khan Serai. The British advanced along with their body of cavalry and fighting as they came reached the Ridge which the mutineer troops had abandoned on hearing of the disaster at [Badli-ke-serai]. A few sepoys it is true remained by the Flag-staff and met the Europeans with a withering volley which killed many and wounded a great number but nothing could stand against the bold spirit and bravery of the British who gained possession of the entire Ridge. Vast numbers of the mutineers, Horse, Foot and Artillery, were killed and still more wounded that day. Heaps of dead were scattered over the battlefield – but most of the wounded either by their own exertions or assisted by their friends managed to reach the city. The false maulvi was taken back a close prisoner and being proved to be a spy was put to death . . .

It has been already stated that strong guards had been stationed at the city gates and the wall manned throughout, guns being laid at the most commanding points. From these . . . the rebels poured a heavy fire of shot and shell on to the Ridge. In this an old Company's artilleryman named Kalah Khan greatly distinguished himself keeping up so hot a fire day and night that even the mounted orderlies on the Ridge found great difficulty in carrying orders and as their only chance of safety had to gallop at top speed from one position to another.

Three or four days after taking the heights the British commenced a desultory fire of heavy guns on the city but were chiefly occupied in strengthening their position to the right and making arrangements for a regular siege. If they had followed up the victory at [Badli-ke-serai] and after seizing the Ridge had immediately pushed on with artillery, cavalry and infantry and at once assaulted the city they would no doubt have lost a large number of men but they would to a certainty have battered in the Kashmir and Lahore gates and entered the city with all the courage and dash which had up to that time distinguished their advances. The rebel troops would have been quite unable to drive them back being few in number and so thoroughly panic-stricken from their defeat as to be incapable of forming any plans or taking advantage of any opporunity.

In the city of Delhi there lived one Mahbub Ali Khan – he was high . . . in the royal confidence but had for a long time been a great invalid. He now determined to check if possible the system of plunder daily carried on by the sepoys and believed that if he could induce them to go and fight the English they would soon lose all heart and energy and their numbers diminish daily. He therefore offered to supply rations if they would go and exterminate the unbelievers. They readily agreed to his proposal, and at noon when the sun was at its strongest, and the heat intense, two or three regiments of infantry, three or four hundred cavalry, and four guns, moved out with the avowed intention of attacking the British batteries, under the impression that the Europeans would not leave their camp on account of the excessive heat. They advanced for a short distance beyond the walls and opened fire with round shot against the Ridge while the sepoys discharged volleys of musketry which were perfectly harmless, the bullets never even reaching the British position, while the Europeans did great execution with a new description of rifle and their artillery fire from the heights was rapid and well directed. The British besides fought under cover while the sepoys had little or none. Numbers fell on both sides but in this and subsequent action the greater loss was on the rebel side. Daily did a mutineer force move out to battle and daily did it return foiled in every attempt to capture the British position. Mahbub Ali Khan did once, for the sake of appearances, send out rations to the troops but subsequently on the plea of illness failed to carry out his promise. While the rebel army invariably returned to the city after sunset the British remained alert with pickets, vedettes, etc., thrown out.

Two or three companies of Europeans were frequently sent from the British entrenchments to oppose and check the advanced . . . rebel troops, and these, sometimes in skirmishing order concealing their advance and so avoiding the artillery and sometimes in close column would start up in their front and charge them. On the mutineers returning to the city some such dialogues as this would be heard among the Cavalry – 'We have carefully examined every portion of the Ridge and are convinced that those who opposed us today form the sole remnant of the British army – not more than 80 or 100 Europeans are now left. Ah, my brother, where can the kafirs [Unbelievers] have gone? They had an army complete in every respect – where is it now? Nowhere! Listen, brothers and reflect – If they had more troops, would they not have come and attacked us? Certainly they would.' How marvellous was this, and how completely did the Almighty for His own wise ends pervert their understanding – so that men of forty years' service and upwards, nurtured and trained by the government, who had fought and conquered on many a battlefield and who were well acquainted with the power, boldness and invincible courage of the British yet accepted, and in their hearts believed, such utter nonsense.

The fact was that the rebel army possessed no really trustworthy information as to the number and position of the British troops – nor had they a single spy on whose word they could rely. On the contrary the Native officers who had not accompanied the troops usually sat in the Diwan-i-khas of the Palace and at intervals sent the King's harkaras [spies] for news of the fight. Those fellows went only a short distance beyond the gates and on their return to the Palace reported: 'Your Highness's army of ghazis [Muslims engaged in religious war] have nearly surmounted the heights and will very shortly return as conquerors.' On this congratulations passed among the assembled officers and they sent congratulatory messages to the King in the zenana to the effect that in a very brief period he might consider himself really a King.

This sort of thing went on daily in the rebel army.

The British now pushed on their batteries and advanced them in front of and below the Ridge, fastening the guns with chains buried deep in the earth, thus effectively preventing them being carried off by any *coup de main*. In this manner they constructed a battery towards Alipur and another at [?] while the mutineers had none outside the walls of the city.

About this period two native infantry corps, the 'Doo' and 'Macdonald' with a park of artillery arrived from Nasirabad and encamped near the Kashmir gate in the houses and grounds of the late Colonel Skinner and were soon followed by the Mehidpur Contingent. This large addition to the rebel troops greatly elated Mirza Moghul and Mirza Khizr Sultan, the King's sons, but proportionately troubled Hakim Ahsanullah Khan who was anxious to discover some means of preventing the mutineer regiments coming to Delhi. But had he made his wishes known he would have been instantly put to death. On one occasion he flew into a passion and abused the sepoys calling out to them: 'Why do you come here making mischief? If you want to fight why don't you go out and do so?' From this the whole of the Delhi people suspected the Hakim to be at heart a friend of the English. Similarly Nawab Amir-ud-din Khan and Zia-ud-din Khan, sons of Nawab Ahmad Baksh, an old jagirdar [holder of a grant of land] of Lord Lake's [commander-in-chief in India 1801–7] were really well-wishers of the British government but how could their inmost thoughts and feelings be known? People could only judge by outward acts. These men did not take any part with the rebels or join the King's sons – and their loyalty was, on the occupation of Delhi by the British army, clearly established. In the same category may be placed Mufti Sudr-ud-din, principal [native judge] of the city, who was repeatedly, both by princes and troops, called on for a fatwa [legal decision or decree] that the crusade they were engaged in was lawful and right and pleasing to the Deity. The Mufti always avoided doing so – indeed no such fatwa was possible as no declaration of the kind is to be found in the Koran or anywhere in the Muhammadan religion. A report was indeed current in the army that [two of the royal family] were also friendly to the British and there is no doubt that they earnestly desired the overthrow of . . . the mutineers, but the story was only partially believed. Had the princes or the troops really believed it during the siege they would have destroyed them root and branch and spared neither age or sex – wives and infants, every one belonging to them would have been slaughtered. Subsequent to the capture of the city the conduct of these men became known.

The well disposed in the city found themselves powerless. As far as they could they had intelligence of the rebel plans conveyed to the English on the [Ridge] – but the only means of getting rid of the sepoys was by killing them and that was clearly impossible as they had possession of every street and lane and did just as they pleased, being supreme. No citizen or outsider who had taken refuge in the capital had any power whatever and if any Europeans fell into the sepoys' hands they were killed on the spot. The truth of all this would have been clearly established if any European officer, Civil or Military, had left Delhi alive. The English would have credited his statements, but who would place reliance on [an Indian's] tale? – For a trifling and perhaps imaginary benefit to himself he lies before [the magistrate] and by so doing brings about the unjust punishment of thousands. As a general rule [Indians] consider it a very trivial offence to cause by false evidence the punishment of an innocent man but as Firdausi [Persian poet, AD 930–1020] writes: 'Every man is not a real man, or woman a perfect woman. All are unlike – God has made all five fingers different.' All [Indians] are not alike – The good are few, the evil many. Moreover quarrels, contention, bitter animosities, prevail among all, gentle or simple, relatives or strangers.

The mutineer chiefs now sent a second [order] to [the] Nawab of Jhujhur on the part of the King couched in these terms: 'Come and join in the plot and be a chief and leader in our army.' The nawab by way of reply sent a hundred troopers to the King under the command of his father-in-law . . . nominally to aid the rebels but in reality for the protection of his grandfather . . . who was in Delhi and was also well disposed to the British.

Four days after the arrival of the Nasirabad brigade their leaders determined to assume the offensive and after sunset the 'Doo' and 'Macdonald' regiments with all their guns left the city, and passing round to the rear of the Ridge held by the Europeans, got close to the old cantonment parade ground and placed their guns there. A heavy artillery fire was kept up between both forces all night and the infantry were engaged almost hand to hand, the men being now and then actually mixed together so that abuse was heaped by the combatants on each other. Great numbers fell upon both sides, the British loss being heaviest. Several of the Europeans' tents were set on fire by the Nasirabad artillery. Day at length dawned and the mutineers began to run out of ammunition. Hakim Ahsanullah Khan had purposely delayed sending further supplies. The result was that the Nasirabad troops were forced to retire and re-entered the city. Had they received it they would very probably have advanced their batteries and fighting with still greater ferocity have cut their way into the British lines. The fire from Selimgarh and from the city walls was incessant against the Ridge which replied with shell and round shot.

The former did considerable damage to the buildings but caused little loss of life – several women were however wounded by them.

The people of Delhi were subjected to two special sources of molestation and distress –

1st. The general pillage by the rebel troops.

2nd. The shot and shell from the British batteries on the Ridge. All without exception whether bad or good, well disposed or hostile to the English, felt that they were shut as it were in a cage from which there was no escape.

The sepoys at the instigation of some citizens seized a man whose brother, Lachman Singh, was in the European camp, accused him of conveying intelligence to the besiegers and without further enquiry struck off his head, and hung up his body in front of the [police headquarters].

The British now further strengthened their advanced batteries by placing three guns a short distance in rear of each so that in the event of the foremost being taken those behind could pour in grape upon the captors. The mutineers on seeing this adopted a similar course and sent two guns to [?] supported by an infantry regiment, and constructed batteries on right and left with an entire regiment at each.

About this period [the chief of police] fell sick and the King hearing that the Thanadar of Mundh [Syed Mubarak Shah] had arrived in the town, summoned him to his presence and ordered him to carry on the duties of [police chief]. This the Thanadur declined on the plea that he was unfit for so exalted a position, but the King replied: 'You will have the title of [chief] but Khadr Baksh Khan whose mother-in-law receives a monthly pension of two hundred rupees from the British government will be your deputy and he will do all the office work. Moreover the other Thanadars retain their positions and carry on the regular duties. Do not therefore refuse the post.' On the Thanadar a second time refusing, the King became displeased saying: 'You must and shall obey', so he was appointed with Khadr Baksh Khan as his deputy. On the sepoys hearing of the above interview they suspected the Thanadar to be in league with the British and by the advice of Mirza Moghul stationed a company of sepoys in the [police headquarters] nominally to keep order but really to watch the [police chief].

So great a number of troops had by this time assembled in the imperial city that the army officers determined to crave [audience of] the King and communicated their intentions and wishes to him. In general he paid little attention to what they said, but in this instance made no objection and on a certain day the entire body of officers met in the Diwan-i-khas and placed the old monarch on the throne. A royal durbar [audience] was held and the chief rebels desired that the King should take an active part in both the civil and military administration. Hakim Ahsanullah Khan perceiving this state of things, did his utmost to stop it, urging the age, bad health and infirmities of the King. On that Mirza Moghul and Mirza Khizr Sultan with a view to the increase of their own power and dignity took the military arrangements into their own hands and declared themselves the chiefs and leaders of the rebel army.

One day a Hindu, apparently a sepoy, but armed with sword and shield and carrying a large bunch of keys went to Hakim Ahsanullah's residence in the Palace, and addressing the old man said: 'These are the keys of the Bareilly Jail. It has been broken up and destroyed. Four regiments of Native Infantry, the 8th Irregular Cavalry and a troop of Horse Artillery stationed there mutinied and killed all the European officers and residents of the place. They have also appointed Khan Bahadur Khan . . . to be ruler of Bareilly and its dependencies . . . Besides the military head of this force Muhammad Bakht Khan has had a great seal engaved: *"Al hukum l'Illah wa mulk l'Illah."** The entire body, Horse, Foot and Artillery with Magazine, Treasure, etc., is marching here accompanied by three or four thousand ghazis under Sarfaraz Ali. The column has already visited Rampur and Moradabad, destroyed the jail at the latter station and released the prisoners. The keys of that jail also are here. Muhammad Bakht Khan commands and it is the intention of the whole body, military and ghazis, to come to Delhi and die at the feet of the King.' On hearing this speech Hakim Ahsanullah Khan was greatly disturbed in mind and replied: 'My brother, I am but a poor hakim and practise the art of healing. I claim neither country or King – go and tell your news to the King or to the royal princes.'

In the meanwhile a further reinforcement of about three hundred of the Sappers and Miners arrived. They had been stationed at Roorki and on hearing of mutinies elsewhere had become greatly excited and eventually had themselves mutinied. Mirza Khizr Sultan recognising the importance of this event kept the men near himself in Selimgarh. Both he and Mirza Moghul were highly elated at the position of affairs and convinced that by the arrival of the great Bareilly column the sovereignty of Hindustan was as good as won – whereas it was the will of the Almighty that every sign and symbol of royalty in Hindustan should henceforth be expunged for ever.

There was great rejoicing over the Sappers and Miners on account of the material aid they would give in mining operations and the erection of batteries and this special work was made over to them – also the strengthening of the defences at the Kashmir gate and the Kala burj which had been literally ground to dust by the fire of the British batteries. They were also directed to prepare a mine running from the Kashmir gate to the Ridge by means of which the rebels might, without any open fighting, blow all the European troops into the air. This mine was placed in charge of Jemadar Munir Khan. The work had been in progress for some days when a party of mutineers went to examine it and perceived that its direction was not to the Ridge but to the Shah burj. The fact was reported to the King and Mirza Moghul who asserted that the Jemadar had so constructed the mine that he could any night destroy the Shah burj and he must be in collusion with the British and should suffer death. On that the two

* 'The supreme authority is the Lord's and the country is the Lord's.'

207

princes had him seized and publicly executed and the idea of constructing a mine to the Ridge was for the time abandoned. On the same day a sepoy of [a Native Infantry Regiment] stationed at Ferozepur reported to Mirza Khizr Sultan that his corps would shortly arrive to join the royal forces. It and the 'Lord Moira' Regiment were in the same cantonment and the recruits of both in consequence of the general disturbance and mutiny had refused to receive or bite the new cartridges on the plea that they had been smeared with bullock's fat and hog's lard. On this the Native officers of both corps met and agreed to mutiny, feeling certain they would sooner or later be required to use these cartridges. Their intentions were suspected by the European officers who very cleverly managed to remove the Native guard from the Fort and replace it by a company of the European regiment. The two Native Infantry corps were ordered to encamp on different sides of the cantonment. The 'Lord Moira' took up the position directed by the [other] unaware that the old garrison composed of their own men had been replaced in the Fort by Europeans, made a rush for the gates, but were repulsed with heavy loss, and during the night they burnt the Church, the officers' bungalows, and committed every kind of violence. The next day they returned to their lines and began to cook their food, but were fired on by the Europeans when they fled from the station proceeding to Delhi via Ludhiana.

A Camel [corps trooper] now arrived with a letter to the King from Bakht Khan telling of the approach of the Bareilly brigade, and a petition from Muhammad Shafi of the 8th Irregular Cavalry requesting that the [Bridge of Boats] over the Jumna should be strengthened. These were passed on to Mirza Khizr Sultan and Moghul who deputed Kadir Baksh Khan of the Sappers to see to the bridge. The Camel [trooper] further reported that thousands of ghazis as well as a large portion of the brigade, intended to attack and capture the Ridge immediately on crossing the river – after which they would present themselves before the King.

When the British learnt that the Bareilly mutineers were near at hand they filled a barrel with gunpowder and floated it towards the bridge intending it to reach at the time the brigade was crossing when it should explode and destroy the bridge with all upon it. The [boatmen] observed it and brought it to the bank, carrying it afterwards to Mirza Khizr Sultan who gave 5 rupees to each man. At 7 a.m. the Bareilly force entered the city and Bakht Khan with the other officers of the brigade sent to the King requesting him to hold a royal durbar when all would do homage.

There was no open space in the city sufficient for this vast assembly so the brigade encamped outside the Delhi gate near the jail. This was found necessary as the crowds of sepoys already in the town were occupying the houses and most of the shops – the entire 73rd Native Infantry being in the Ajmir Bazaar – five or seven sepoys in every shop. These scoundrels had . . . defiled the buildings and looted all they could find. They had stained themselves with the blood of Euro-

208

pean gentlemen, ladies and children and were enjoying their ease and passing their time in every species of debauchery.

A European sergeant whom they called Abdullah was with the Bareilly brigade, as well as two or three Christians, half castes of the poorest class. Mr John Powell, son of Mr Powell of Saharanpur, whom they had seized and brought from Moradabad, was also with them but under surveillance. The 29th Native Infantry were favourably disposed to these persons and would let no one molest them, saying that they had made them Muslims.* The regiment indeed took considerable care of them, provided for their wants and would not permit the sepoys of other corps or the townspeople to approach them.

A few hours later Bakht Khan in his uniform as [an officer] of Artillery, and the rest of the officers, also in full dress, to the number of about two hundred and fifty, all mounted, repaired to the Palace, to present [gifts] to the King. Bakht Khan sent a Camel trooper to summon [Syed Mubarak Shah] to give immediate information regarding the state of the city...

On the Camel [trooper] announcing the police officer's arrival he was called up and dismounting awaited orders – Bakht Khan addressed him in these words: 'I have been informed that you were in the British service so no dependence can be placed on you.' The [chief of police] replied: 'I have been in service for only one year on Rs. 30 a month. Your Excellency was [an officer] receiving Rs. 80 a month and have been 40 or 45 years a servant of the English.' On which Bakht Khan called out: 'Shut your mouth or it shall be filled up with musket balls.' [Syed Mubarak Shah] then said: 'I am not fit for the position of [police chief]. In opposition to my own wish but by the desire of the King I remain ... but am powerless to protect the city.' Bakht Khan replied: 'I am convinced you want to get out of the city so that you may go and tell the English the state of things inside Delhi.' At that moment [one of the attendants] of the King's said: 'General Sahib, there is a company of sepoys stationed at [police headquarters].' Bakht Khan answered: 'It is well. I will place 25 [troopers] there also that they may carry out the business of my camp and watch the conduct of the [chief of police] and report the same to me.' Then turning to [Syed Mubarak Shah] he said: 'Be present morning and evening at my tent and carry out my orders in every respect – you may now go.' He and the rest of the assemblage then entered the Palace.

The King seated on the throne held a royal durbar that day. All offered [gifts], kissing the throne and crying out: 'After the lapse of centuries our wishes are accomplished. God has restored the [empire] to Hindustan. Reign undisturbed and without anxiety. We will do all that is needful.'

Bakht Khan then begged the King to have all the military officers assembled to enable him to issue orders to each, remarking at the same time: 'This system of going out daily fighting and retiring is

* A company of the 29th N.I. had formed the Treasury Guard at Saharanpur.

utterly useless. The troops will move out on the day and hour appointed by me and without my sanction must not move a step. If any other chief or leader claims supreme command let him take all the responsibilities of the army on his head or I do now.'

The King answered: 'I have heard all you have said, but alas, in my opinion the last days of the house of Timur [the Moghul dynasty] have arrived – though it is just possible that the time for the elevation of my throne and Kingdom has now come. The truth is that whereas I was before in ease and comfort and in no way harassed by anxiety – I am now in my old age subjected to all manner of discomfort and annoyance since the arrival of this vast collection of troops. Not only am I in constant trouble of mind, but my very life is uncertain for I have no confidence in you, as up to the present hour your men are engaged in pillage, murder, and all manner of oppression, maltreating the people of my capital. On this account I have written [a list of grievances] and will have it read to all your officers tomorrow in full durbar – you will then perchance feel some pity for the people and put a stop to the tyranny and oppression with which they are now burdened.'

On hearing the King's speech, Bakht Khan, Muhammad Shafi and Nurdad Ali sent for a Koran and taking up the book swore an oath saying: 'May God desert us if we desert this throne and forsake your Highness. Your Highness is our King. This is our solemn oath which we swear on the Koran the symbol of our faith.'

The King remained silent. All then took leave and retired to their several quarters.

On that same evening, Bakht Khan and Muhammad Shafi unaccompanied by any escort went to the King . . . and the former said: 'If your Highness will appoint me commander-in-chief of the whole army and direct all the troops to carry out my orders and have a commander-in-chief's seal engraved for me I will on my part appoint Muhammad Shafi, General, and Nurdad Ali, Captain, and your Highness will confirm them in these posts.' To this the King consented.

Soon after this Maulvi Sarfaraz Ali, chief of the ghazis, by the advice of Bakht Khan came and met the King . . . [and] the King, because he was a high Maulvi, desired him to be seated. Sarfaraz Ali then said: 'Your Highness, I see no one here deserving of being taken into your confidence and counsel. If you consider it expedient nominate me as [chief minister]. After that you will have no anxiety or trouble – and I will keep you acquainted with the affairs of the kingdom. Be pleased also to confer some title on me which will add to my dignity.' The King remained silent for some time and then merely remarked: 'We shall see about it.' Upon this those two individuals departed.

Mirza Moghul and Mirza Khizr Sultan who had for some time regarded the empire as virtually their own, and ever since the arrival of the Bareilly brigade had considered themselves masters of Hindustan, were greatly displeased at Bakht Khan and Maulvi Sarfaraz Ali having thus interviewed the King. They determined that their authority, not that of the Bareilly leaders, should be paramount, and to this end, and that the people should look up to them as the real heads of the state, they conspired with the officers of the regiments which had been first to Delhi and without the sanction or even knowledge of the King had seals engraved. Mirza Khizr Sultan's seal bore the inscription 'Colonel of the Army' while Mirza Moghul was . . . commander-in-chief. Both princes were anxious to prevent either Bakht Khan or Sarfaraz Ali being raised to high position or special honour by the King – indeed Mirza Moghul conspired against the life of the former and plotted with certain sepoys to waylay and kill him. But Bakht Khan's position was too strong, surrounded as he was by so large a force of Horse, Foot and Artillery so that the intention was never carried out.

Quarrels and dissensions daily increased among the leaders of the mutineers who were all more or less jealous of each other. Two days after the above-mentioned interview between Bakht Khan and the King a great durbar was held by the King at whose express desire all the [leading men] of the city and the officers of the army were present. The King was seated on the [throne] in the Diwan-i-am and produced the [list of grievances] which he had been preparing for several days. It was written in a fair and legible hand, was at least [eighteen inches] in length and nearly as broad. The monarch handed it to Hakim Ahsanullah Khan and desired him to read it in an audible voice. He did so. The following were the contents.

'When Nadir Shah [of Persia] in accordance with the summons of the Nizam-ul-mulk [chief minister] to Muhammad Shah, King of Delhi, came from Ispahan to the capital [in 1739] and ordered a general massacre of the people and pillage of the place he stopped it after a few hours.

'Again in the time of [the emperor] Shah Alam, when Ghulam Kadir Khan . . . put out the King's eyes [1788], he permitted the plunder of the city for only a short time and then imperatively put a stop to all violence on the part of the Rohillas and Pathans.

'Again during the reign of Farruksiyar when Husain Ali Khan . . . strangled the King [1719] when pretending to put an amulet round his neck, the pillage of the city was carried on for only a brief period. Moreover when Ahmad Shah Durain came from Ispahan and some three [hundred thousand] Maratha Horse arrived from the Deccan and gained a footing in the city the plunder was not continued for long. All over the world during a change of dynasty, although rulers have, either by way of example or to instil fear, permitted pillage and bloodshed to exist for a time – still there was an earnest desire to stop it as soon as practicable and restore quiet and order. But this has not been so here. It is a matter of surprise, indeed amazement, that murder and robbery are still carried on by you although upwards of two months have now elapsed and though you profess to be fighting for the faith and to have come to do me homage as sovereign of Islam

– mercy and pity have no place among you. Robbery and murder prevail in every bazaar in this city.'

The King had prepared a very lengthy document much to the above effect – all of which he caused to be read to the assembled [audience]. On hearing it, all bowed their heads from shame and left the presence. But the sepoys continued to carry on the same system of robbery, and to such an extent that when one of them went to a shop for supplies he would call out: 'Give me a seer [about $2\frac{1}{2}$ lb] of sweetmeats for a pice [copper coin of low value]', on which the poor merchant would answer: 'Ah, Maharaj [Lord] – a seer of sweetmeats for one pice! No one has ever asked for so much – Jemadar Sahib, such a thing would be quite improper in Your Excellency.' On which the sepoy by way of reply generally raised his musket and shot the poor man. No one asked who had done the deed – no one listened to any complaint. Each sepoy was then a king in his own estimation, each [trooper] a [chief minister].

[Two landowners of Ghazi-ud-din Nagar] were in high favour with the King who made over [that] district to them on the understanding that no ordnance stores or provisions of any description should pass through their country to the British camp.

A jagirdar of Lord Lake's was ordered to arrange matters on behalf of his Majesty in Ferozepur Lahari – but he excused himself saying he was unequal to so difficult a duty being a great invalid and subject to epileptic fits . . .

Maulvi Fazl Huq of Khairabad who was in the Alwar raja's service on a monthly salary of Rs. 450 now arrived in Delhi. As the Maulvi was celebrated throughout Hindustan for his wisdom and sagacity the King made him one of his aides-de-camp. His arrival was highly displeasing to Hakim Ahsanullah Khan as so well known a Maulvi would certainly influence the King. But Fazl Huq did not pronounce a [judgement] in favour of a [holy war] or in any way mislead the King, though he was known to be in his counsels.

Bakht Khan had now command of the army in the field, but Mirza Moghul, Mirza Khizr Sultan . . . and Mirza Abu Bakr all in their several ways took a lead in military arrangements. The King's council was composed of Bakht Khan and Sarfaraz Ali, and in a lesser degree of Fazl Huq, but though the King wished it, the last was not permitted to be present in the council.

For some time Bakht Khan and the leading officers met in a tent pitched in front of the former [military] quarters and arranged all military matters, but the majority finding this unsatisfactory shifted to premises near the Delhi Gate. But neither Bakht Khan nor Mirza Moghul would attend though summoned by the others. Bakht Khan was displeased at their having left the vicinity of his camp and Mirza Moghul considered it derogatory to his rank to sit in any house in the city and wanted the assembly to meet in his own palace.

About this period Bakht Khan and some Cavalry and Infantry officers when attending the royal durbar recommended the King to send [a royal letter] to the several rajas of Hindustan to the following effect. 'It has pleased the most high God, after the lapse of a hundred years to restore the sovereignty to Hindustan [i.e. the Moghul empire]. It is your duty therefore to rule your several territories with circumspection – and in accordance with ancient usage to present [ceremonial gifts] and pay tribute to the Emperor and to send aid in men and money until the royal forces have defeated the British and driven them from the Ridge. Consider yourselves allies in this army of ghazis and ready to give even your lives for the establishment of the emperor's throne. Remain therefore no longer supine, and as if asleep, but awake and rouse yourselves.'

One of these [letters] was sent to Raja Gulab Singh of Kashmir and Jammu, another to the Maharaja of Patiala – a third to the Maharaja Sindhia at Gwalior – a fourth to the [deposed ruler of Oudh] . . . [and others to] the nawab of Tonk and . . . the raja of Jaipur. All were despatched by Camel [troopers] belonging to the rebel army or by the King's [messengers]. Those for Jammu, Patiala and Jaipur fell into Hakim Ahsanullah's hands who tore them up and said he had forwarded them. It was at this time that Muhammad Yusuf Khan, nawab of Rampur, after consulting with the Commissioner of Bareilly, sent a petition to the King through his [agent], tendering his allegiance and presenting a [ceremonial gift] of one gold mohur [coin]. The King was pleased and highly complimented the bearer of the petition. [The nawab was, in fact, loyal to the British.]

About three weeks after the arrival of the Bareilly brigade an attack on the British lines was determined on and the rebel troops advanced beyond their battery in Taliwara [just outside the Kabul gate] with two heavy guns drawn by bullocks. Fire commenced from the British batteries and some companies of Gurkhas led by the Adjutant of the regiment advanced to oppose the mutineers.

An exceptionally heavy fire of musketry was maintained on both sides with severe loss, when the Adjutant with his Gurkhas made a sudden rush on the guns, the officer with great bravery going in front laid his sword on one of the rebel guns but received a severe wound . . . The Gurkhas however followed up their advantage, seized the guns and dispersed the rebel troops who fled in utter confusion, some back to their own batteries, others inside the city, while the victors withdrew the captured guns into their own lines. The following day Bakht Khan and the other chief officers waited on the Emperor, and concealing the loss of the guns pointed out that disaster and defeat had resulted in consequence of the troops having left without his [Bakht Khan's] permission.

The fire of round shot, shell and shrapnel from the batteries on the Ridge greatly increased. Shells of very large calibre were fired by the rebels also, but with an inferior aim to that of the English, though the ammunition was the same. Considerable loss in killed and wounded resulted from this artillery fire.

Sometimes Muhammad Shafi of the 8th Irregulars or Nurdad Ali would take out a party of cavalry, and proceeding beyond their own batteries would advance close to those of the British. On one occasion

... with about 150 [troopers they] managed to get up to the British batteries and surprised the Europeans who were scattered about off duty, drinking tea. The English sprang up and rushed to their guns when one or two hand to hand encounters took place, but the majority of Muhammad Shafi's men occupied themselves with looting, and when a party of officers and a few mounted Europeans came against them they fled. During their flight, Nurdad Ali had an encounter with an English officer [Lieutenant James Hill] who attempted to use his pistol but it missed fire, then he threw it at Nurdad Ali striking him on the face. On this Nurdad Ali fled and when he got back to his camp proclaimed his own prowess and pointing to his black eye said: 'Look – my face bears witness to my having been in the thick of the fight. If the troopers had not commenced looting, the heights were as good as won, but what can be done when troops will not obey orders.'

A few days after this, a man dressed as a fakir [religious beggar] was seen to go two or three times back and forth between the Magazine and the Palace. He appeared to be insane. He was seized as a spy and brought into the Palace and large numbers of sepoys were sent to recognise him if possible as he was believed to be a European officer. A sepoy among the crowd cried out: 'I know him – I was with him for years in Afghanistan – look if he has the mark of a wound near the waist.' Such a mark being found, the sepoy said: 'This is Lawrence Sahib – I recognise him perfectly.' On this they took the fakir to the Lahore gate of the Palace and cut him to pieces. Nothing further was ever known about the man but the sepoys spread a report that they had washed a portion of the body when the colouring matter disappeared and showed the white skin of a European. Many however wholly disbelieved this story.

A scarcity of gunpowder and percussion caps began to be felt, the natural result of the indiscriminate plunder of the Magazine at the commencement of the disturbance – besides vast quantities had been expended in the engagements which had been going on daily since the arrival of the British on the Ridge. Many sepoys would take a quantity of cartridges and go beyond the walls in the direction of the batteries, sit down and bury them in the sand, then returning to their comrades would say: 'My brothers, my ammunition is all expended. I am going back to the city for more and will return immediately.' Hundreds, yes thousands of sepoys acted in this way – so how was it possible that the supply could last?

Mirza Moghul and Mirza Khizr Sultan represented to the army chiefs that Magazine stores were running short and that arrangements should be made without delay for further supplies. These two princes then selected a suitable house in Taliwara for a powder manufactory. Thirty maunds [about 3,000 lb] were made daily with about a quarter of a maund [about 25 lb] of percussion caps and duly stored or distributed to the several regiments.

Akbar Khan, then a resident of Meerut, went to the princes and offered to make a projectile of such size and power that it would

214

destroy a whole section of men. Convinced of his ability to do so, they advanced him Rs. 4,000 for expenses and ordered him to commence the work at once in the Palace. Thousands of rockets were already in the Magazine and men were busy manufacturing others.

At this period the mutineer army began to clamour for pay and loudly abused the King, Hakim Ahsanullah, Zinat Mahal, Bakht Khan and Mirza Moghul, saying: 'How can we fight when we are starving?' A small quantity of gold mohurs and rupees were consequently distributed to the officers and men, with the exception of the Bareilly brigade, and an urgent order issued to [the revenue official] of Kote Kasim, directing him to remit treasure immediately to the King. The revenue of the [district] of Kote Kasim had been made over in perpetuity to the King by the British in addition to His Highness' monthly pension of one lac and 25,000 rupees [Rs. 125,000]. The [revenue official] reported his inability to collect the revenue owing to the disturbances, but renewed orders were sent, and Bakht Khan promised to despatch some men and officers to aid in the work. Eventually, Sher Khan, a resident of Kairana in [the Muzaffarnagar district] was deputed with twenty-five [troopers]. On arrival at Pataudi the party was feasted by the nawab and Jagirdar Abdur Ali Khan, whose father . . . had received the jagir for distinguished service in the field with Lord Lake. Sher Khan refused the dinner and detained the sons who had been sent by the nawab to present it, and demanded a large sum of money and in case of refusal threatened to kill the sons there in his camp. The nawab sent Rs. 5,000 but they were not released, on which he collected his retainers telling them to kill the [troopers] if necessary, but anyhow to rescue his sons. They did their utmost to effect their object peacefully but in vain – on which they rushed on the troopers, got hold of the sons, and sent them to their father. Only two of the whole number of [troopers] escaped to Delhi and they were severely wounded. When this news reached the city there was a great stir among the rebel chiefs. The nawab was declared to be a friend of the British, to be destroyed. It was further determined that a force should be sent against him without delay but Hakim Ahsanullah prevailed on the King to use his influence against such a course and it was at length abandoned.

The approach of the Nimach brigade was now reported. At that place the 72nd Native Infantry, the Artillery, a regiment of Regular Cavalry, as well as [outlying] detachments . . . and the 7th regiment Gwalior contingent had mutinied on hearing of the events at Meerut and Delhi . . . This force commenced operations by seizing the guns, they then plundered the Treasury, and after breaking into the jail and releasing the convicts, marched for the capital.

The [British] officer commanding at the neighbouring cantonment of Mahidpur sent his Hindustani regiments against the Nimach men with orders to capture the guns, but these troops on arrival fraternised with the mutineers. Their next move was to have been Ajmir which they intended to plunder but were dissuaded by [a man from Deoli]

215

who told them they would find [at Deoli] two guns, a large Magazine and considerable treasure, and only twenty-five troopers to oppose them.

When Lawrence Sahib [Colonel George Lawrence], Resident at Ajmir, heard of the mutineers' intentions he deputed a party of Johdpur cavalry to bring away the [British] women and children. These men conducted them in safety to the village of [?] and made them over to the [local landowners]. When they entered Deoli they . . . found a company of recruits stationed there and proceeded by regular marches to Fatehpur Sikri.

One of the Alwar raja's regiments and four guns were also sent by the Resident at Ajmir to surprise the Nimach troops, but they, hearing of its approach, turned the tables and surprised their pursuers when the entire regiment with the guns joined the mutineers, who were soon after reinforced by a regiment of the Kotah contingent with 240 Horse.

The Nimach brigade strengthened as above mentioned arrived at [a place] about seven-and-a-half miles from Agra where five companies of the 3rd Europeans and a troop of Horse Artillery moved out to oppose them. The action commenced with a very heavy artillery and musketry fire. The Europeans and artillery soon began to retire and the mutineers to pursue. At length the Europeans reached Agra and by degrees entered the Fort – the mutineers following them up through the city and even to the Fort gates. When the lower classes heard of the defeat of the English they began to slaughter the Christians in the city.

Faiz Ahmad [head clerk] of the Board of Revenue was in a mosque close to the gate of the Fort and called out to the Nimach troops: 'Go slowly and cautiously, take great care, the ground in front is mined.' The pursuing mutineers stopped at once. Had they not done so the Fort gates could not have been closed, so great was the rush of people, and they would have gained possession of the place though it would no doubt have been with heavy loss.

A shot from one of the British guns took off one of the hands of [the leader of the mutineers] and four fingers of the other, causing him to drop his reins. The mutineer army, seeing their [leader] wounded and helpless, was seized with panic and retired to the old encampment . . . but hearing that the Europeans were advancing with fresh guns they moved off towards Mathura being short of ammunition.

After the Nimach brigade had disappeared from the neighbourhood [of Agra] the Europeans sallied out and inflicted severe punishment on the city people, executing many. The magistrate, whose temper had been excessively crusty since the proclamation of martial law, recommended all government servants to fly while they could. The majority did so and joining the mutineers accompanied them to Delhi. Among them was old Faiz Ahmad. He reached the capital along with the Nimach brigade and was at once appointed Chief Criminal Judge by the King, the [chief of police and his subordinates] being directed to send their reports to him for orders. Faiz Ahmad though of great age retained his courage to the last.

The magistrate of Mathura on hearing of the approach of the Nimach troops left for Agra with an escort of four [troopers] and arrived in safety. He gave each man a present of Rs. 100 with a promise of promotion on the cessation of hostilities and let them depart. The Nimach men found forty government elephants at Mathura and took possession of them. During their halt of seven days they mulcted [the bankers and merchants] of [one hundred] and seventy-five thousand rupees and then marched for Delhi on receipt of urgent orders from the King, going via Ballabgarh but not interfering with the raja as he had sent a contingent of a hundred Horse to the royal army.

The Nimach brigade encamped to the south of that of Bareilly and on the following day the leaders, viz. Sirdhana Singh, Hira Singh, and Ghaus Muhammad Khan accompanied by all the other officers went to the Palace to do homage to the King and present the usual [ceremonial gifts]. Sirdhana Singh was a stupid and ignorant fellow, but the other two were able men and the real leaders and instigators of the meeting.

His Majesty complimented them on their brilliant deeds at Agra – but these officers unlike those of the Bareilly brigade did not kiss the throne or swear to support it. The entire Nimach column was estimated at eight thousand men of all arms.

Bakht Khan, since his appointment as commander-in-chief, had daily issued orders to the other officers of the rebel army and to the [chief of police] and city police officers. He had also, in conjunction with Maulvi Sarfaraz Ali, who was styled [chief minister], been carrying on the affairs of the country generally, and the two had nominated Fazl Huq to be [governor] of the Doab [the country lying between the Jumna and the Ganges rivers]. The latter however declined the appointment and the King who had not been consulted represented that he had given the post at the beginning of the outbreak to Walidad Khan of Malaghur ... who had been carrying on the duties ever since. From this statement which was undoubtedly correct, it is manifest that the King had designs on the empire very soon after the arrival of the Meerut mutineers in Delhi ...

Bakht Khan and Sarfaraz Ali having obtained the royal permission to nominate the [governors] of Banaras and Allahabad appointed two illiterate mean-looking [men from Oudh] who during a durbar quarrelled and fought in the royal presence to the great scandal of the assembled nobles, calling for the sarcastic remarks of [one of the latter] who pointed them out as the distinguished individuals whom Bakht Khan and Co. had made nazims [governors] ...

Information reached Bakht Khan that the British siege train numbering nine hundred carts was in progress to the Ridge via Bajputad and from another source that it was coming by Ambala and Karnaul and had already reached Rao Serai. On this he sent three separate notices to the King but receiving no reply went in person to

His Majesty and said: 'Give me a thousand volunteer Horse and I'll go and either blow up or loot the [siege train].' No one listened to him, for though he was nominally commander-in-chief by the King's orders, the King never treated him as such, because his sons Mirza Moghul and Mirza Khizr Sultan were so violently opposed to him. The consequence was that the [siege train] arrived in safety in the British camp.

The artillery combat between the British and rebel batteries continued without cessation day or night. Sometimes the rebels would advance close to the English batteries – on others the Europeans would rush down from the Ridge and the fight be near the rebel guns. On most days Bakht Khan inspected the several batteries escorted by a body of horse and once had a narrow escape, a piece of shell striking his [turban] and setting it on fire – an inch or two lower and that day would have been his last.

It was now within a few days of the Bakr-Id festival. Bakht Khan therefore sent orders to the [chief of police] and other city officials directing them to assemble the entire Muhammadan and Hindu population of the capital as he wished to address them. This was done and Bakht Khan came as he had promised and spoke as follows: 'Listen to me, my brothers – I regard the Hindu and Muslim religions alike. There are great numbers of Hindus in the several regiments in this city – so let no Muslim sacrifice [a cow or bullock] on the approaching Id – whoever does shall be put to death. Speak my Hindu brethren. Does this order meet with your approval?' All replied: 'We are much gratified – your Highness' policy is excellent and you are a person of exalted wisdom.' All then departed quietly to their homes.

The company of sepoys stationed in the [police headquarters] were mustered and [Syed Mubarak Shah] was informed in their presence that if a single bullock or goat was sacrificed in the city he should be put to death. Bakht Khan further ordered a guard to be supplied to the [chief of police and his deputy] and sent four of the town criers to publish the following order by beat of drum in every lane, street and alley of the city.

'The people are the Lord's – the country is the King's – the decree is that of Bakht Khan, Chief of the Army. If any man high or low sacrifice bullock or goat he shall suffer death.'

The result was that not even a kid was sacrificed on the Id. Indeed these precautions were absolutely necessary because the sepoys had already murdered certain [Muslim] butchers who had been rash enough to expose their meat [beef] for sale.

It was about this time that Iltaf Husain arrived with an imposing retinue bearing presents for the King from the Begum [Hazrat Mahal] of Lucknow who had commenced a general massacre of the English throughout Oudh and was then fighting with them in Lucknow itself. The gift for Zinat Mahal consisted of a jewelled necklace of great length – a pair of jewelled armlets, and another smaller necklace. For the King there was a jewelled headpiece worth about [100,000]

218

rupees, a magnificent Koran, and 101 gold mohurs. The King was greatly pleased on being informed of the arrival of the [emissary] from the Begum whose kingdom had for ages paid fealty and allegiance to the throne of Delhi, and directed that he should be presented on the following day in full durbar. As it had been arranged the King came forth next day and after seating himself on the throne of his ancestors became impatient for the [emissary's] arrival and sent to hasten him. The King's attendants then represented to his Highness that Nawab Ali Khan, a [provincial governor] in Oudh and a very powerful noble of that state, was coming with the [emissary]. On hearing this the monarch was so elated that he promptly composed [a poem] . . . and had it read out by Mirza Khizr Sultan and Ahmad Kuli Khan, the father of the queen, Zinat Mahal. Ahmad Kuli Khan loudly praised it on which Mirza Khizr Sultan added three verses of his own and read them out to the King.

In this manner the time passed but still the [emissary] did not appear. The monarch became angry and said pettishly: 'Why does he not come?' and summarily dismissed the durbar. On the following day Nawab Hamid Ali Khan brought the [emissary] to the King, when the former made obeisance and presented the [ceremonial gifts] in the [hall of audience]. It subsequently transpired that the delay of the previous day was caused by Hamid Ali Khan who was anxious to exchange the jewelled ornaments of immense value for others of a greatly inferior description which he intended to make over to the King – but the contemplated exchange could not be effected in time . . .

Soon after the departure of the Begum's [emissary], Bala Rao brother of Nana Sahib, the murderer of the English, arrived via Malaghur where he had been detained for some days by Walidad Khan, son-in-law of the King, who had feasted him in his fort near Bulandshahar.

Towards the latter end of July a man of mean appearance, in sorry plight and resembling a [robber], came to the [police headquarters] and enquired for the [chief of police]. The sepoys on guard asked who he was and why he wanted the [chief of police] On this he became so frightened only stammering out unintelligible replies that they suspected and imprisoned him and on [Syed Mubarak Shah's] arrival said they believed him to be a spy from the British camp – but after a careful search they had found no letter or paper about him. The [chief of police] going privately to the fellow enquired whence he had come and was told he had been sent to . . . the King's confidential priest by Inazet Ali Khan, nephew of Mahbub Ali Khan [a judge] in the Muzaffarnagar district but that he had failed to find him and hearing that the [chief of police] was a [man from the same district] had come to obtain the requisite information. On this the [chief of police] whispered: 'Have you any letter?' – He replied: 'Yes, in my stick – one for the King, one for [his priest] and Muhammad Naki, and I would no doubt have been given one for you also had the writers known of your being [chief of police] here.' On this [Syed Mubarak

Shah] told the sepoys that the man had been sent by [Mahbub Ali Khan to the King's priest] which satisfied them and they let him depart – at the same time telling the [chief of police] that his head should answer for it if they afterwards found he had deceived them. On the sepoys going below the [chief of police] cut the stick open in a private room and found the letters as stated.

The petition to the King asked for aid in men, describing the writer's readiness to arm in his cause. The letters to the other two men begged them to use their influence to have his prayer to the King granted. The [chief of police] tore up the papers and told the bearer he had found only one in the stick. The man was in great fear of the sepoys and on obtaining their permission to go and see some ... men in the Bareilly camp took the opportunity of escaping from the city ...

On one occasion the rain fell in torrents and about two hundred sepoys at the Taliwara battery in the Subzimundi were lying in the sheds for shelter from the wet, the rest of the men being in the battery, when the Europeans believing it was empty or nearly so advanced against it with a company firing as they came on. About eighty sepoys were sent to Hades by a volley and the others left their guns and fled. The Europeans pursued when the mutineers who were inside the sheds and had escaped notice came out and fired a volley knocking over between thirty and forty men and officers, on which the English retired to their own batteries.

The lower classes of the city people, Hindus, Muhammadans and ghazis, who generally hung about the batteries in considerable numbers, now rushed forward and beheaded some of the dead Europeans, and after fixing the heads on poles took them into the city, followed by enormous crowds. The bearer of every head brought to the King received five rupees. Those who took them to Mirza Moghul three or four – Mirza Khizr Sultan also rewarded those who brought any heads to him ...

After consultation with the principal officers of the Nimach brigade and those leaders who had been in Delhi previous to the arrival of that column, it was settled that it should be placed under the command of Mirza Kobash, heir presumptive to the throne, and he stated his intention of accompanying it on all expeditions against the British – as the failure of the royal troops was very generally attributed by both people and army to the fact that no prince of the Royal House had ever led them or been present during the engagements. Mirza Kobash kept to his agreement and frequently went out with the column to attack the British batteries and returned to the city in the evening – a desultory fire having been kept up for hours but with no decisive result.

About five hundred men arrived about this period from Tonk, the [ruler] of that place having been unable to restrain them. Their stated object was a crusade against the infidel, their real one plunder. In this manner fully five thousand men from various quarters poured into Delhi as ghazis, the majority armed merely with [battle-axes] –

dressed in blue tunics and green turbans. All these ghazis including the Tonk men received two annas a day from the King. They usually joined in the attacks on the British lines, returning with the troops. Several of these fanatics engaged in hand to hand combat and great numbers were killed by the Europeans.

Frequently two old withered Muslim women from Rampur led the rebels, going far in advance with naked swords and bitterly taunting the sepoys when they held back, calling them cowards and shouting to them to see how women went in front where they dared not follow – 'We go on without flinching among the showers of grape while you flee away.' The sepoys would excuse themselves saying: 'We go to fetch ammunition', but the women would reply: 'You stop and fight and we will get your ammunition for you.' These women frequently did bring supplies of cartridges to the men in the batteries and walked fearlessly in perfect showers of grape, but by the will of God were never hit. At length one of the two was taken prisoner and brought before Mr Greathed, Civil Commissioner, who after enquiring into the state of the city and the rebel army gave her five rupees and released her, at the same time issuing strict orders that no man should molest her. As she never returned to the mutineers she was considered by many to have been a British spy. When the band of ghazis moved off to the assault the women invariably went in advance of all.

It was about this time that the officers of the Nasirabad, Nimach and Bareilly brigades held a council of war when it was determined to erect a battery in the Kudsia Bagh, such an arrangement being considered necessary as the British batteries had now reached the Racket Court. A large body of ghazis, a regiment of Cavalry, two regiments of the Nasirabad Infantry – about 250 men of the 20th Native Infantry from Meerut, a like number of the 72nd Native Infantry, with five guns were stationed there. The shower of shell, case and round shot which now poured into the city from the British batteries terrified both the people and the rebel army. Large numbers were killed and so great was the force of the shells that they passed through and utterly destroyed the old . . . buildings which were of great strength, with roofs of three layers of stone.

About 8 o'clock one morning, before the King had come out of his apartments, thirty or forty of the nobles were seated round the ornamental Tank [pool] in the Palace square, waiting his arrival. Just as the monarch emerged from his private room three shells fell directly in front and behind him and burst, but without injury to any one. The King immediately retired and all the others who had been seated there got up and left. That same evening the King called up the chief officers of the army and thus addressed them: 'My brothers – there is no longer any safe place for you, or the citizens, or even for me to sit – the ceaseless showers of shot and shell have already prevented that – for, as you see, by the very [pool] where I was in the habit of sitting every day, the round shot and shell are now falling. You say you came here to fight – can you not do so even so far as to stop this rain of shot and shell pouring into the Palace?'

On hearing this the Nimach, Nasirabad and Bareilly brigade commanders held a second council of war and settled that when the rains had to some extent abated a force should be despatched to Najafgarh to attack the enemy in the rear, while another strong column should assault and carry the Ridge where it was believed only a small number of European troops would be left, the main body having previously left to oppose the advance from Najafgarh.

These plans having been agreed on, a party of officers waited on the King and asked His Highness to wait for a week or ten days and he would then see what gallant deeds would be done by his faithful army to advance his cause.

It was at this period that the following incident took place at the Kudsia Bagh battery. About midnight the majority of the men with the guns were asleep while the rest were lying about in scattered groups without their arms or accoutrements – in fact so careless and off their guard that they might as well have been asleep – and the troops on picket were in the same condition. A servant of one of the English officers observing this state of things, gave information to the English on which a Captain sahib took a party of Europeans and Ghurkas from the Racket Court battery and massing them on the road advanced with light and noiseless footsteps to the Kudsia Bagh. Some of the Gurkhas running on in advance came upon the sleeping sepoys and attacked them with their kukris [knives]. On opening their eyes the sepoys found themselves in the claws of death and fate and pretended to be asleep on which the Gurkhas commenced to behead them and killed nearly one hundred. When the other mutineers in the battery were roused and stood to their arms the Gurkhas rejoined their own party and the Europeans fired a volley killing about one hundred and fifty more of the mutineers, while none of the British received a scratch. The latter then carried off three out of the five guns in the battery, but the rebels replaced them a few days after and planned an ambuscade. With this object they lay in concealment on both sides of the road, the battery appearing empty. Again the British were informed that though the captured guns had been replaced, the man were again all [off their guard] – so two companies of Europeans and one of Gurkhas started at once from the Racket Court post but when close to the Kudsia Bagh the sepoys fired a deadly volley killing or wounding about forty, on which the party retired removing their dead.

The plan of engaging the British at Najafgarh was repeatedly debated but nothing was done.

Abdul Wahid [chief clerk] of Mr Fraser, the Chief Commissioner's Court, came one day to [Syed Mubarak Shah] and told him that Mr Powell, Postmaster of Moradabad, son of old Mr Powell of Saharanpur, with three other Christians and a European sergeant, had been brought to Delhi by the 29th Native Infantry and though prisoners were protected by the corps, at the same time asking if he could devise any plan for obtaining Mr Powell's release. After deliberating together they determined to offer a sum of money to Bakht Khan to

222

liberate him. That officer however demanded a sum of Rs. 10,000 to be paid beforehand, which he would, he said, share with the officers and men of the 29th – but added that Mr P.'s life was in no danger and they need not imagine it was, as the regiment had made him a Muslim and would no doubt eventually release him, the corps having protected him hitherto from the men of other regiments who would otherwise have to a certainty murdered him.

Some days later the officers of the 29th represented to Bakht Khan that the sahibs who were in their lines were much inconvenienced owing to its being the rainy season and asked him to arrange for their removal to a house in the city as all had embraced the Muslim faith. Bakht Khan on this spoke to Shaib-ud-din, who had been stationed in the [police headquarters] to attend to the requirements of the Bareilly brigade, and he had them placed in an unoccupied room under a strong guard of ghazis, the sepoys remaining in the lower storey of the building. Only the men of the 29th and these ghazis were permitted to hold any communication with the prisoners – but both Abdul Wahid and the [chief of police] managed now and then by bribing the guard to pass sweetmeats and other comforts to them but were never allowed to approach near enough to admit of conversation. One day however Mirza Moghul came to the [police headquarters] and through his servant directed the [chief of police] to present a gift to him as the King's son. The [chief of police] having received no pay had to borrow Rs. 2 from one of the [militiamen] and presented them to the prince accompanying him afterwards to see the sahibs. As the [prince] was seated on one side, the [chief of police] managed to get close to Mr Powell who whispered: 'Mubarak Shah, shall I live to see Saharanpur again?', on which [he] replied in the same low tones: 'God alone knows, but keep up your heart, for Abdul Wahid and I have been scheming for your return there and the release of these other sahibs also.' The ghazis perceiving what was going on peremptorily stopped it saying all talking was forbidden and that the [chief of police] had been allowed to approach the prisoners only on account of his having accompanied the prince.

When the sepoys of the other mutineer regiments heard of the Europeans being in the [police headquarters] they charged the [chief of police] with being in league with the English and of being a Christian, threatening to attack the place and put him and the prisoners to death. They came several times to put these threats into execution but were told that the men were under the protection of the 29th and the [troopers] and others stationed at the police office prevailed on them to depart.

About the 26th August it was finally settled in council that a column should be sent round to Najafgarh consisting of the entire Nimach brigade with its guns and the Nasirabad brigade and its artillery, while a reserve under the immediate command of Bakht Khan should bring up the rear composed of two Infantry Regiments, four hundred Cavalry and four guns. This force marched on the 27th. On reaching the Jumna canal the bridge was found to have been destroyed by the British but Bakht Khan had it repaired but so inefficiently that it again gave way on the troops attempting to cross. During the time it was being made serviceable the rebel troops were exposed for a whole day and night to the inclemency of the season and thoroughly drenched with rain. At length the bridge being reported safe, the column moved on to [a] village . . . about [12 miles] from the city and along the bank of an extensive swamp, the Bareilly brigade as reserve bringing up the rear.

Previous to the arrival of the rebel army at Najafgarh, intelligence of the movement had reached the British who without delay despatched a comparatively small column consisting of two troops of artillery and a body of infantry who proceeding along the dry side of the swamp were ready to oppose the mutineers.

The Nimach troops arrived greatly fatigued at the swamp . . . but had no time to rest and refresh themselves. Besides the wheels of the gun carriages sunk so continually in the swamp that the progress was very slow and the sepoys had to wade through water which was above their knees. While thus struggling in the morass the British guns opened upon them and Bakht Khan hearing them halted the reserve. The real fact was that he and the officers of the Nimach force were not on good terms. They had been displeased at his having been given the chief command and he was angry with them for having openly shown their dissatisfaction. On this account one party desired the ruin and degradation of the other. Each leader wanted his own name alone to be famous, and himself hailed as victor.

The grape from twelve guns now poured into the Nimach troops and infantry and artillery became helplessly fixed in the marsh – they could neither advance or retreat and numbers began to fall. To make matters worse they were unable to see the British guns which were dealing such destruction in their ranks, as they were hidden by trees and high standing crops, but notwithstanding the extreme difficulty of their position the rebel artillery fired repeatedly and the sepoys also.

When men can neither advance or retire there is no help for them – the brave man and the coward have nothing for it but to stop and die. On that day 470 of the Nimach brigade, Horse, Foot and Artillery, were killed by grape alone.

The Nasirabad brigade had in the meantime advanced on the right and their fire proved fatal to upwards of a hundred of the British thereby enabling the remaining portion of the Nimach men to get out of the swamp. Had it not been for this not a man, not even an animal belonging to that brigade would have escaped alive. Their six guns fell into the hands of the British and the mutineer army fled in utter disorder while the round shot increasingly harassed them in their flight. At length staggering along exhausted and totally disorganised they reached Bakht Khan's fresh troops and retired along with them – while the Europeans took the captured guns to pieces, placed them on elephants and carried them to their camp on the Ridge.

The rebel troops had been practically starving for three days on this expedition. Bakht Khan therefore sent a company in advance to Mirza Moghul and Jemadar Shahbahadur urging them to send parched grain, sweetmeats, etc., for the men with all possible haste. The [prince] told the Jemadar to see to it. The latter suggested that orders be issued to the [chief of police] and the [parchers of grain] but the city Thanadars refused point blank to execute the orders saying it was not their duty to arrange for supplies . . . While matters were in this state the near approach of the troops was announced, when Mirza Moghul . . . warned the Thanadars that in the present temper and hunger of the troops, they would in all probability be killed if the supplies were not forthcoming. The prince further declared that the [chief of police] was the person really in fault and deserved to be killed. Consequently the [commander] of the Hariana Regiment . . . took a company to the [police headquarters] for that purpose. The [chief of police] suddenly discovering the plot against his life escaped through a dark passage in [the] rear of the [police headquarters] and eventually arrived safely at the home of Abdul Wahid who has already been mentioned. The sepoys after searching in vain for the [chief of police] left for the Palace taking the [deputy chief] along with them after giving him a severe beating – they would have killed him but Shahbahadur prevented them. Fazl Huq then collected sweetmeats and other supplies and despatched them to the troops outside the walls of the city. The beaten army at last reached their own tents, but so great had been their panic, so complete their defeat that they did not fully recover their senses for three days. The prestige of the rebel army had waned materially previous to their defeat at Najafgarh but after that it was completely and for ever lost.

The sepoys began to renew their charge against the [chief of police] declaring he was injuring the cause and in collusion with the British, so he left his office and took shelter with Hakim Ahsanullah Khan who recommended his keeping out of the way for a few days until the matter blew over, saying that he would report his being indisposed. On Bakht Khan hearing this he sent a guard to bring him, as from his remaining in hiding he suspected he was tampering with the enemy, and at the same time telling him that if really was ill he could live just as well at the [police headquarters] as elsewhere and if he died he, Bakht Khan, would have him decently buried. The [chief of police] was therefore taken back to [police headquarters] by the guard.

Four days after the fight at Najafgarh some [robbers] informed Bakht Khan that a number of carts containing supplies for the British camp were halted [at a travellers' resting place] near Alipur. He, in consequence, despatched a force consisting of 500 Volunteer Horse, in addition to the Nimach Cavalry, two regiments of infantry and three guns, to Alipur. These troops arrived during the night and after having killed and wounded several of the escort and dispersed the rest, looted the supplies, and seeing no enemy, determined to halt for the night and take the carts next morning to Delhi. One of the escort however who had escaped conveyed intelligence of the disaster to the British camp when two troops of European Cavalry, a battery of guns, and a regiment of Gurkhas marched at once for [Alipur] and arriving before sunrise opened fire. The rebels who had a village between them and the English kept up a heavy fire until their ammunition was expended – but the mutineer Horse had commenced to retire immediately the British guns opened and were loudly abused by their infantry who kept shouting: 'You infernal cowards and pigs. Where are you going to – what can the [Europeans] do to you? You brutes, look at us – we will not retreat one step until the last breath comes into our throats.' No one paid any attention and the Foot soon followed the Horse. The British advanced and took possession of the [travellers' resting place] which they found deserted and made immediate arrangements for the removal of the carts with the supplies to their own camp on the Ridge. The rebel force, though their loss had been small, re-entered Delhi in a state of complete panic. The Europeans had only three or four killed, all by the enemy's round shot. On the return of the successful force into camp the British advanced the Racket Court battery to the Kudsia Bagh and held that position. On this the rebel army lost all heart for whenever the British had captured any position no efforts on the part of the mutineers had ever succeeded in retaking it. Moreover the Kudsia Bagh battery was close to the city wall.

The simultaneous discharge of six guns from [the Kudsia Bagh] quickly spread terror among the rebel artillerymen on the walls and their condition rendered them unable to work their guns; indeed it became evident to the mutineers generally that the British troops would very shortly enter the capital. Hakim Ahsanullah Khan seeing their state of panic bribed a [woman], through one of his own servants, to mix some percussion powder with the sulphur and other ingredients which she was grinding in the manufacture of gunpowder. This woman was one of a large number employed making powder for the troops. She carried out his instructions towards sunset when the powder made during the day was collected in a large heap. A spark from her millstone fell on it and the whole exploded killing about four hundred and fifty persons and utterly destroying the houses in the neighbourhood.

Mirza Moghul led the sepoys to believe that Hakim Ahsanullah Khan was at the bottom of the business and recommended their putting him to death. The rumour spread like wildfire through the city and the sepoys pouring out of every street, lane and alley rushed fully armed to the Palace. The King was at the time returning from Lelunghur and Ahsanullah Khan with him, but the majority of the sepoys did not know the Hakim by sight. They surrounded the royal palanquin, which was a kind of throne borne on men's shoulders, and one of their number recognising Ahsanullah was about to cut him down when the King stretched out his arm and prevented him, on which Shah Samad Khan, one of the King's orderlies, seized the Hakim by the hand and drawing him out of the crowd placed him in one of the royal apartments from which he was transferred into one of the private rooms, while the infuriated sepoys rushed into the [Royal Treasury] with their muskets and pressing on the royal palanquin shouted: 'We will leave when you deliver Ahsanullah Khan into our hands – until then we don't budge.'

Other parties of sepoys ran to the Hakim's residence, set the buildings on fire and destroyed or looted an immense amount of property. The women of the family escaped and concealed themselves in the neighbours' houses.

As soon as the King heard of the plunder and burning of his friend's house he sent his bodyguard consisting of four hundred Afghan Horse, in whom he placed implicit reliance, to suppress the fire and stop the plunder. These men went as directed but on arrival joined the sepoys and townspeople in the general pillage. In the meantime Mirza Moghul had sent a trooper to bring the [chief of police] to the palace and kept him there under surveillance asserting that he was an accomplice in the explosion of the [gunpowder].

When 8 o'clock had struck the King saw that there was no chance of the sepoys leaving the Palace until the Hakim was made over to them so he earnestly implored both Mirza Moghul and Mirza Khan Sultan to make them swear not to put the old man to death. As it was Mirza Moghul who had originated the accusation . . . his heart relented when thus supplicated by the King his father, and he induced the sepoys to take the oath, after which he, accompanied by Mirza Khizr Sultan and Mirza Abu Bakr, took Ahsanullah Khan and handed him over to the troops at the same time sending the [chief of police] back to [police headquarters] under an escort.

The mutineers placed the Hakim in the room he usually occupied in the Palace and stationed a guard over him. For four days he was thus confined and during the whole of that time the King never once left his private apartments, replying to all remonstrances on the part of the rebel officers: 'I am sick and ill – Ahsanullah Khan was my medical man. You have imprisoned him – henceforward it will be very difficult for me to live.' On this the chief military officers consulted together and eventually took the Hakim from the sepoys and brought him to the King, who placing his hand on his friend's shoulder remained weeping for some time. Then in accordance with his usual practice he left his apartments and held a state durbar. After it was over Mirza Moghul and Mirza Abu Bakr placing Ahsanullah Khan [on their own elephant] escorted him to his burnt dwelling where they left him on receiving a gift of two gold mohurs.

The sepoys also attacked and plundered the house of Raja Jait Singh, uncle of the [ruler] of Patiala, believing that he conveyed intelligence of city affairs to the maharaja. Not content with plundering his palace they disgraced him and led him with bare feet through the main bazaars to the royal Palace. The King, who was sitting in the Diwan-i-khas, saw the raja being thus hurried along by the sepoys and rose up at once, [clasping] him to his bosom and consoling him to the best of his ability and expressing regret at the treatment he had met with. He bemoaned also his own helpless position and the power

227

and unbridled licence of the soldiery. The King then sent Mirza Moghul and Mirza Abu Bakr with the raja and had him taken with all respect and honour to the Akla Mahal within the Palace.

On the following day the sepoys seized a Christian, name unknown, and took him to the Fort with the intention of killing him. The [chief of police] hoping that if he could get him from them in their excited and bloodthirsty state he might eventually be able to save his life begged that they would spare him for the moment so as to obtain from him all particulars of the enemy on the Ridge – adding: 'Although I am well aware that you regard me as an enemy, I still consider the course I propose the best. It is in your power to act on the advice or reject it.' Hyat Muhammad Khan, Daffadar [corporal] of Gall's Irregulars who happened to be standing near remarked: 'Yes, my brothers, leave him here and we'll make a Muslim of him. Keep him in the [police headquarters] where everything is under your own eye.' The sepoys agreed to this proposal. Parties of them came every second or third day saying: 'You ought to kill that man' – when the [chief of police] and the Daffadar would reply: 'We are instructing him in the Muhammadan faith, and he will soon recant.' They would then send for the man and tell him he must turn Muslim without delay, but he invariably refused and was sent back to [one of the city jails] along with the thieves and pickpockets of the city who were confined there – both [chief of police] and Daffadar asserting 10 or 15 days more would see him a Muhammadan while at heart they hoped that in the meantime the city would be assaulted and the prisoner escape in the confusion. It was the will of the most high God that such should be the case and he escaped on that day. His name is not known but if he ever turns up he will confirm the above statement.

By this time the British battery at the Kudsia Bagh had greatly damaged the city wall and damaged the muzzles of most of the mutineers' guns rendering them wholly unserviceable and killed nearly all the artillerymen. The guns on the Kala Burj were completely silenced. The gunners dared not raise their heads above the parapet, indeed the fire was so incessant that the disabled guns could not be removed and replaced by others.

On that same day, Friday, the ghazis collected in great numbers, prepared for action and took the most solemn oath that they would go out and fight and if necessary die, but would never retreat. This large assemblage made a brave show and when passing the [police headquarters] called out: 'If the [chief of police] is a true Muslim let him come with us. We go to die.' [Syed Mubarak Shah] tried to excuse himself saying his duties lay in the city and he had no call to go out to battle – but they replied: 'No – today we will put you to the proof and if you do not join our crusade against the unbelievers we shall include you in the [holy war] and put you to death.' As a last resource he agreed to go, saying: 'I will bathe and dress. Proceed and I will follow immediately.' Deceiving them in this way he induced them to depart, saying to himself: 'Most of these fellows will be killed and those who survive will not remember to come for me.'

The ghazis marched along the Chandni Chowk shouting out: 'Citizens, citizens, all who would be martyrs for the faith, come, follow us.' Several of the townspeople, just for the name of the thing, accompanied them but returned from the main gate. By the grace and power of God two hours had barely passed when the entire body of ghazis returned and on the people enquiring the reason, said: 'The hour of prayer had arrived and evening approached hence our return.' But the real cause was that the fire from the batteries and the ceaseless volleys of musketry prevented any advance. Only a few sepoys attempted to go on – none of the others dared raise their heads – and if out of a thousand men only ten are willing to fight, what good can they do – they will not be even noticed.

The King became greatly depressed when he heard that the guns on the city walls had been silenced and taking up a Koran opened it to see what it would declare. The first passage his eye fell on was to the following effect: 'Neither you nor your army but those who were before.' The old King remained silent but Hakim Ahsanullah Khan tried to persuade him that it really meant he would conquer in the [end]. The fact being that he dared not give the real interpretation from fear of Bakht Khan, Maulvi Sarfaraz Ali and Fazl Huq.

Now that the rebel army had become panic-stricken and knew that the British would soon gain an entrance into the city they publicly declared their intention of evacuating it and plundering the neighbouring districts on the plea that they had received neither pay or means of subsistence from the King and were starving. A sum of Rs. 32,000 received from Tuli Ram of Rewari was in consequence distributed among the troops and it was resolved in council that the balance necessary to pay up the arrears to the troops should be raised by a house tax and by contributions from the [landowners] and well-to-do residents – but no violence or undue pressure to be allowed in the collection of the cess. From men known to own upwards of [100,000 rupees], a contribution of Rs. 25,000 was demanded – but those assessed at this amount went to Mirza Moghul and giving him a present of five or six hundred rupees succeeded in having the call reduced to Rs. 1,500 or even Rs. 1,000. The result was that only about Rs. 6,000 were levied under the general tax and a similar amount from the [richer residents] of the city.

The mutineers now began to construct a large [earthwork] inside the Kashmir gate with the view of intercepting the fire from the Kudsia Bagh and other batteries – but it was of little effect as the British fire was so fearful and continuous that the very earth shook.

The sepoys of the 29th Native Infantry recollecting the sergeant whom they had brought with them from Muradabad and hoping to benefit by any skill he might possess, took him in a [litter] to the Taliwara battery and after flattering his courage and ability asked how the effect of their artillery fire could be increased. He in consequence laid and fired the guns against the English batteries. The shot struck fair and true and so delighted the sepoys that they presented gifts to the sergeant who replied: 'It is too late – I can do nothing now – if you had acted on my advice at the commencement, the British batteries could not have advanced a foot. Now that matters are hopeless you want me to stop their further progress – it is impossible but I will die along with you.'

Only three rebel batteries remained at Taliwara. The fire from the city walls had ceased and the English now chiefly concentrated their fire on the Kashmir gate and its immediate neighbourhood. They also placed a couple of guns close to the wall, in advance of those at the Kudsia Bagh and completed and strengthened this new battery notwithstanding the most strenuous opposition on the part of the mutineers who made repeated sallies from the Kashmir gate.

When the English were satisfied that the proper time for assault had arrived they determined that it should take place at 4 a.m. on the 14th September . . . At that hour one division marched against the rebel battery at Taliwara which it succeeded in capturing though met with a terrible fire of round shot, shell, grape and musketry. All the heavy field guns fell into the hands of the British – but the rebels managed to remove all the Horse Artillery pieces. A mass of ghazis from the Bareilly and Nimach camps hastened to Taliwara and hurled themselves upon the British who, overmatched, fell back with the loss of two guns and their ammunition waggons. In this engagement about three hundred men fell on either side. On retiring the British made for the Kala Burj and took it by assault when the rebels evacuated the position at Taliwara.

The attack on the Kala Burj [a fortified tower] was as follows:

The troops placed a ladder against it and a European officer mounted first. He was killed instantly, his body falling back into the ditch. Ten or a dozen ladders were then planted against both sides of the Burj when several other officers, European soldiers and Gurkhas mounted them and rushing on the defenders and singling out the gunners and killing them, captured the guns, on which the sepoys fled leaving the Burj in the hands of the British.

The other division of the English which had advanced from the Kudsia Bagh had by this time entered the city by means of scaling ladders – while the third division which had moved on the Kashmir gate found it closed and barricaded – on which some European officers fastened bags of gunpowder against it and blew up the entire gate with its defenders when the troops rushed in and thus penetrated into the city.

[Two] regiments of the Nasirabad brigade with part of the 20th Native Infantry and two guns were in Colonel Skinner's house near the Kashmir gate and met the advancing British column with such a deadly fire of grape and musketry that between three and four hundred men were killed or wounded including over sixty officers. The column wavered and partially retired but the officers with wonderful gallantry stood their ground and in the midst of that deadly fire took counsel together what should be the next move.

After a short time the officers prevailed on their men to advance and they proceeded to clear the way by firing every now and then from two guns of a field battery which they had procured. On seeing the bold advance of the British column the Nasirabad troops retired with their guns, many flying in such panic that they mistook the way and rushing madly through several houses leapt over the city walls. The English then occupied the vacated position in Colonel Skinner's house and grounds and planted a battery there.

A party of European cavalry with indomitable courage advanced as far as Nawab Khan's gateway but encountered a heavy volley from sepoys concealed in the adjoining houses. Several of the troopers fell dead and the rest retired, ten or twelve passing through the ruined gateway of [a] house whence they galloped into the Chandni Chowk where the mutineer cavalry had picketed a large number of their horses. These they hamstrung and then retired. In the meantime a party of European infantry led by a Captain advanced with invincible bravery to the Palace, determined to get possession of the King or perish in the attempt – while another party went to the [police head-quarters] – a third into the gardens surrounding the Begum Sumru's palace – and a fourth worked their way through every difficulty to the Jama Masjid. This last party which had, in addition to their regular arms, a small mortar with plenty of ammunition was attacked with great ferocity by the sepoys, ghazis and city people and being without support was forced to retire with a loss of about forty Europeans. The party in the [Begum Sumru's gardens] had about fifteen killed. Those who had gone to the [police headquarters] gained entrance by means of ladders planted against the walls. The three Eurasian clerks who had as already mentioned been brought from Moradabad by the 29th Native Infantry were still in confinement under a ghazi guard. On entering the place two of the townspeople who were in [the cells] were shot by the Europeans who spared all the others on their pray-ing for mercy. The three Christian clerks were also killed but it is not known by whom – one account stating that the ghazis put them to death before their own flight – the other that they were shot by the European soldiery in mistake for . . . rebels. [Syed Mubarak Shah] was fortunately absent that day having gone to Bakht Khan's camp to enquire for a friend who was sick. A large body of ghazis assem-bling from various points advanced on the [police headquarters] on which the Europeans came down and engaged them but were so greatly outnumbered that they were obliged to fall back on their main body at the Kashmir gate after sustaining considerable loss. The Christian who, it will be remembered, had been seized by the sepoys at the batteries and whose life had been spared by the inter-vention of the [chief of police] and the Daffadar Hyat Muhammad Khan, managed to escape uninjured in the confusion.

The rebels and mutineers had by this time become thoroughly dis-organised and with the exception of the Nasirabad brigade began to evacuate the city. The rest of the sepoys closed the gates, but were in many instances attacked by the townspeople, who in return for the bad treatment to which they had been subjected at their hands de-prived them of their arms, beat them with shoes and disgraced them

231

in every possible way, crying out: 'Where is your boasted courage? What has become of your power that you can no longer oppress and tyrannise over us?'

The British had now entire possession of the block of houses in the vicinity of the Kashmir gate and had erected a battery there. The Shah Burj was also in their hands. One side of the city extending from the Kashmir gate to the Magazine on one side and to the Shah Burj on the other, was occupied by them while abundant stores of all kinds were constantly being brought in from their old camp on the Ridge.

When news of the assault reached the Palace the main gates were closed and two large guns charged with grape placed in front of the principal entrance. It is beyond the power of words to express or describe the courage and dash of the party of Europeans who went first to the Palace and who were nearly all killed nor indeed is a correct account possible of those who went to the Jama Masjid – the pen of a man is unable to record it – for there were at least sixty thousand mutineers, ghazi and rebel troops in Delhi and about an equal number of city people. The last it is true were not all enemies but the British at the time believed them to be so. Officers and men pressed on regardless of the numbers opposed to them, thinking only of gaining entrance into the Palace and if necessary sacrificing their lives within it. About three hundred sepoys and ghazis fell that day in the city. After the Europeans had made good their entry they were followed by Sikhs and Gurkhas whose loss amounted to over 150 men. A company of Europeans and one of Gurkhas held the Shah Burj, a detachment of Sikhs being placed in support with a couple of guns. Three thousand rebel troops with two guns attempted to retake it but were met with so terrible a fire that they hurriedly retired.

By 12 o'clock on the day most of the rebel army reached their tents but the two Nasirabad regiments . . . took up a strong position in the Magazine. Up to this time the King had been led to believe that the fighting was confined to the quarter of the city in the vicinity of the Kashmir gate.

Despair now fell on the rebel army in Delhi and elsewhere. They had no longer any hope of success or of driving the English out of the country and only thought how they could save their own lives.

The Europeans held a council of war to determine how the Magazine should be assaulted.

About 1 p.m. a mixed crowd of sepoys [troopers] of various regiments and ghazis assembled but finding it impossible to proceed along any of the streets as all the approaches were held by the British who shot down all who dared to show themselves, they commenced a sharp fire from the tops of the houses which they maintained until dusk but it was all to no purpose – they had effected nothing when night came on. Only two guns now remained with the mutineers and along the whole of the Chandhi Chowk to the Palace and even to the

Lahore gate only scattered parties of sepoys and ghazis were to be seen – all the rest had fled.

The greater part of the [two Nasirabad] regiments occupying the Magazine, believing that the Europeans had got into their rear and would assault during the night when no support could possibly reach them evacuated the position and dispersed.

The same sort of thing already described continued the following day. Whenever the Europeans saw an opportunity they made their way into the main streets and bazaars and shot all who opposed them. The spirit of the mutineers now completely deserted them and they contemplated entire evacuation of the capital.

On the third day the English effected a break in the Magazine wall through which they managed to enter and overcoming the sepoys . . . took possession of the place after which they raised batteries in commanding positions outside.

As a last resource several of the principal officers of the mutineer army accompanied by Sarfaraz Ali and Maulvi Faiz Ahmad went to the King and besought him to mount and lead the troops assuring him that the entire army, the citizens of Delhi and the people of the surrounding country would all follow, fight and die for him, and expel the British. The King, afraid of his life, hesitated. On which they more earnestly entreated him saying: 'Your end is now approaching – you will be captured – why die a shameful dishonourable death? Why not die fighting and leave an imperishable name?' The King replied that he would place himself at the head of the troops at 12 o'clock that day.

As soon as the Royal intention of leading the army to battle was known, masses of mutineers, ghazis and townsmen collected in front of the Palace, not less than seventy thousand men. Presently the royal [sedan chair] was seen slowly issuing forth from the great gates – on which the troops and citizens advanced towards the Magazine but halted about two hundred yards from it as all who went further fell by the British bullets which poured down the street like rain. The King's [sedan chair] had by this time almost reached another of the gates of the Palace and he sent continually to ascertain how far his army had advanced, but they were no nearer the Magazine – when Hakim Ahsanullah Khan, forcing his way to his royal master, told him that if he went any further he would to a certainty be shot as European riflemen were concealed in the different houses. 'Moreover,' added the Hakim, 'if you go out with the army to fight how can I possibly explain your conduct tomorrow to the British. What excuse can I advance for you after you have joined the mutineers in battle?' On hearing these words the King left the procession and re-entered the Palace on the plea of going to the evening prayer. The mass of the people and troops now became confused, then alarmed, and eventually dispersed.

During the night the English shelled the Palace and the rebel encampments outside the walls. That same night the King left the Palace by the back entrance to the river, crossed in a boat and went to Humayun's tomb about two miles from the city and there remained. The mass of the people, Hindu and Muslim, began to leave the city but the rebel officers alone knew of the King's flight. A party of European soldiers more or less intoxicated entered the house of Ramji Das Mahajur on pretence of protecting the women of the family but treated them in a shameful manner.

During the night the King sent to Bakht Khan for two hundred [cavalrymen] as a personal guard and at 3 a.m. on the morning of the 20th September 1857 . . . they were about to start under the command of Maulvi Nurdad Ali, when the rest of the regiment seeing the horse saddled suspected that all was not right and got ready also. The infantry observing the cavalry prepared for a move, followed suit – while the artillery on hearing that the sepoys were fully accoutred and ready to march made immediate arrangements for flight, remarking: 'God knows what's in the wind now.' When the Nimach brigade saw that of Bareilly about to start they followed their example – so did the Nasirabad column – the result being that when the 200 troopers moved off in front intending to proceed to the King, the entire rebel army's Horse, Foot and Artillery commenced their retreat in a confused broken mass, leaving all their tents and baggage behind. No one attempted to stop them – not a man even asked his neighbour where they were going – all were alike broken in spirit and apathetic, because flight had for some time been the uppermost thought in each man's heart. The rebel army proceeded by the direct road to Balabgarh and Farukhabad. On arrival at Humayun's tomb Bakht Khan and Muhammad Shafi went to [the King] and asked him to accompany them. He prepared to do so but was stopped by Hakim Ahsanullah Khan who said: 'Recollect that you are the King. It is not right for you to go. The army of the English mutinied against their masters, fought with them and have been utterly routed and dispersed. What has your Highness to do with them? Be of good courage. The English will not regard you as guilty.' With such words he restrained the King from accompanying the army in its flight, on which Bakht Khan and Muhammad Shafi left and rejoined it on the march to Balabgarh. It went via Mathura and crossing the river Jumna reached a place not far from Aligarh. There it separated into two divisions, the Cavalry going towards Bareilly, the Infantry moving to the eastward but wherever the army went it was defeated and scattered and sent to Hades as the object of God's displeasure.

When the English on the Ridge saw that the entire mutineer army had abandoned their baggage and were flying in panic and confusion thinking solely of saving their own worthless lives, and in disorderly and disgraceful retreat, were hurrying along the road to hell, they assumed the entire government of the city and without fear or favour proceeded to reward the friends and well wishers of the British government and to punish the evil doers.

The following day Mirza Alahi Baksh . . . father-in-law of the late Heir Apparent, after an interview with Hodson Sahib went to the King at Humayun's tomb with the intention of bringing [him]

234

back into Delhi. Outside the tomb he was met by Hodson Sahib, who took charge of the King and placed him under surveillance in the Palace.

Hodson Sahib subsequently brought the princes Mirza Moghul, Mirza Abu Bakr and Mirza Khizr Sultan in a [bullock cart] as prisoners and when near the jail shot all three and had their bodies taken to the [police headquarters].

After the lapse of a year and a half when the contract of the Company Bahadur [East India Company] was broken and the Queen of England took the country under her own rule, she proclaimed a general amnesty and forgiveness for all past offences.

May the High God ever protect and shield so great and merciful a Sovereign and preserve her people in the East from all tyranny and oppression.

NOTES AND SOURCES

The full titles of printed books, pamphlets and newspapers, and the location of unpublished material quoted in the Notes can be found on pp. 244–47.

PART ONE: A CLOUD IN THE INDIAN SKY

1 *Seeds of discontent*

1 Bjornstjerna, p. 18
2 Grant, *Observations*, p. 220
3 *ibid.*
4 Mill, *History*, vol. 5, p. 543
5 Macaulay, T. B., *Minute on Education* (1835). Macaulay was Law Member of the governor-general of India's Executive Council, 1834-38.
6 Baird, *Dalhousie*, p. 372
7 Education in India: Minute of the lieutenant-governor of Bengal ... P.P. 52 (35), para. 44 (1860)
8 Distributed in 1855. Quoted by Sayyid Ahmed Khan, Appendix 1, p. 55
9 Grant, J. P.: Correspondence with Indian government, showing progress of Measures ... for carrying out the Educational Despatch of 19 July 1854. P.P. 47 (72), 1857–58, p. 81

2 *The chapati and the cartridges*

1 Kaye, *Sepoy War*, vol. 1, p. 335
2 'A Resident in the North-Western Provinces of India', p. 34
3 Holmes, *Mutiny*, pp. 79–80
4 P.P. (30) 1857. p. 3, Enclosure 6 in Letter to Court of Directors, 7 Feb. 1857
5 Deposition of Sheikh Karim Baksh, P.P. (30), 1857, p. 50
6 *The Friend of India*, 5 March 1857
7 Quoted in Trevelyan, *Competition Wallah*, p. 337
8 Home Miscell., vol. 725, p. 1052
9 Pearse, *The Hearseys*, p. 377
10 Description based on the autobiography of Sir John Hearsey, in Pearse, pp. 382–86

3 *The breaking of the storm*

1 Canning to Lord Granville, 9 April 1857. Quoted in Fitzmaurice *Granville*, vol. 1, p. 245
2 *Delhi Gazette*. Quoted in Trevelyan, *Competition Wallah*, p. 337–38
3 *ibid.*, p. 338
4 Correspondence in *The Englishman*, Calcutta. 22 April 1857

5 Letter from Lucknow, quoted in Trevelyan, *Competition Wallah*, p. 340
6 Quoted in Kaye, *Sepoy War*, vol. I., p. 566
7 Captain Craigie, quoted in Forrest, *History*, vol. 1, p. 32
8 Report of the court-martial, quoted in Kaye, *Sepoy War*, vol. 2, p. 49
9 *Further papers*, vol. 1, pp. 4–5
10 Quoted in Campbell, *Memoirs*, vol. 2, p. 372
11 Edwardes, M., *Bound to Exile*, pp. 112–14. Narrative based on Gough's memoirs.
12 Kaye, *Sepoy War*, vol. 2, p. 115
13 *The Friend of India*, 28 May 1857
14 Kaye, *Sepoy War*, vol. 1, pp. 654–55
15 Quoted *ibid.*, vol. 2, p. 118
16 Journal of a Lady, quoted *ibid.*, vol. 2, p. 119
17 *ibid.*
18 Canning to Robert Vernon Smith, 20 May 1857
19 Letter of 26 May 1857. Quoted in Cunningham, *Canning*, p. 115

PART TWO: THE CITY AND THE RIDGE

1 *Navel of the world*

1 Thorn, *Memoir*, p. 236
2 For the background, see Edwardes, M., *King of the World* and *Glorious Sahibs*.
3 Edwardes, William, *Reminiscences of a Bengal Civilian*. Quoted in Kaye, *Sepoy War*, vol. 2, p. 662
4 Letter to Sir Charles Metcalfe, 2 June 1836. Translation from *Records of the Delhi Residency*, p. 47
5 Sayyid Ahmed Khan, p. 4
6 Minute of 10 February 1849. Kaye, *Sepoy War*, vol. 2, p. 21
7 Heber, *Narrative*, vol. 2, p. 290
8 Anonymous writer in *The New Monthly Magazine*, London. October 1858
9 Steel, *On the Face of the Waters*, pp. 135–36
10 Munshi Jivanlal in Metcalfe, *Two Native Narratives*, p. 86
11 For the composition of the court and its functions, Mutiny Papers Bundle 57, Nos. 509–511, National Archives of India
12 Translation of the full text in Ball, *History*, vol. 1, p. 459

2 *The mind of General Nicholson*

1 Quoted in Edwardes, E., *Memorials*, vol. 1, p. 58
2 Cust, *Pictures*, p. 247
3 It is surprising but, as far as I am aware, true that no major authority has examined in detail what might be called the sexuality of imperialism. It is perhaps also interesting that when I first suggested that Nicholson was homosexual (in *Bound to Exile*) in 1969, the reaction in Northern Ireland, where it seems Nicholson remains something of a cult figure – and to where his statue, formerly erected outside the Kashmir gate at Delhi, was removed after the Indian government had proposed to demolish it – was almost as violent, and certainly as abusive as one would have expected in the late nineteenth century.

4 Taylor, *Life*, pp. 116–18
5 Trotter, *Nicholson*, p. 197
6 Letter from Peshawar, in *Blackwood's Magazine*, November 1857
7 Edwardes, E., *Memorials*, vol. 1, p. 394
8 *Lahore Chronicle*, 21 May 1857
9 Greathed, *Letters*, p. 94
10 Hodson, *Twelve Years*, p. 258. This heavily edited version of Hodson's letter was produced by his clergyman brother in an attempt to convince readers that Hodson was an innocent and maligned Christian gentleman.
11 *History of the Siege of Delhi, by an Officer who served there*, p. 223
12 Bosworth-Smith, *Lawrence*, vol. 2, p. 207
13 Roberts, *Forty-One Years*, p. 130
14 Edwardes, E., *Memorials*, vol. 2, p. 50

3 *A signal vengeance*

1 Captain Waddy, quoted in Cooper, *Crisis*, p. 201
2 Metcalfe, *Two Native Narratives*, p. 170
3 Young, *Delhi 1857*, p. 171
4 Griffiths, *Siege*, p. 174
5 Quoted in Kaye, *Sepoy War*, vol. 3, p. 621
6 Hodson, *Twelve Years*, p. 275
7 *ibid.*, p. 316
8 Criticism of Hodson's behaviour at Delhi soon surfaced, and it became the subject of considerable and acrimonious controversy throughout the remainder of the nineteenth century. Only the principal figure was missing from the roster of those who supported or condemned him. Hodson was killed during the final attack on the city of Lucknow in March 1858. When his trunks were opened, they were found to be stuffed with loot. For an exhaustive rehearsal of the case against Hodson, see Holmes, *Mutiny*, Appendix N, pp. 591–617.
9 Kaye, *Sepoy War*, vol. 3, p. 636
10 Bourchier, *Eight Months' Campaign*, p. 156
11 Letter in the *Bombay Telegraph*, September 1857, quoted in Martin, *Rise and Progress*, p. 188
12 Anonymous letter in *The Times*, 16 November 1857
13 Roberts, *Letters*, p. 71
14 Coopland, *A Lady's Escape*, p. 269
15 Hare, E., *Memorandum of the Siege of Delhi*, in Kaye Papers, Home Miscell., vol. 726
16 Coopland, *A Lady's Escape*, p. 273
17 Report quoted in Muir, *Records*, vol. 1, p. 239
18 Griffiths, *Siege*, p. 233
19 Bosworth-Smith, *Lawrence*, vol. 2, pp. 245–46
20 Ghalib, *Dastambu*. Translated in Krishanlal, 'The Sack of Delhi 1857–58 as witnessed by Ghalib', in *Bengal Past and Present*, vol. 74, 1955, pp. 104–7.
21 Letter of Ramchandra to Colonel Burn, military governor of Delhi, 27.11.57. Foreign Secret Consultation No. 524, 29 January 1858. National Archives of India.
22 Bosworth-Smith, *Lawrence*, vol. 2, pp. 256–57

PART THREE: THE WELL AND THE WALL

1 *The Dream of Dhondu Pant*

1 William Morland, commissioner of Bithur. Foreign Political Consultation No. 9, 3 Oct, 1851
2 For. Pol. Cons., No. 8, 3 October 1851
3 *ibid.*
4 For. Pol. Cons., No. 106, 28 Jan. 1853
5 Thomson, *Cawnpore*, p. 54
6 Shepherd, *Personal Narrative*, p. 14
7 Roberts, *Letters*, p. 120. 'While searching over the Nana's Palaces at Bithur the other day, we found heaps of letters directed to that fiend Azimullah Khan by ladies in England, some from Lady —— ending *"your affect. Mother"*. Others from a young girl at Brighton named ——, written in the most lovable manner. Such rubbish I never read, partly in French, which this scoundrel seems to have understood; how English ladies can be so infatuated.'
8 Russell, *Diary*, p. 33
9 Lang, *Wanderings*, p. 114
10 Deposition of Sitaram Bawa, in Home Miscell., vol. 726, p. 1157
11 See Edwardes, M., *Battles*, p. 59
12 Captain Fletcher Hayes. Quoted in Kaye, *Sepoy War*, vol. 2, pp. 300 1
13 Parts of the text of this remarkable document are given in Gupta, *Nana Sahib*, pp. 85–87. The complete version is in For. Pol. Cons., No. 27 and 28. 26 November 1858.
14 Wheeler to Lawrence, 24 June 1857. Quoted in Edwardes and Merivale, vol. 2, p. 353
15 Thomson, *Cawnpore*, pp. 148–50
16 The explanation suggested here was first given in Edwardes, M., *Battles*. It is not supported by the evidence of the only survivor who made a detailed report on what he believed had happened. Mowbray Thomson (*Cawnpore*, pp. 166–67), however, does state that 'the native boatmen . . . all jumped over and waded to the shore. *We fired into them immediately'* (my italics). Evidence from native informers given after the rebellion confirmed that the boats were fired upon first, but by this time the British propaganda version of events at Cawnpore was firmly established. It seems highly unlikely that the truth will ever be known. For a survey of the existing evidence, see Gupta, *Nana Sahib*, pp. 104–15.
17 Kaye, *Sepoy War*, vol. 2, p. 393
18 Shepherd, *Personal Narrative*, pp. 155–56. Shepherd was in prison at this time and his evidence is based on what he heard from some of his jailers.
19 Forbes-Mitchell, *Relief*, p. 94
20 Gordon-Alexander, *Recollections*, pp. 194–95
21 Roberts, *Forty-One Years*, p. 217
22 Russell, *Diary*, p. 271
23 *ibid.*, p. 278
24 For. Pol. Cons., No. 66. 27 May 1859
25 *ibid.*, No. 68. 27 May 1859
26 For. Pol. Proceedings, No. 33. October 1861

27 *ibid.*
28 Foreign Department Political (A), No. 177. August 1861
29 *ibid.*, Nos. 17 and 18. December 1861
30 Quoted in *The Times*, 11 February 1864
31 Northbrook to Salisbury, 6 November 1874. For. Dept. Pol. (A), No. 83. November 1874
32 Elgin to secretary of state for India, 14 August 1894. Elgin Papers, India Office Library.
33 See, for example, Savarkar, V. D., *The Indian War of Independence of 1857* (London 1909 and Bombay 1947). Even a quarter of a century after India achieved independence, the myths of 1857 seem as durable as ever. In 1972 the Nana Sahib was made the hero of a novel, *The Devil's Wind*, by the Indian writer Manohar Malgonkar.

2 *The madness of Colonel Neill*

1   Kaye, *Sepoy War*, vol. 2, pp. 130–31 f/n
2   Holmes, *Mutiny*, p. 211
3   Kaye, *Sepoy War*, vol. 2, p. 130
4   *ibid.*
5   Kaye, *Lives*, vol. 2, pp. 366–67
6   Kaye, *Sepoy War*, vol. 2, p. 209
7   Canning to the President of the Board of Control, 20 June 1857. 'A portion of the regiment of Sikhs was drawn into resistance who, had they been properly handled would, I fully believe, have remained faithful.' Quoted in Kaye, *Sepoy War*, vol. 2, p. 226
8   Quoted *ibid.*, vol. 2, p. 233
9   *ibid.*, p. 236
10 See Appendix 2, pp. 157–58
11 Kaye, *Sepoy War*, vol. 2, pp. 236–37
12 *ibid.*, p. 237
13 *ibid.*, p. 235
14 *ibid.*, p. 263
15 Holmes, *Mutiny*, p. 220. For details see P.P. (54) 1858, and Martin, *Indian Empire*, vol 3
16 Kaye, *Sepoy War*, vol. 2., p. 268 f/n
17 Chunder, *Travels*, vol. 1, pp. 103–4
18 *ibid.*
19 Kaye, *Lives*, vol. 2, p. 374
20 *ibid.*, p. 376
21 Russell, *Diary*, pp. 281–82
22 Forrest, *History*, vol. 1, p. 372
23 Swanston, *My Journal*, p. 23
24 North, *Journal*, p. 76
25 Forbes-Mitchell, *Relief*, pp. 24–25
26 Kaye, S*epoy War*, vol. 2, p. 388
27 Home Miscell., vol. 726
28 Forrest, *Selections*, vol. 2, p. 96
29 Home Miscell., vol. 726
30 Forrest, *Selections*, vol. 2, p. 155
31 Maude and Sherer, vol. 1, p. 482
32 Neill to Havelock, 27 July 1857. Quoted in Kaye, *Sepoy War*, vol. 2, p. 399
33 Forbes-Mitchell, *Relief*, p. 26
34 Kaye, *Sepoy War*, vol. 2, p. 400

35 Forbes-Mitchell, p. 26
36 Maude and Sherer, vol. 1, pp. 251–52
37 Campbell, *Memoirs*, vol. 1, p. 281
38 Leckey, *Fictions*, pp. 166–68
39 Malleson, *History*, vol. 1, pp. 502–3 f/n
40 *ibid.*
41 'A Soldier of the 73rd Highlanders.' Quoted in Trotter, *Bayard of India*, p. 165
42 Malleson, *History*, vol. 1, p. 538

PART FOUR: THE SIEGE AND THE SYMBOL

1 *Great nursery of sepoys*

1 Sleeman, *Journey*, vol. 1, Appendix
2 Minute to Council, 21 November 1854
3 Minute of 15 March 1855. Quoted in Kaye, *Sepoy War*, vol. 1, p. 141
4 Quoted in Trotter, *Bayard of India*, p. 134
5 Henry Lawrence to Lord Canning, 18 April 1857
6 Quoted in Morison, *Lawrence*, p. 299
7 H. Lawrence to J. R. Colvin in Agra. Quoted in Morison, p. 307

2 *The Maulvi and the dancing girl*

1 Martin Gubbins. Quoted in Morison, *Lawrence*, p. 317
2 Eye-witness quoted in Rees, *Personal Narrative*, p. 88
3 Inglis, *Letter*, p. 52
4 Edwardes and Merivale, vol. 2, p. 361
5 Only the barest details of military operations in Oudh are given in this chapter. For operations outside the Residency, see Edwardes, M., *Battles*, pp. 57–141. A full, almost day-to-day treatment of life inside the Residency, based on eye-witness reports, can be found in Edwardes, Michael, *A Season in Hell: The defence of the Lucknow Residency* (London and New York, 1973).
6 Quoted in Malleson, *History*, vol. 1, pp. 407–8
7 See especially Chaudhuri, S. B., *Civil Rebellion*. For a rather different Indian view: Majumdar, R. C., et al., *British Paramountcy and Indian Renaissance*, Part I. (Delhi, 1963). This work is vol. 4 in *The History and Culture of the Indian People*.
8 For. Pol. Cons., No. 197. 8 October 1858. A version of this proclamation was published in the *Delhi Gazette* of 29 September 1857, when it was assumed to be one issued by the king of Delhi.
9 Chaudhuri, *Civil Rebellion*, p. 31
10 Quoted in Ball, *History*, vol. 2, p. 337 f/n
11 Canning to Sir Colin Campbell, 20 December 1857
12 Malleson, *History*, vol. 2, pp. 397–98
13 Anonymous. 'The campaign of 1857–8', in *Calcutta Review*, March 1859
14 For the full text of the proclamation, see Maclagan, *Clemency Canning*, pp. 183–85
15 Russell, *Diary*, p. 115
16 *ibid.*, p. 103
17 Forbes-Mitchell, *Relief*, pp. 134–35
18 Khan Bahadur Khan of Bareilly. Quoted in Russell *Diary*, p. 72

19 Malleson, *History*, vol. 2, p. 544. Malleson, of course, assumed that the Maulvi had been born in Oudh.
20 For. Pol. Cons., No. 413. 15 July 1859. Quoted in Sen, *Eighteen Fifty-seven*, p. 367

PART FIVE: THE FORTRESS AND THE PYRE

1 *The Jezebel of India*

1 For. Pol. Cons., No. 283. 30 December 1859 (Supp.)
2 *ibid.*
3 Parasnis, *Maharani*, pp. 43–44
4 Lang, *Wanderings*, pp. 93–94
5 Kaye, *Sepoy War*, vol. 1, p. 91
6 See Godse, *Majha Pravas*
7 For. Pol. Cons., No. 354. 31 July 1857
8 *ibid.*
9 *ibid.*
10 Lowe, *Central India*, p. 236
11 Godse, *Majha Pravas*, p. 67
12 Lowe, *Central India*, p. 200
13 Sylvester, *Recollections*, p. 98
14 *ibid.*, pp. 102–3
15 Godse, *Majha Pravas*, p. 82
16 Lowe, *Central India*, p. 236
17 *United Service Magazine*, October 1918–March 1919
18 Godse, *Majha Pravas*, pp. 100–4
19 The description of the attack and capture of Jhansi is based on that in Edwardes, M., *Battles*, pp. 159–72
20 See Edwardes, M., *King of the World*
21 Quoted in Varma, *Rani Lakshmibai*, p. 198

2 *The last rebel*

1 Lang, *Wanderings*, pp. 410–11
2 Anonymous. 'The pursuit of Tantia Topee', in *Blackwood's Magazine*, August 1860, p. 173
3 *ibid.*, p. 181
4 Malleson, *History*, vol. 3, p. 523
5 Firuz Shah was a direct descendant of the first Bahadur Shah, who reigned from 1707–12. He left Delhi in 1855 to visit Mecca and returned to Bombay in May 1857. He was the only rebel leader to publicly condemn the murder of innocent women and children (in a proclamation issued in February 1858, For. Pol. Cons., No. 122, 30 April 1858). In 1864 a Muslim sect known as the Wahabis was said to be in touch with him and using his name in an attempted uprising. In November 1881, a pension of Rs. 5 a month was granted by the government of India to his widow on condition that she did not return to Delhi. This was later raised to Rs. 100 a month.
6 Malleson, *History*, vol. 3, p. 376 f/n
7 *ibid.*, p. 377
8 For. Pol. Cons., No. 166. 22 April 1859
9 After the Nana Sahib's departure from Cawnpore Tantia Topi was in possession of a duplicate seal and issued letters in his master's

name. It is also possible that he was responsible for the issuing of an interesting proclamation which, though it is undated, must have been written after the fall of Delhi to the British. The proclamation was directed in the Peshwa's name to 'various office-holders and the whole population of the Deccan and the Carnatic', and claimed that the Peshwa had conquered substantial territory north of the Narbada river. 'At the present time,' it went on, 'the English having disagreements among themselves about their religion are quarrelling and fighting and killing each other. The French and Russians who entertained from a long time a hatred against the British and a design to turn them out of Hindustan have thought this a proper time to carry it out and with this intention they have been sending armies by sea these three months past. The Chinese also have declared war against the Kaffers [literally, "infidels"] and the latter having no armies to send against the Chinese are much alarmed. The Persians, Afghans and Baluchis, moreover, are ready with arms collected to aid us. In short, this is the golden time to root out the English from this country. The Kaffer English in order to discourage the population, fabricate false information of their having retaken Delhi, and other places and having defeated us and make it known to the public, but such ought not to be believed.' For. Secret Proceedings, No. 18. 22 October 1858.

10 Malleson, *History*, vol. 3., p. 379
11 Voluntary Deposition or Statement made by Tantia Topi on 10 April 1859. Malleson, *History*, vol. 3, p. 515–16
12 Quoted in Ball, *History*, vol. 2, p. 602
13 *ibid.*

PART SIX: THE QUEEN'S PEACE OVER ALL

1 *A king on trial*

1 Ball, *History*, vol. 2, p. 168
2 *ibid.*
3 *The Friend of India.* 1 October 1857
4 Quoted in Ball, *History*, vol. 2., p. 169
5 Coopland, *A Lady's Escape*, p. 275
6 Russell, *Diary*, pp 170–71
7 *ibid.*, p. 171
8 *ibid.*, p. 175–76
9 *ibid.*, p. 176
10 Extracts from the charges and all quotations from the transcript of the trial that follow are quoted from P.P. 1859 Session 1 (18) and Session 2 (25).
11 Quoted in Ball, *History*, vol. 2, p. 179
12 Officiating Civil Surgeon, Delhi. Quoted in Ball, *History*, vol. 2, pp. 179–80
13 Lieutenant E. S. Ommanney to Chief Commissioner, Delhi. 9 October 1858
14 For this see Buckler, F. W., 'Political Theory of the Indian Mutiny', and Dewar, D. and Garratt, G. T., 'Reply to Mr F. W. Buckler's Political Theory of the Indian Mutiny', in *Transactions of the Royal Historical Society*, vol. V, 1922, and vol. VII, 1924.
15 Quoted in Toye, *Springing Tiger*, p. 103

2 *The white mutiny*

1 Russell, *Diary*, p. 209
2 Quoted in Maclagan, *Clemency Canning*, p. 227
3 Quoted in Morison, *Lawrence*, pp. 182–83
4 Sir Hugh Rose to Sir Edward Campbell, Military Secretary to the viceroy, 24 September 1860

3 *A fettered land*

1 For the full text of the proclamation, see Maclagan, *Clemency Canning*, p. 232
2 Memorandum on the Elimination of all Unchristian Principle from the Government of British India. Quoted in Edwardes, E., *Memorials*, vol. 2, p. 90.
3 Russell, *Diary*, p. 151
4 Canning to secretary of state for India, 16 October 1859. Wood Papers, India Office Library
5 *ibid.*, 13 June 1860
6 This was awarded to the Raja of Jhind, the only native ruler who actually led his own troops at the capture of Delhi. He was also given territories producing revenue of over Rs. 1 million a year, and a house in Delhi. The salute of ceremonial guns for his state was raised from nine to eleven, and the number of trays of ceremonial gifts increased from eleven to fifteen.
7 *Memoir of L. B. Bowring*, Indian Office Library. Bowring was Canning's private secretary.
8 Canning to secretary of state. Wood Papers, 12 November 1859
9 The address of the talukdars and Canning's reply are in P.P. (47) 1861, pp. 475–79
10 Sir James Fitzjames Stephen, quoted in Trevelyan, *Macaulay*, p. 302

BIBLIOGRAPHY

Unpublished material

India Office Library, Foreign and Commonwealth Office, London:
 Home Miscellaneous Series, vol. 725 and 726
 Papers of Sir Charles Wood, MSS. Eur. E.78
 Papers of the 8th Earl of Elgin, MSS. Eur. C.145
 Memoir of L. B. Bowring
National Archives of India, New Delhi:
 Mutiny Papers
 Foreign Department Secret Consultations, 1851, 1858, 1859
 Foreign Department Political Proceedings, 1861
 Foreign Department Political (A), 1861
 Foreign Department Political Consultations, 1857, 1858, 1859
 Foreign Secret Proceedings, 1858
Parliamentary Papers (P.P.):
 1857 (30), 1857–8 (47), 1858 (54), 1859 (18) (25), 1860 (52), 1861 (47)

Newspapers and periodicals

Bengal Past and Present, Calcutta
Blackwood's Magazine, Edinburgh
Calcutta Review

Daily News, London
Delhi Gazette
The Englishman, Calcutta
The Friend of India, Serampur and Calcutta
Lahore Chronicle
The New Monthly Magazine, London
The Times, London
Transactions of the Royal Historical Society, London
United Service Magazine, London

Published material

BAIRD, J. G. A.   Private Letters of the Marquess of Dalhousie. London 1911
BALL, C.   History of the Indian Mutiny. 2 vols. London n.d. (c. 1860)
BJORNSTJERNA, Count Magnus   The British Empire in the East. London 1840
BOSWORTH-SMITH, R.   Life of Lord Lawrence. 2 vols. London 1883
BOURCHIER, Col. G.   Eight Months' Campaign against the Bengal Sepoy Army during the Mutiny of 1857. London 1858
CAMPBELL, Sir G.   Memoirs of my Indian Career. 2 vols. London 1893
CHAUDHURI, S. B.   Civil Rebellion in the Indian Mutinies. Calcutta 1957
CHUNDER, Bholanauth   Travels of a Hindu. 2 vols. London 1869
COOPER, F.   The Crisis in the Punjab. London 1858
COOPLAND, Mrs Ruth   A Lady's Escape from Gwalior. London 1859
CUNNINGHAM, H. S.   Earl Canning. London 1892
CUST, R. N.   Pictures of Indian Life. London 1881
EDWARDES, E.   Memorials of the Life and Letters of Major-General Sir Herbert B. Edwardes. 2 vols. London 1886
EDWARDES, H. B., and MERIVALE, H.   Life of Sir Henry Lawrence. 2 vols. London 1872
EDWARDES, Michael   Battles of the Indian Mutiny. London and New York 1963. New edn 1970
   Bound to Exile: The Victorians in India. London 1969, New York 1970
   Glorious Sahibs: The Romantic as Empire-Builder. London 1968, New York 1969
   King of the World: The Life and Times of Shah Alam, Emperor of Hindustan. London 1970, New York 1971
FITZMAURICE, Lord   Lord Granville. 2 vols. London 1925
FORBES-MITCHELL, W.   The Relief of Lucknow. Ed. M. Edwardes. London 1962
FORREST, G.   History of the Indian Mutiny. 3 vols. Edinburgh 1904–12
   Selections from the Letters, etc., preserved in the Military Department . . . 4 vols. Calcutta 1893–1912
Further Papers Relative to the Mutinies in the East . . . 2 vols. Calcutta 1901
GRANT, Charles   Observations on the State of Society among the Asiatic Subjects of Great Britain, particularly with Respect to Morals and the Means of Improving it, written during the Year 1792. Privately printed, 1797
GREATHED, H. H.   Letters written during the Siege of Delhi. London 1858
GRIFFITHS, C. J.   The Siege of Delhi. London 1910
GODSE, Vishnu   Majha Pravas. Poona 1948 (In Marathi)

GORDON-ALEXANDER, W. Recollections of a Highland Subaltern. London 1898

GUPTA, P. C. Nana Sahib and the Rising at Cawnpore. Oxford 1963

HEBER, R. Narrative of a Journey through the Upper Provinces of India. 3 vols. London 1828

History of the Siege of Delhi, by an Officer who served there. London 1861

HODSON, G. H. (ed.) Twelve Years of a Soldier's Life in India. London 1859

HOLMES, T. Rice History of the Indian Mutiny. London 1898

INGLIS, Hon Julia Letter containing Extracts from a Journal kept by Mrs Inglis during the Siege of Lucknow. London 1858

KAYE, J. W. History of the Sepoy War. 3 vols. London 1880
Lives of the Indian Officers. 3 vols. London 1880

LANG, J. Wanderings in India and Other Sketches of Life in Indostan. London 1859

LECKEY, E. Fictions connected with the Indian Outbreak of 1857 Exposed. London 1859

LOWE, Thomas Central India during the Rebellion. London 1860

MACLAGAN, Michael Clemency Canning. London 1962

MALLESON, G. B. History of the Indian Mutiny. 3 vols. London 1878

MARTIN, Montgomery The Indian Empire. 3 vols. London 1858–61
The Rise and Progress of the Indian Mutiny. London 1859

MAUDE, F. C., and SHERER, J. W. Memories of the Mutiny. 2 vols. London 1894

METCALFE, T. G. Two Native Narratives of the Mutiny in Delhi. London 1898

MILL, James History of British India. 6 vols. London 1820

MORISON, J. L. Lawrence of Lucknow. London 1934

MUIR, Sir William Records of the Intelligence Department of the North-Western Provinces of India during the Mutiny of 1857. 2 vols. Edinburgh 1902

NORTH, Lieut. Journal of an English Officer in India. London 1858

PARASNIS, D. B. Maharani Lakshmi Bai Saheb Hyanche Charita. Satara 1894. (In Marathi)

PEARSE, Hugh The Hearseys, London 1905

Records from the Delhi Residency and Agency. London 1911

REES, L. E. R. A Personal Narrative of the Siege of Lucknow. London 1858

'Resident in the North-Western Provinces of India, A'. The Rebellion in India. London 1858

ROBERTS, Field-Marshal Lord Forty-One Years in India. London 1898

ROBERTS, Fred Letters Written During the Indian Mutiny. London 1924

RUSSELL, William Howard My Indian Mutiny Diary. Ed. M. Edwardes. London 1957

SAYYID AHMED KHAN Asbab-e-Bhgawat-i-Hind. 1858. English translation: The Causes of the Indian Revolt. Banaras 1873

SEN, S. N. Eighteen Fifty-seven. New Delhi 1957

SHEPHERD, W. J. A Personal Narrative of the Outbreak at Cawnpore . . . during the Sepoy Revolt of 1857. Lucknow 1879

SLEEMAN, W. H. A Journey through the Kingdom of Oude in 1849–1850. 2 vols. London 1858

STEEL, Flora Annie On the Face of the Waters. London 1897

SWANSTON, W. O.   My Journal. Uxbridge 1890

SYLVESTER, J. H.   Recollections of the Campaign in Malwa and Central India. Bombay 1860

TAYLOR, A. C.   Life of General Sir Alexander Taylor. London 1913

THOMSON, Captain M.   The Story of Cawnpore. London 1859

THORN, W.   Memoir of the War in India. London 1818

TOYE, Hugh   The Springing Tiger: A study of Subhas Chandra Bose. London 1959

TREVELYAN, G.   The Competition Wallah. London 1895

Life and Letters of Lord Macaulay. London 1908

TROTTER, L. J.   The Bayard of India. A Life of General Sir James Outram. London 1919

The Life of John Nicholson. London 1898

VARMA, Vrindavanlal   Rani Lakshmibai. New Delhi n.d. In Hindi)

YOUNG, Keith   Delhi 1857. London 1902

INDEX

THE WASHING OF THE SPEARS
The Rise and Fall of the Zulu Nation
Donald R. Morris

A brilliant account of the life of the Zulu nations under the great ruler Shaka, and its tragic fall under Cetshwayo in the Zulu war of 1870. The Great Trek by the Boers in the 1820s brought them face to face with the expanding power of the Zulus – then the most formidable nation in Black Africa. This confrontation produced a prolonged struggle culminating in the Zulu war, when, armed only with their assegais, the Zulus challenged the right of Victorian England. Their startling success at the battle of Isandhlwana carried with it the seeds of their ultimate and humiliating destruction.

'The author's style is quiet and unobtrusive, well suited to his torrid material; he knows how to tell a good story; and his numerous character-sketches of Bantus and Britons alike are always sympathetic and often perceptive. Particularly well done is his account of Shaka, the ruthless giant whose powerful will united the Zulu tribes into a ferociously disciplined nation, and whose grotesque disregard of human life and suffering resulted in his own murder in 1828. . . . Commander Morris's thorough and understanding book provides a sad commentary on the enduring attitudes of mind that have made the solution of such problems so intractable'

Christopher Hibbert, The Spectator

£1

THE GREAT TREK
Oliver Ransford

Oliver Ransford has a considerable reputation as a writer of popular works on Southern African history and has now turned his attention to the Great Trek of 1834–5, the search by a few thousand dedicated Afrikaners for their Promised Land. By their trek the Afrikaner pastoral farmers of the Cape thrust white settlement deep into Southern Africa and set in motion the interaction between Boer and African that has been the major theme of subsequent South African history. Mr Ransford's sympathies lie with the Boers: he deals with the exploits of Potgieter, Retief and Pretorius; the Battle of Vegkop at which 33 musket-armed Boers defeated 5,000 Matabele; the successful laager formation of the wagons in battle; the cruelty and craftiness of Dingaan, the Zulu chief who was responsible for Retief's tragic death; and the events which led up to the Boer submission to the British crown in 1842, to Boer independence in the Transvaal a decade later and shortly afterwards in the Orange Free State.

Mr Ransford has written a memorable book about a people who are little-liked and little-known. He writes well, while the romance and colour of the story he tells lend vigour to his telling of it and help make his book eminently suitable to the general reader.

£1 *Illustrated*

IMPERIAL ADVENTURER
Emperor Maximilian of Mexico and his Empress
Joan Haslip

When Ferdinand Maximilian, Hapsburg Archduke, accepted the throne of Mexico in the nineteenth century, he little knew the tragedy and disaster that were to follow. Mexico had disintegrated through anarchy and misrule and those European powers with commercial interests in the country agreed that only a European monarchy would put an end to the grim, bitter struggle that was draining the life-blood of the nation and destroying the economy. This European intervention in Mexican affairs brought hostility from the United States; the support promised by Napoleon III was withdrawn when Maximilian refused to meet the French Emperor's demands; and so determined was his wife, Charlotte, to be an Empress that she persuaded her unhappy husband to retain his position when abdication could possibly have saved his life.

Maximilian has always been regarded as a complex character, artistic and liberal on the one hand, autocratic and traditional on the other. Even his relationship with his wife is a subject for speculation. Joan Haslip's magnificent portrait of Maximilian is drawn against a detailed background as she moves with authority from the courts of Europe, with their surface of grandeur and pomp, to the dusty heat of Mexico, and follows the drama to its climax of betrayal, madness and death.

£1·60 *Illustrated*

QUEEN VICTORIA
Her Life and Times
Volume One: 1819–1861
Cecil Woodham-Smith

In this magnificent account of the first forty-two years of
Victoria's life, Cecil Woodham-Smith has produced a narrative which not only presents new facts relating to the Queen,
but reveals her as a character to whom history has failed to do
justice. The unfavourable circumstances of her upbringing,
years of suffering and frustration during which she was virtually kept a prisoner, developed what has been described as 'a
vein of iron in her most extraordinary character'. She was
more intelligent, more reasonable, more generous and lovable,
far shrewder than has been recognised. With her lively and
receptive mind, her judgment of personalities and politics
matured quickly and she was able to combine the arduous
duties as Head of State with the rearing of a large family, the
only queen regnant in British history to do so.
Volume one of the definitive work on Victoria presents the
most detailed life of the Queen yet written. With the aid of
her personal correspondence, we are able to gain an intimate
knowledge of the young Queen's formative years, of her
marriage, and of the impact of the Prince Consort on court
and society. An important aspect of this biography is that
Victoria is shown in relation to her times; the European background is skilfully painted in, outlining the issues leading up
to the Crimean War, the Indian Mutiny, and the major
events of the first half of Victoria's reign.

£1·50 *Illustrated*

THE DRAGON EMPRESS
Life and Times of Tz'u-hsi 1835–1908
Empress Dowager of China
Marina Warner

' "I have often thought," the Empress Tz'u-hsi is reported to have said, "that I am the cleverest woman who ever lived." This five-foot-high daughter of a mediocre Manchu civil servant of small means, who deserted his post, contrived by luck and unscrupulousness to manoeuvre herself into a life-long term as absolute monarch of 400 million people, and a multi-millionairess.

Imperfectly educated, vastly ignorant both of the outside world and of the miseries of her own subjects, she lived, a monstrous queen bee, in isolated splendour, with an entourage of 3,000 eunuchs. Though she reigned over China, she can hardly be said to have governed it. China was a corrupt bureaucracy weighed down by a complex of outdated belief, custom, hierarchy, pomp and ritual. The Japanese quickly learned to defeat the West with its own weapons; the Chinese, with all their wonderful qualities, collapsed.

There was Tz'u-hsi, with her "keen sense of enjoyment at the troubles of other people", playing people off against each other, crying "Off with his head!" in malice or in some real or imagined expediency, growing ever vainer and greedier. Tz'u-hsi, though she had her points, is not lovable in retrospect. There is a horrid fascination about her life and times, and Miss Warner's conducted tour of them is highly recommendable and strikingly illustrated'

The Sunday Telegraph

£2·50 *Illustrated*